PEOPLE AND PLANNING

SOCIETY TODAY AND TOMORROW

General Editor: A. H. Halsey

*Fellow of Nuffield College and Head of the Department
of Social and Administrative Studies, Oxford*

*

People and Planning

THE SOCIOLOGY OF HOUSING
IN SUNDERLAND

NORMAN DENNIS

London
FABER AND FABER

First published in 1970
by Faber and Faber Limited
24 Russell Square London WC1
Printed in Great Britain by
Western Printing Services Ltd., Bristol
All rights reserved

SBN 571 09011 7

CONTENTS

7

PLATES

9

Plates 1, 2, 3, 5, 6 and 8 are reproduced by kind
permission of the Sunderland Museum Collection
and plate 19 by the *Sunderland Echo*. Plates 7 and
9 are the author's photographs and the remainder
were taken at the expense of Sunderland's Housing
Needs Study for the author by the Department of
Photography, University of Newcastle upon Tyne.

DIAGRAMS

11

TABLES

ACKNOWLEDGEMENTS

This research was financed by a grant from Sunderland Corporation. My first debt of gratitude, therefore, is to the council for making this work possible. I have had to spend much of my time in Corporation departments, and I should like to express my appreciation of the warm and unstinted co-operation I have received from officials and staff at all levels. I hope that nothing I have to say about the problems of policy and administration seems to show an insensitivity to the dilemmas they face, or will be interpreted as detracting from my high personal regard for the officers with whom I have come into contact. Miss Joan Vipond and Mrs. Joan Wood have been my co-workers and I cannot speak too highly of them. Among my colleagues at the University of Newcastle upon Tyne I should particularly like to thank Professor Peter Collison, Mrs. Kathleen Bell and Jon Davies for their most valued support and stimulation. The research has depended most of all, however, on the willingness of hundreds of my fellow-townspeople to be questioned (sometimes for hours on end) about their housing needs. I hope that they will not feel that their generous hospitality has been wasted.

N.D.

INTRODUCTION

This book is about planning and about people. The planning is of housing; the people are the inhabitants of Sunderland. Here, a discussion which all too easily presents itself in simplified and inert abstractions comes vividly to life. This is more than an absorbing account of the history and present state of housing in a particular town. It goes much further to raise general moral and political questions about the relation between government and individuals. In the twentieth century we have grown accustomed to the idea of planning as a necessary adaptation to changing circumstances and as a means of using scarce resources for the optimal or efficient pursuit of future goals. A book about planning therefore is a book about ends and means. What follows is a penetrating examination of public and private aims in communities which are leaving behind their struggle for physical survival and emerging into a world where only a small part of what is consumed is necessary for the maintenance of life. It is also an authoritative analysis of the planning process and its effectiveness in realising the aspirations of communities and families.

Planning is associated with left-wing politics. 'The hidden hand' is, of course, also 'a planner' with the market as its instrument. But socialist and labour parties have attacked this form of 'planning' as one which is vitiated by unequal distributions of power, wealth and income between citizens; planning by the hidden hand does not accurately reflect the preferences of citizens in community as opposed to individuals in a market. These arguments are nowhere more relevant than in the sphere of housing which is both costly, amounting usually to four times the average annual earnings of an individual

worker, and also durable, affecting the lives of future generations.

An enquiry of this kind often turns out to be a more or less
sophisticated attack on socialism and a plea to 'return to the
market'. Here, however, if the discussion is critical of the
policies and methods of housing authorities, the criticism is
directed to the planner's indifference to egalitarian notions of
income and power, and his ignorance of the preferences and
values of the community he is appointed to serve. Remedies are
to be sought not only in an improvement of the knowledge and
technique of the planning organisation, but also in new forms
of democratic political procedures. Both the political and
scientific lessons which emerge from the analysis are brought
out clearly in the body of the work and summarised in the
conclusion.

Sunderland itself is a large county borough at the mouth of
the Wear on the north-east coast of England. In population it
ranks fifteenth among the towns of England and Wales. It was
the product, not of the early industrial revolution, but of a
highly developed technology of steel and steam engineering in
the last quarter of the nineteenth century. Although the
complex of towns along the Clyde is more important taken as a
whole, Sunderland until very recent times frequently produced
a higher annual tonnage of ships than any other single town or
city in the world.

The twentieth century, however, brought structural changes
in the international economy which halted Sunderland's
growth. In the nineteen thirties it suffered the fate of its smaller
shipbuilding neighbour on the Tyne, Jarrow, and went
through the agony of large scale and prolonged unemployment.
Compared with the industry elsewhere in this country, shipbuilding has been tenaciously successful on the Wear, but with
a much reduced demand for labour. In the nineteen fifties and
sixties Japan and other foreign competitors have posed increasingly severe problems, and unemployment in Sunderland
has persistently exceeded national and regional rates. Net
outward migration has been continuous; in the nineteen sixties
this outflow ceased to be counterbalanced by a large excess
of births over deaths and population began to decline.

Sunderland, as a town, has a distinct character. It is geographically set off by its position on the river and the coast. Centred visibly and closely on its productive work it is the antithesis of suburbia: housing is an annexe to the workplace and the community is a working community. It is, in a double sense, a working-class town. Sunderland also has a social distinctiveness which is part reflection and part cause of its physical isolation. There is the shared dialect and accent of the Wearsider, local patriotism for the town's football team, the community and neighbourhood pubs and social clubs, and the collective consciousness of a harsh industrial history and of present competition for survival in an advanced industrial world.

Equally Sunderland is a distinctive civic entity and, since the end of the second world war, its housing policies have been outstanding in both aims and achievements. In proportion to its population Sunderland has a comfortable lead over the other large county boroughs of England and Wales in the number of its post-war council houses. Among the main reasons for this is the long dominance of the Labour party.[1] The Labour-dominated council secured power on the same wave of war-time radicalism which gave the Labour party a majority in the House of Commons. It worked against a background of pre-war depression in the town's heavy industries and within the context of the far-reaching town-planning and housing legislation of the post-war period.

Because of its housing record and the extent to which the local authority has become the principal provider of dwellings, Sunderland is a particularly useful case to study; and Norman Dennis, who is already widely known for his contributions to the sociology of the family and of communities and who is, furthermore, a loyal local patriot, is especially well qualified to study it. His contribution is also particularly valuable because of his inside experience as a full-time local government planner for over a year before undertaking this research.

The reader will sense for himself the intimate knowledge both of the families and communities affected by the planning policies and of the procedures themselves. Here I want to draw attention to the fundamental question which is posed through-out the book: on what grounds can we accept or reject the

[1] From 1945 to 1967.

theory or principle by which an organisation is guided in its planning of action? Sociologists call these grounds the 'legitimation' of the organisation and its activities. Contemporary sociological discussion owes this usage to the German sociologist Max Weber who pointed out that organisations differ greatly when they come to decide whether what they are doing is 'morally right' and based upon 'the correct and relevant data'. One type of organisation accepts the word of its leader on both these matters. This is Charisma. *Ipse dixit*–the sayings of the leader are the criteria of both truth and worth. A second type of organisation rests its activities upon a piety for what has actually, allegedly or presumably always existed and upon a belief in the every day routine as being the inviolable norm of conduct. This is organised authority based on tradition. Thirdly, there are organisations to which Weber gave the term bureaucratic, which appeal to the rule of general laws applying to all within the jurisdiction of the organisation without regard to differences of race, age, family background or social condition. The legitimacy of such an organisation's authority does not depend upon the actual benefits given to particular persons, but upon the legality of the general rule which has been purposely thought out and enacted. Authority here is based on formal as distinct from substantive justice.

Bureaucratic routine administrations have emerged where the same service can (and especially where it must) be provided day after day in an identical way to large numbers of people. This is the case with, for example, gas, water and electricity supplies and transport and postal services. Bureaucratic administration is also appropriate to the production of houses when, because of chronic shortage, large numbers of identical dwellings must be produced. It is appropriate to the demolition of houses where a few formal characteristics–for example, whether the house is at all damp or possibly where a measurable amount of dampness is present–enable an official to distinguish unequivocally between a slum house and a non-slum house.

Fourthly and finally there is a type of legitimation which is increasingly important in the modern world. The activities of an organisation are not 'proved' right and good because they are the command of a charismatic leader, or because of tradition, or because they can be subsumed under some

24

general rule, but because they are so certified by the trained members of the organisation whose special function it is to evaluate the particular issue. This is professional authority. Decisions, characteristically in the form of 'advice', are made by those who have been appointed to a 'sphere of competence' on the basis of qualifications attested by a professional group of peers.

As long as the group of professionals make claims only in the technical sphere; as long as they merely say 'this is the given task, we know the most economical means of accomplishing it', the organisation will show many bureaucratic characteristics. But it is also possible for professionals to make claims in such a way or to such an extent that their legitimation resembles that of the inspired leader. These claims to legitimation typically take the form of a kind of group charisma. Each case is adjudicated not by an appeal to strictly formal conceptions unambiguously established, made public and safely recorded 'in the files', but by informal judgments rendered by the personal incumbent of the professional status in terms of concrete ethical or practical valuations. These valuations may be quite opaque to those outside the profession. The professional, by definition, is absolved from justifying his decision; he does not need to reveal his basis in theory or fact or value.

Mr. Dennis examines the planning process in these terms, and is thereby enabled to study the legitimations of decision makers. These legitimations are partly bureaucratic. In part too they are professional, though still located in the markedly bureaucratic atmosphere of local government and therefore encrusted with and obscured by bureaucratic attitudes and sentiments. At the same time the context of the study is that of two sets of decisions about housing in Sunderland. First is the decision to add to the town's housing stock of about 60,000 a further 6,000 houses in the form of a large self-contained estate – 'Silksworth New Township'. The second decision is that which resulted in the proposal to demolish about 2,000 old houses between 1965 and 1970. The background and the consequences of these decisions are described in detail in the following chapters.

These facts are then evaluated from the point of view of two special systems of value. The first of these systems is one which gives high priority to the proposition that decisions ought to be made in the light of ascertainable knowledge. From this point of view Mr. Dennis is able to offer a critical examination of planning as an expertise. The second system emphasises the capacity of ordinary people to reach rational decisions about matters which directly affect them, including the capacity to judge the all round suitability of their own home to the present and prospective circumstances of themselves and their families. But even more it emphasises the moral proposition that the exercise of personal discretion is itself a social and personal good. When such discretion has to be abbreviated, as is unavoidable on countless grounds, the case of those who desire to impose restrictions must be well based in fact and convincing in terms of political, social and moral argument. From this point of view Mr. Dennis clarifies the nature of citizenship and points to new ways in which the social scientific survey can be used in the service of democracy.

In short, two questions are raised about community decisions. How well are they supported by investigation of the relevant facts, and from what standpoint of social value can they be defended? This detailed study of a particular town as a microcosm of politics and administration gives fresh understanding of the age-old problem of the proper relation between government and the governed.

A. H. HALSEY

PART ONE

THE DECISION TO BUILD

CHAPTER I

POPULATION GROWTH
AND HOUSEHOLD FISSION

The problems of measuring a town's current housing needs are slight when compared with assessing what they will be in the future. The Milner Holland Report, the authoritative study of London's housing, reached the same conclusion. The original intention was 'to attempt some forecasts and estimates of future needs and developments'.

After the committee had looked in detail at the problem it saw that any forecasts would depend for their validity upon a number of essentially unknowable factors, such as:

1. The trend of population numbers, including a detailed analysis of migration as it affects the particular locality;

2. The likely future pattern of households, their number, sizes and rates of formation and dissolution;

3. Future decisions of the central Government on the scope and role of local housing authorities, housing associations and private landlords, and decisions as to the future long-term preservation, improvement or replacement of older houses;

4. Decisions about the future pattern and volume of employment, which is of crucial importance in determining patterns of migration;

5. The amount of money households will be able and willing to make available for housing, not in terms of forecasts of national economic growth, but in terms of the future of occupational groups and income distribution in the particular town or city for which the housing forecast must be made.

Not only is the demand for housing highly complex. The

components of the demand, the committee argued, social groups, income groups, the age, size and marital status of the members of households are constantly changing. 'In the circumstances, we have not included any assessment of the future.'[1]

There are several reasons, however, for wishing to look at one of these unknowns, population. The first is that, whatever may be feasible, the total population (as it is organised in households) defines the number of dwellings which would ideally be required. Thus, if it were certainly known or highly likely that there would be a large flow of population into a borough in the next few years, a myriad of housing decisions would be affected. This is roughly the situation in which towns in the Midlands and South East England now find themselves. Decisions could be made because population would not be the only known quantity. For the immediate future as compared with the future measured in quinquennia or decades it is possible for the decision-maker to be relatively well-informed about many of the other factors relevant to the situation such as, for example, the productive capacity and expansion potential of the building industry locally and nationally; the amount and nature of Exchequer support for housing programmes; official and unofficial housing policies in the borough itself; the number, competence and views of professional personnel employed by the local authority; and the likely incomes and levels of rent acceptable to the prospective tenants.

On the basis of such information a housing policy could be adumbrated, indicating the number of houses which the local authority would build, the number it would allow private builders to supply, the location and size of the houses and the social characteristics of the eventual tenants.

There are other decisions which have to be made to-day and which are governed by knowledge of, or guesses at, future population size and structure. Such decisions concern the infra-structure of the housing stock rather than housing itself– investment in house-building plant, sewerage works, electricity and gas installations and reservations of open space for public recreation.

Still supposing that accurate projections were a technical possibility, it is nevertheless necessary to recognise that the outcome of the decisions could not be known. Too much else is uncertain. Even with the accurate population projection which is being postulated, the decision maker would have to gamble on a particular combination of contingencies and hope for the best. Thus knowledge of a population expansion may lead a local authority to encourage a private firm to invest in an industrialised building plant. It may even guarantee the firm a market for its products. But whether the product is acceptable five years hence as the particular year's addition to the housing stock cannot be known. Economic depression may have intervened, the firm's products may have been superseded by another superior to them, and certain other major assumptions may have been falsified by events—for example, owner-occupation may have risen still further in public estimation and a particular form of dwelling (e.g. high flats) which the firm must supply if it is to remain solvent may not be suitable for sale to individual householders.

In this longer term the decisions based upon knowledge or estimates of population numbers tend to relate to the population itself. If population is shown to be increasing then this fact may be used to argue the case for population dispersion, to prevent pressure on scarce housing resources in any particular region of the country. Where population is shown to be declining it may be argued, as it was argued in connection with Washington New Town, County Durham, that an exemplary and large-scale expansion in the number of up-to-date dwellings in surroundings designed by trained town-planners and architects would be necessary to attract population and to dissuade potential emigrants from leaving the region.

The further into the future that the population estimate is pushed the more restricted becomes its usefulness in making decisions in the here-and-now. But there is additional reason for taking population projections seriously. The local planning authority is obliged by statute and by various regulations to prepare a development plan for its area, indicating the manner in which the land covered by the plan is to be used and the stages by which the development is to be carried out, and this development plan has to be reviewed at least once every five years. The amount of land which will be marked on the development plan as available for housing use in fifteen or twenty years' time clearly depends upon a prognosis of population growth or decline.

NOTE TO CHAPTER 1

1 Ministry of Housing and Local Government, *Report of the Committee on Housing in Greater London*, Cmnd. 2605, HMSO 1965, pp. 3, 4.

CHAPTER 2

THE FUTURE POPULATION OF SUNDERLAND

The Official Projections

The official estimates of the population of Sunderland in 1971 and 1981 are based on two sets of assumptions: those of the MHLG (Ministry of Housing and Local Government) and those of the LPA (local planning authority). The assumptions about the birth-rate, the death-rate and the age and sex structure of the population are those of the Ministry. The Ministry does not take migration into account, and the migration assumption is therefore that of the LPA.

Birth-rates up to 1981 are assumed to follow the rising trends which were predicted in 1961 for England and Wales as a whole. The rates for Sunderland, however, would continue to exceed the national rates by the same proportion as in the base year. The pattern of the fall in the death-rates would be the same as predicted in 1961 for England and Wales, with Sunderland again retaining its proportionately higher death-rates of the base year.

These rates are age specific. The death-rate, that is, is not a single figure for the whole population of the town. There is a death-rate for infants in their first year, a rate for young men of 20–24, a rate for old people of say, 80–84, and so on throughout the age range. Similarly, the birth-rates are age specific. There is one rate for women in their early 20s and another for women in their early 40s. The rate most used is that calculated per thousand fertile women, women in the age-range 15–44 or 15–49. To arrive at a future population size using these rates, therefore, it is necessary to apply them to a population of a known age and sex composition. The age and sex structure of Sunderland which forms the starting point of the population prediction of the MHLG is that given in the Census volumes.

The migration assumption most frequently favoured in local authority documents in recent years has been a version of the migration trend mentioned in the Hailsham report.[1] For the Northern Region as a whole this said that by 1981 the rate of net migration would be five-sixths of the rate experienced in the intercensal period 1951–61. The LPA's version was a slight modification of this–five-sixths of the 1951–61 rate for the full period 1971–81.

There is, therefore, the official MHLG projection which takes no account of migration, and the LPA's semi-official modification of the MHLG projection which takes into consideration the Hailsham migration assumption. According to the MHLG estimate the population of Sunderland CB will be 207,400 by 1971, and 231,300 by 1981 (Table 2.1). According to the LPA estimate the population will be 199,400 by 1971 and 215,300 by 1981 (Table 2.2).

A refinement of the LPA's Projections

The local authority's calculation assumes that migration between 1951 and 1961 took place, and between 1961–71 and 1971–81, will take place evenly throughout the age range. It is however possible to refine this procedure. By applying local age-specific death-rates to Sunderland's population and by consulting Census tables generally available it is quite simple to obtain the age and sex structure of the migrants from Sunderland between 1951 and 1961. It is merely a matter of following each age cohort through the ten years from 1951 to 1961 (e.g. the cohort '0–4 in 1951/10–14 in 1961', or the cohort '45–49 in 1951/55–59 in 1961'), calculating how many, according to the age-specific death-rate for the town, would have been expected to die, and deducting these from the 1951 figure for the cohort. If the number in the cohort in 1961 were larger than the number in the cohort in 1951, less deaths, then there would have been net immigration. If after taking account of deaths the cohort in 1961 were smaller than it was in 1951,

34

then there would have been net emigration from the cohort. (Tables 2.3 and 2.4.)

The Population in 1971, Using the Assumptions of the MHLG and LPA, with Age-Specific Migration

The loss of population between 1961 and 1971 by net migration from the population which was alive in 1961 can be estimated from the 1951–61 numbers of migrants.

Using the local authority's assumption of five-sixths of the 1951–61 number of migrants, together with these age-specific rates of migration, the MHLG's official projection for 1971 is amended in the manner shown in Table 2.5.

But there would be a further loss between 1961 and 1971. Some children born in Sunderland between 1961 and 1971 would emigrate with their parents. This loss will be ignored in these calculations. Even ignoring the fact, however, that there will be parents with children under 10 years of age among the net emigrants, there is still a loss of population in the 0–9 age groups by 1971. This is because some of the emigrants are fertile women. It is only over the longer period to 1981 that this fact makes itself felt, but it is necessary to trace the process stage by stage.

In the ten years 1961–71 2,790 women who are fertile in 1961 (aged between 15–49) will emigrate. On the further assumption that migration takes place evenly throughout the decade, this is an annual loss of 279.

According to figures supplied by the General Register Office, the average annual birth-rate of Sunderland women aged between 15–49 in the years 1960, 1961 and 1962, was 86·9 per thousand per annum. The 279 fertile women who were net migrants in 1961–2 would therefore give birth to 24 children in each of the years 1961–2, 1962–3, 1963–4, 1964–5 and 1965–6–a total of 120 children. Meanwhile a further 279 women would have migrated in 1962–3 and would have given birth to 24 children in each of the years 1962–3, 1963–4, 1964–5 and 1965–6–a total of 96. The fertile women who were net migrants in 1963–4 would give birth to 72 children, the migrants of 1964–5 to 48, and the migrants of 1965–6 to 24. Between 1961 and 1966, therefore, there is a loss to Sunderland of 364 births.

35

Assuming infantile mortality to remain at the 1960–2 average annual level of 24·06 per thousand, the loss to the 5–9 age-group in 1971, the survivors of these births 1961–6, is 355.

What is the loss to the 0–4 age-group due to these 'migrants-in-the-womb', i.e. the babies who would be born to fertile women who were net migrants during 1966–71?

First, births would still be being lost to Sunderland because of the net migrants of 1961–6 who would be fertile in the period 1961–71. The 175 women aged 45–49 in 1961 (and who migrate at the rate of 17·5 a year) would be no longer fertile by 1966, but the 504 girls who were 10–14 in 1961 (and who migrate at the rate of 50·4 a year) would now be in the fertile age-group 15–19. Of the 1961–6 migrants, 1,560 would be fertile in 1966–71 (i.e. the 279 fertile women in 1961 who migrated each year 1961–6 minus the five years' migration of the 44–49s who migrated at the rate of 17·5 per year, plus the five years' migration of 50·4 of the 10–14s who migrate each year).

Assuming that fertility is rising at the rate of about two per cent every five years (which would make the birth-rate 88·6 per thousand in the quinquennium 1966–71) these 1,560 fertile women would give birth to 691 babies in the five years 1966–71. There would be a loss of 18 of these babies in their first year, due to infantile mortality, so that there would be a net loss of 674 to the 0–4 age-group of 1971.

There is, of course, a further loss due to the net migration of fertile women in the years 1966–71. Of the women who are fertile in 1966–71, there is a net loss by migration of 312 a year. With a birth-rate of 88·6 per thousand fertile women, they will give birth to 414 babies, of whom 404 will survive their first year to become the 0–4 age group of 1971. (Table 2.6.)

The Population in 1981, Using the Assumptions of the MHLG and the LPA, with Age-Specific Migration

Adding migrants-in-the-womb to the migrants expected during 1961–71 on the 'five-sixths of the 1951–61 numbers' assumption gives a result which is little different from that obtained by merely taking five-sixths of the 1951–61 numbers. Indeed, because of deliberate underestimates of losses (children under ten emigrating with their parents have been ignored) this calculation is very slightly higher than the LPA figure.

The effects of the migration of fertile females are, however, cumulative. Between 1961 and 1981, what will be the number of migrants-in-the-womb, using the MHLG and LPA fertility and migration assumptions?

First consider the years 1971–6. Of the women who were net emigrants from 1961 to 1971, 3,143 would be fertile (15–49) in this period. On the assumption that fertility rises by 2 per cent per quinquennium, the birth-rate by 1971–6 would be 90·4 per thousand. Therefore, when allowance is made for infant mortality, these fertile net emigrants would have given birth to 1,387 children. These children will be 5–9 in 1981. To these must be added children of the 5–9 group in 1981, lost to Sunderland because of the net migration of fertile women 1971–6. These children number 369. This makes a total loss of 5–9s in 1981 of 1,756.

The children born in the five years 1976–81 are the 0–4s of 1981. Of the women who migrated during 1961–71, 3,251 are now fertile, and the birth-rate is now 92·2 per thousand. Allowing for infant mortality, they give birth to 1,463 children who will survive to be 0–4 in 1981. Of the women who were net emigrants during 1971–6, 1,873 are fertile in the period 1976–81. They give birth to 852 children who survive to be members of the 0–4 age-group in 1981. Due to the net migration of fertile women in the years 1961–76, therefore, this age-group is smaller by 2,315 than the MHLG estimate shows. Finally, there is a loss to the town of 422 children due to the net emigration of potential mothers in the five-year period 1976–81. This makes a total loss of 2,737 children aged 0–4 in 1981.

An adjustment must be made to the 10–14 age-group of 1981. These were the 0–4s of 1971, of whom 1,078 were lost due to the migration of fertile women 1961–71. A slight adjustment must also be made to the age-group which is 15–19 in 1981 – the 436 5–9s of 1971 who were the children of emigrant mothers. These can be distributed to the male and female age-groups in the ratio of ·5146: ·4854 (=224 males, 211 females).

Age-specific migration for other age-groups is shown in Table 2.7 and 2.8. This refinement of the LPA's calculation therefore amends the MHLG's figures for 1981 in the way shown in

Table 2.9. In total there are 18,000 fewer people in Sunderland in 1981 than the MHLG estimate shows. It is also considerably in excess of 2,000[2] less than the LPA shows on precisely the same assumption of migration at five-sixths of the numbers of net migrants in the decade 1951–61. This amounts to a difference of 8 per cent in the two estimates of the increase in the population of Sunderland CB between 1961 and 1981.

New Migration Assumptions

The MHLG recognises that the official estimates must be adjusted in the light of local evidence. The ambition and hope expressed in the Hailsham report was that the annual number of net migrants 1951–61 would be reduced by one-sixth by 1981.

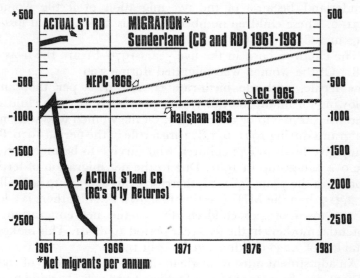

Diagram 2.A

The Northern Economic Planning Council aimed to reduce it to zero by 1981. The only possible basis for any statement about future migration trends, however, is knowledge of past and present migration and of the factors which influence it. What has been Sunderland's actual experience in recent years?

Annual net migration has proceeded at a much heavier rate in the 1960s than in the 1950s. The annual average loss due to net migration from Sunderland CB in the years 1951–61 was 960. The annual average net loss from the borough from 1961 to 1965 was 1,915. It was 1,800 from the borough and the rural district taken together.[3] (Table 2.10 and Diagram 2.A.)

Is this likely to continue? The extent to which new industrial development, partly under the impetus of state assistance, has counteracted the decline of the town's original industries is summarised in two sets of figures. The first shows the number of jobs available. (Table 2.11 and Diagram 2.B.) New employment

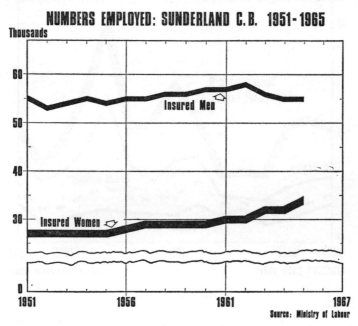

NUMBERS EMPLOYED: SUNDERLAND C.B. 1951-1965

Source: Ministry of Labour

Diagram 2.B

in the form of trading-estate factories has kept pace with the job opportunities lost elsewhere, but has favoured women rather than men. These factories, too, are at the extremities of long hierarchical systems of industrial production and therefore are not the type which generate a great deal of subsidiary employment.

The second set of figures shows the rate of unemployment from 1953 to 1967 in the Employment Exchange areas of Sunderland CB. (Table 2.12 and Diagram 2.C.) The nineteen

sixties show no improvement in either the percentage of unemployed or in the position of Sunderland in relation to other
areas of the country. Moreover, because of their status as branch
factories (in the main) employment established since the second
world war tends to be unstable, because adjustments are made
here rather than at the more important central locations.

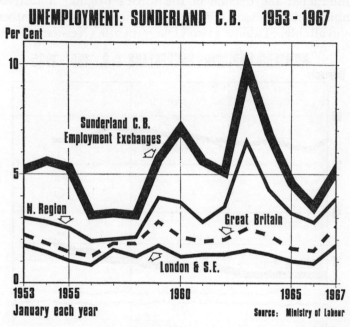

UNEMPLOYMENT: SUNDERLAND C.B.   1953-1967

Diagram 2.C

An examination of the natural history of Sunderland as a
town shows that its main development took place in the second
half of the nineteenth century when a vast expansion in international sea-borne trade, together with its own natural
advantages, established its pre-eminence as a centre for the
construction of steel-hulled steam ships and for the mining and
export of coal. (See Table 2.13 and Diagram 2.D.)

Shipbuilding and marine engineering still employ nearly one
out of every five adult males in Sunderland.[4] Out of a total of
employed males of 56,852, the mid-1966 figure of males
employed in this industry[5] was 9,808 (17 per cent). The extent

to which Sunderland has lost its differential advantage in ship-building is indicated, however, by the fact that in the week ended 5 September 1967, for example, Japan reported ship-building orders for 1,405,000 tons; the whole of the United Kingdom was able to report only one order for 9,000 tons. (Table 2.14.) At this time there is, therefore, no evidence to

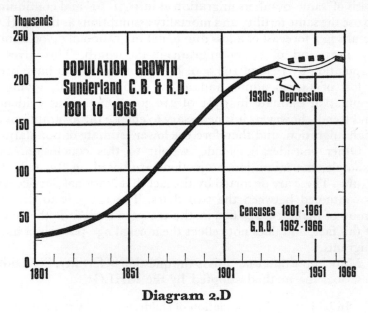

Diagram 2.D

support the official projections which suggest that a period of growth as rapid as that of Sunderland in its heyday is now in prospect.

While such a rate of future growth may be a desirable goal, it is not possible to incorporate it into any realistic estimate of what the population of Sunderland is likely to be by 1971 or 1981. Rather, it must be regarded, if anything, as optimistic to assume that the annual numbers of net migrants up to 1971 and 1981 will be as low as half as many again as the average annual numbers during the ten years 1951–61.

Retaining the MHLG fertility and mortality assumptions, supposing that migration will run at one-and-a-half times the 1951–61 numbers and following the above methods of cal-culating losses the result is a population by 1971 which is 6,300

41

below that of the LPA and 14,200 below that of the MHLG. (Table 2.15.) The result of carrying the calculation forward to 1981, is a population 15,900 fewer than in the LPA estimate and 31,900 fewer than in the MHLG estimate. (Table 2.16.)

In principle a very large number of assumptions can be used as the basis of the population projection. Calculating on the basis of 'same-numbers migration as in 1951–61' and continuing to use the same fertility and mortality assumptions as the MHLG results in a forecast of a loss due to net migration of 7,700 adults by 1971 and of 1,700 migrants-in-the-womb. This gives a population by 1971 of 198,000. By 1981 there would have been a loss of 14,300 adults and a loss of 6,600 births, giving a population estimate in 1981 of 210,300. On present evidence and trends, however, it is necessary to choose the assumptions of high migration, and therefore the lower estimate of population.

Other considerations add weight to this conclusion. For example, the migration projections are based on the 1951–61 figures. These are distorted by the fact that National Service was discontinued between the two dates. The net *gain* to the age group of males 15–24–699 in the ten-year period–is the result of this fact, and does not reflect the normal age-pattern of male migrants.

More important than this is the question of fertility. Schneider describes the method adopted by the MHLG:

> In projecting the population of children . . . it was necessary to allow for differential fertility. . . . Differential fertility was measured by the average of the birth-rates . . . standardised for the sex-age composition of the local population by the appropriate area comparability factor (birth ACF).[6]

The MHLG therefore assumes that Sunderland will share in the increased fertility rates of the country as a whole, and that its traditionally high fertility differential will be maintained.

Sunderland's actual experience again contradicts this supposition. In comparison with the country as a whole the fertility of Sunderland women, far from rising, has dropped steeply in recent years. It was 26 per cent above the national rate in 1957. By 1965 it was 4 per cent below it. (Table 2.17, Diagram 2.E.) This fall in the birth-rate is related to the improvement in the opportunity for Sunderland women to work outside the home,

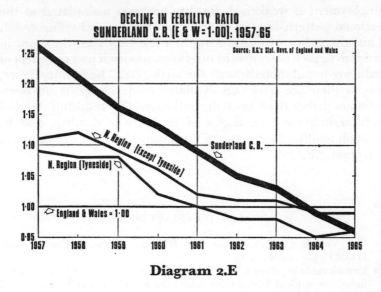

DECLINE IN FERTILITY RATIO
SUNDERLAND C.B. (E & W = 1·00): 1957-65

Source: R.G.'s Stat. Revs. of England and Wales

- N. Region (Except Tyneside)
- Sunderland C.B.
- N. Region (Tyneside)
- England & Wales = 1·00

Diagram 2.E

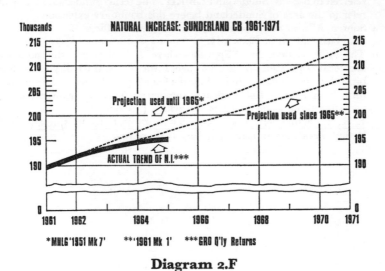

Thousands   **NATURAL INCREASE: SUNDERLAND CB 1961-1971**

Projection used until 1965*

Projection used since 1965**

ACTUAL TREND OF N.I.***

*MHLG '1951 Mk 7'   **'1961 Mk 1'   ***GRO Q'ly Returns

Diagram 2.F

43

for as the social structure geared to predominantly male employment is weakened, fertility becomes assimilated to the national pattern instead of reflecting the general rising trend. Thus the policy of introducing new industry into the town in order to reduce net outward migration has itself had the effect of reducing population through the birth-rate. The fertility figure, too, is therefore likely on available evidence to be an over-estimate rather than an under-estimate. The resulting trend of natural increase (the excess of births over deaths), and its relation to official estimates of the natural increase are shown in Diagram 2.F.

NOTES TO CHAPTER 2

1 *The North-East, A Programme* (the Hailsham Report), Cmnd. 2206, HMSO 1963, paras. 9, 13.
2 Considerably in excess of 2,000, because the calculation which gives the figure has ignored live children under the age of 10 who have migrated with their parents.
3 Sunderland CB and Sunderland RD were amalgamated in April 1967 to form the new Sunderland CB. The new enlarged county borough is referred to here as 'Sunderland CB/RD'. The term 'Sunderland CB' will refer to the area of Sunderland before this boundary extension.
4 Source: Ministry of Labour Northern Regional Office.
5 Standard Industrial Class VII.
6 The $\mathrm{ACF} = \Sigma FP \times \Sigma p \div \Sigma Fp \times \Sigma P$—where P and p are the national and local populations by sex and age, F the national fertility rates (live births by age of mother divided by the female population of the age concerned) and sigma sign indicates summation over all sex-age groups, including those (such as males) for which F is zero.
J. R. L. Schneider, 'Local Population Projections in England and Wales', *Population Studies*, X, 1, July 1956, p. 105.

Table 2.1

The Official MHLG Projection to 1971 and 1981*

Sex	Age	Projection to mid-1971	Projection to mid-1981
Persons	0–4	21,100	22,200
Persons	5–9	19,000	21,900
Persons	10–14	17,900	21,000
Males	15–44	41,100	46,600
Males	45–64	21,200	23,100
Males	65+	8,500	9,900
Females	15–44	41,500	46,700
Females	45–59	17,500	18,200
Females	60+	19,700	21,800
Persons	All ages	207,400	231,300

Source: MHLG
* New Series [1961 Base] Mark One
Sunderland CB pre-April 1967 boundaries

Table 2.2

The Semi Official Projection of the LPA

Projection to 1971: MHLG's population projection to 1971 minus five-sixths number of migrants from Sunderland 1951–61: 199,400

Projection to 1981: MHLG's population projection to 1981 minus ten-sixths of the number of migrants from Sunderland 1951–61: 215,300

Source: Sunderland LPA

Table 2.3

Net Migration of Males by Age: Sunderland CB 1951–61

Age of cohort mid-1951	Age of cohort mid-1961	Number in cohort mid-1951	Calculated deaths 1951–61	Actual number in cohort in 1961	Calculated net migration in 1951–61
Born 1956–61 0–4					
Born 1951–56 5–9					
0–4	10–14	9,237	54	8,611	− 572
5–9	15–19	7,180	45	6,534	− 601
10–14	20–24	7,153	55	5,896	−1,202
15–19	25–29	6,215	75	6,326	+ 186
20–24	30–34	6,185	92	6,606	+ 513
25–29	35–39	6,959	129	6,714	− 116
30–34	40–44	5,912	190	5,662	− 100
35–39	45–49	6,045	245	5,734	− 66
40–44	50–54	6,036	359	5,498	− 179
45–49	55–59	5,738	620	4,970	− 148
50–54	60–64	5,042	980	4,074	+ 12
55–59	65–69	3,995	1,250	2,910	+ 165
60–64	70–74	3,525	1,380	2,180	+ 35
65–69	75–79	2,791	1,393	1,299	− 99
70–74	80–84	2,250	1,279	745	− 226
75–79	85–89	1,441	1,028	265	− 148
80–84	90–94	684	726	35	+ 77

Source: Census and special calculations

Table 2.4

Net Migration of Females by Age: Sunderland CB 1951–61

Age of cohort mid-1951	Age of cohort mid-1961	Number in cohort in 1951	Calculated deaths 1951–61	Actual number in cohort in 1961	Calculated net migration in 1951–61
Born 1956–61 0–4					
Born 1951–56 5–9					
0–4	10–14	8,848	29	8,437	− 382
5–9	15–19	7,075	35	6,800	− 240
10–14	20–24	7,119	41	6,473	− 605
15–19	25–29	7,387	48	6,375	− 964
20–24	30–34	7,346	75	6,370	− 901
25–29	35–39	7,239	98	6,576	− 565
30–34	40–44	6,363	120	5,999	− 244
35–39	45–49	6,382	186	5,943	− 253
40–44	50–54	6,256	262	5,780	− 214
45–49	55–59	6,279	351	5,718	− 210
50–54	60–64	5,798	540	5,057	− 201
55–59	65–69	5,010	782	4,234	+ 6
60–64	70–74	4,454	1,084	3,312	− 58
65–69	75–79	3,784	1,327	2,320	− 137
70–74	80–84	2,879	1,439	1,247	− 193
75–79	85–89	1,812	1,345	450	− 17
80–84	90–94	1,105	922	92	− 91

Source: Census and special calculations

Table 2.5

The Official MHLG/LPA Projection Amended to Take Account of Age-Specific Migration to 1971

Sex	Age mid-1971	MHLG Projection for 1971	Migration 1961–71 at 1951–61 numbers	Five-sixths of 1951–61 numbers	Population mid-1971
Persons	0–4	21,090			
Persons	5–9	19,027			
Persons	10–14	17,901	− 954	− 795	17,100
Males	15–44	41,063	−1,320	−1,100	40,000
Males	45–64	21,167	− 381	− 317	20,900
Males	65+	8,506	− 196	− 163	8,300
Females	15–44	41,498	−3,519	−2,932	38,600
Females	45–59	17,501	− 677	− 564	16,900
Females	60+	19,652	− 691	− 576	19,100

Source: Special calculations

Table 2.6

Population 1971 Taking into Account Age-Specific Migration and 'Migrants in the Womb': Sunderland CB

Sex	Age in 1971	MHLG projection to 1971	Migration 1951–61	Five-sixths Migration 1951–61	'Migration in the womb'	Population mid-1971
Persons	0–4	21,100			−1,100	20,000
Persons	5–9	19,000			− 400	18,700
Persons	10–14	17,900	−1,000	− 800		17,100
Males	15–44	41,100	−1,300	−1,100		40,000
Males	45–64	21,200	− 400	− 300		20,900
Males	65+	8,500	− 200	− 200		8,300
Females	15–44	41,500	−3,500	−2,900		38,600
Females	45–59	17,500	− 700	− 600		16,900
Females	60+	19,700	− 700	− 600		19,100
Persons	All ages	207,400		− 6,400	−1,400*	199,500

Source: Special calculations

* Where figures in tables are rounded, a rounded total may not correspond exactly with the sum of the rounded items. In this case, for example, the actual numbers are 1,078 + 355 = 1,433.

Table 2.7

Net Migration 1961–81 of Males: Sunderland CB

Age of cohort in 1961	Age of cohort in 1971	Migration 1961–71 five-sixths of:—	Age of cohort in 1981	Migration 1971–81 five-sixths of:—	Calculated migration 1961–81 five-sixths of:—
	Born 1976–81		0–4		
	Born 1971–6		5–9		
Born 1966–71	0–4		10–14		
Born 1961–66	5–9		15–19	− 601	− 601
0–4	10–14	− 572	20–24	−1,202	−1,774
5–9	15–19	− 601	25–29	+ 186	− 415
10–14	20–24	−1,202	30–34	+ 513	− 689
15–19	25–29	+ 186	35–39	− 116	+ 70
20–24	30–34	+ 513	40–44	− 100	+ 413
25–29	35–39	− 116	45–49	− 66	− 182
30–34	40–44	− 100	50–54	− 179	− 279
35–39	45–49	− 66	55–59	− 148	− 214
40–44	50–54	− 179	60–64	+ 12	− 167
45–49	55–59	− 148	65–69	+ 165	+ 17
50–54	60–64	+ 12	70–74	+ 35	+ 47
55–59	65–69	+ 165	75–79	− 99	+ 66
60–64	70–74	+ 35	80–84	− 226	− 191
65–69	75–79	− 99	85–89	− 148	− 247
70–74	80–84	− 226	90–94	+ 77	− 149
75–79	85–89	− 148			
80–84	90–94	+ 77			

Source: Special calculations

Table 2.8

Net Migration 1961–81 of Females: Sunderland CB

Age of cohort in 1961	Age of cohort in 1971	Migration 1961–71 five-sixths of:—	Age of cohort in 1981	Migration 1971–81 five-sixths of:—	Calculated migration 1961–81 five-sixths of:—
	Born 1976–81		0–4		
	Born 1971–76		5–9		
Born 1966–71	0–4		10–14		
Born 1961–66	5–9		15–19	− 240	− 240
0–4	10–14	− 382	20–24	− 605	− 987
5–9	15–19	− 240	25–29	− 964	−1,204
10–14	20–24	− 605	30–34	− 901	−1,506
15–19	25–29	− 964	35–39	− 565	−1,529
20–24	30–34	− 901	40–44	− 244	−1,145
25–29	35–39	− 565	45–49	− 253	− 818
30–34	40–44	− 244	50–54	− 214	− 458
35–39	45–49	− 253	55–59	− 210	− 463
40–44	50–54	− 214	60–64	− 201	− 415
45–49	55–59	− 210	65–69	+ 6	− 204
50–54	60–64	− 201	70–74	− 58	− 259
55–59	65–69	+ 6	75–79	− 137	− 131
60–64	70–74	− 58	80–84	− 193	− 251
65–69	75–79	− 137	85–89	− 17	− 154
70–74	80–84	− 193	90–94	− 91	− 284
75–79	85–89	− 17			
80–84	90–94	− 91			

Source: Special calculations

Table 2.9

Population 1981 Taking into Account Age-Specific Migration and 'Migrants in the Womb': Sunderland CB

Sex	Age	MHLG Projection to 1981	Calculated migration 1961–81	'Migrants in the Womb'	Calculated population 1981
Persons	0–4	22,200		−2,700	19,500
Persons	5–9	21,900		−1,800	20,100
Persons	10–14	21,000		−1,100	19,900
Males	15–44	46,600	−2,500	− 200	43,900
Males	45–64	23,100	− 700		22,400
Males	65+	9,900	− 400		9,500
Females	15–44	46,700	−5,500	− 200	41,000
Females	45–59	18,200	−1,400		16,700
Females	60+	21,800	−1,400		20,400
Persons	All ages	231,300	−12,000	−6,000	213,000

Source: Special calculations

Table 2.10

Annual Net Migration: Sunderland CB/RD 1951–61 and 1961–65

Mid-year to mid-year	Sunderland CB	Sunderland CB/RD
1961–62	− 761	− 546
1962–63	−1,763	−1,648
1963–64	−2,471	−2,356
1964–65	−2,667	−2,552
Annual average 1961–65	−1,915	−1,800
Annual average 1951–61	− 960	− 882

Source: *Registrar General's Quarterly Return for the Quarter ended 31st March,* for years 1961–65 and Census 1961

Table 2.11

Insured Population: Sunderland CB 1951–65

Date	Insured Males	Insured Females
1951	54,700	26,600
1952	53,500	26,600
1953	53,700	26,800
1954	54,600	26,900
1955	53,600	27,200
1956	55,100	27,900
1957	55,300	28,500
1958	56,000	29,200
1959	56,500	29,000
1960	57,300	28,900
1961	56,800	30,400
1962	57,800	29,900
1963	55,600	31,900
1964	54,600	32,300
1965	55,200	34,300

Source: Ministry of Labour Northern Regional Office

Table 2.12

Unemployment: Sunderland CB 1953–67

Date	Unemployed on Live Register	Date	Insured population (Employed and unemployed)	Percentage unemployed
1953	4,235	mid-1951	81,364	5·2
1954	4,480	mid-1952	80,064	5·6
1955	4,307	mid-1953	80,530	5·3
1956	2,494	mid-1954	81,518	3·1
1957	2,562	mid-1955	80,802	3·2
1958	2,558	mid-1956	82,954	3·1
1959	4,793	mid-1957	83,839	5·7
1960	6,075	mid-1958	85,211	7·1
1961	4,788	mid-1959	85,460	5·6
1962	4,388	mid-1960	86,145	5·1
1963	8,592	mid-1961	87,212	9·9
1964	6,051	mid-1962	87,750	6·9
1965	4,019	mid-1963	87,484	4·6
1966	3,053	mid-1964	86,949	3·5
1967	4,377	mid-1965	89,481	5·2

Source: *Northern Region Monthly Digest of Statistics*, for January of each year, Ministry of Labour Northern Regional Office

Table 2.13

Population Growth: Sunderland CB/RD 1801–1961

Date	Persons	Date	Persons
1801	26,565	1881	139,848
1811	27,657	1891	158,418
1821	33,895	1901	182,074
1831	43,145	1911	195,008
1841	56,211	1921	205,569
1851	70,568	1931	209,992
1861	87,920	1951	206,601
1871	113,260	1961	217,921

Source: Successive Censuses

Table 2.14

Shipyard Orders Reported During the Week Ended 5 September 1967

Country	Yard	Orders (Tons deadweight)
JAPAN	Kawasaki	215,000
	Ishikawajima Harima	210,000
		210,000
	Mitsubishi	210,000
	Mitsui	210,000
	Nippon Kokan	130,000
		130,000
		23,000
		23,000
	Uraga	22,000
		22,000
	TOTAL JAPAN	1,405,000
UNITED KINGDOM	Cammell Laird	9,000
	TOTAL UNITED KINGDOM	9,000

Source: *Lloyd's List and Shipping Gazette*

Table 2.15

Population of Sunderland CB in 1971 on Assumption of One-and-a-half 1951–61 Migration Numbers

Sex	Age in 1971	MHLG's population projection to 1971	Calculated migration 1961–71	'Migrants in the womb'	Calculated Population in 1971
Persons	0–4	21,100		−1,900	19,100
Persons	5–9	19,000		− 600	18,400
Persons	10–14	17,900	−1,400		16,500
Males	15–44	41,100	−2,000		39,100
Males	45–64	21,200	− 600		20,600
Males	65+	8,500	− 300		8,200
Females	15–44	41,500	−5,300		36,200
Females	45–59	17,500	−1,000		16,500
Females	60+	19,700	−1,000		18,600
Persons	All ages	207,400	−11,600	−2,600	193,200

Source: Special calculations

Table 2.16

Population of Sunderland CB in 1981 on Assumption of One-and-a-half 1951–61 Migration Numbers

Sex	Age	MHLG's population projection to 1981	Calculated migration 1961–81	'Migrants in the womb'	Calculated population 1981
Persons	0–4	22,200		− 4,700	17,600
Persons	5–9	21,900		− 3,200	18,700
Persons	10–14	21,000		− 1,900	19,000
Males	15–44	46,600	− 4,500	− 300	41,700
Males	45–64	23,100	− 1,300		21,800
Males	65+	9,900	− 700		9,200
Females	15–44	46,700	− 9,900	− 300	36,500
Females	45–59	18,200	− 2,600		15,600
Females	60+	21,800	− 2,500		19,300
Persons	All ages	231,300	−21,500	−10,400	199,400

Source: Special calculations

Table 2.17

Ratio of Local Adjusted Birth-Rate of Sunderland CB and Sunderland RD to National Rate

Date	Sunderland CB	Sunderland RD
1956	1·23	1·23
1957	1·26	1·29
1958	1·21	1·18
1959	1·16	1·16
1960	1·13	1·16
1961	1·09	0·99
1962	1·05	1·06
1963	1·03	0·96
1964	0·99	1·03
1965	0·96	0·95

Source: *Registrar General's Statistical Reviews of England and Wales*, Table E, for the years shown

57

CHAPTER 3

THE WEAKNESSES OF POPULATION FORECASTS

National Projections

Population projections refer to five, ten, fifteen or even more years into the future. They depend upon variables which change unpredictably and independently of each other. The inherent difficulties of a figure of future population which can give guidance to present decisions can be seen most convincingly by looking at variations in estimates of national population where, as compared with local projections, forecasting is simple.

The best-known set of population estimates were those of the Royal Commission on Population, which reported in 1949. No study before or since has had the resources to examine the problem as thoroughly, or marshalled so distinguished a team of demographers. The Royal Commission was appointed against a background of concern throughout the 1930s with falling population numbers (in contrast to the concern with the rising population trends in the 1960s).

Each of the factors which determine population trends is a variable, so that the number of possible projections is very large indeed. The Statistical Committee considered in detail only two mortality assumptions, and five each for marriage, family-size and net migration—giving a total of 250 possible combinations. From these, sixteen were chosen. The highest gave Great Britain's population by 2002 as 55·5 million and the lowest a population of 40·9 million. (Table 3.1.) The Report itself narrowed its examination to three projections, the assumptions of which differed only with regard to the size of the completed

58

family. Series 'A' shows a gentle fall to 50 million by 1977 and 49 million by 2007, Series 'B' a gentle rise to 52 million by 2007 and Series 'C' a substantial fall to 41 million by 2007. (Table 3.2.)

As is well known, recent forecasts by the Government Actuary's Department (published in the annual reviews of the Registrar General and the Registrar General for Scotland) have painted an entirely different picture of the future. In 1964, for example, the population estimated for 1980 was 60 million. (Table 3.3.)

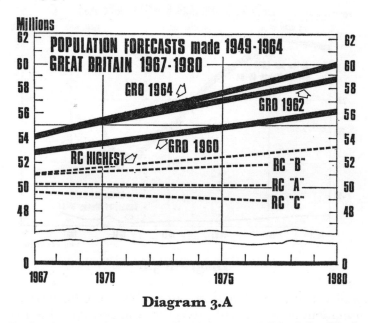

Diagram 3.A

Projections to about 1971 have been published for England and Wales annually since the review of the year 1955, and for Scotland since the review of the year 1959. The estimate of the population of England and Wales by 1971 has varied from 47·4 million to 50·3 million. This 2·9 million difference is equivalent to 6 per cent of the 1964 population. (Table 3.4.) The estimate of the population by 1981 has varied from 46·7 million to 54·5 million—a difference equivalent to 17 per cent of the 1964 population of England and Wales. (Table 3.5.) The difference between the highest and lowest estimates for 1991 is equivalent

59

to 19 per cent of the 1964 population, and the difference between the highest and lowest projections for the year 2001 is equivalent to 30 per cent of the 1964 population. (Diagram 3.A.)

In attempting to assess the reliability and usefulness of local population projections, three points can be made about these figures. The first is that in spite of the large differences between successive Reviews of projections to a particular year, it appears to be thought that there is something rather certain about the

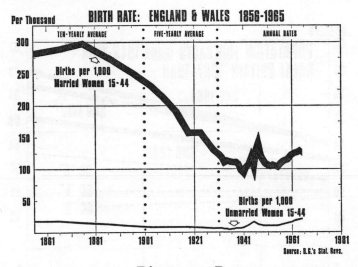

Diagram 3.B

newest calculation—that it is perceptibly more likely that the assumptions of the current projection will correspond to reality than the assumptions of previous projections. The second point of interest is that the method[1] of producing forecasts does not give sufficient weight to the advice of the Royal Commission on Population:

> It is clear that the size of the (completed) family will be decisive for the future number of births . . . there will almost certainly be considerable fluctuations from year to year in marriage rates and also in marital fertility rates. . . . A rapid decline in one decade may be succeeded by a rapid recovery in the next . . . even though the fundamental conditions may remain approximately constant.

60

There is a danger that opinion may be unduly impressed both by the declines and by the recoveries. The most thorough statistical analysis of the trend of the fundamental factors is necessary before attempting to assess the significance of the movement in the number of births.[2]

It is interesting to see that fertility, the fundamental variable for national projections whose rising trend has been the basis of the extrapolations which give such large increases in population, showed a downturn in 1965. (Table 3.6, Diagram 3.B.) The third point is that local population projections 'are a breakdown of the national projections of England and Wales',[3] and this means, in effect, that the shortcomings of the national projections are built into the projections for the local authority area.

The Projections for the Northern Region

The figures for the Northern Region bear directly on Sunderland as part of the region. In projecting the national population the main problem is changes in fertility. In regional projections fertility remains as large a problem as it is for the country, but migration now becomes a very serious problem also. (Even so it is not as serious as it is in forecasting Sunderland's population, for a policy to hasten or discourage migration is much more applicable to the region than to a particular county borough within it.) A study of the projections for the Northern Region demonstrates still further the extremely tentative nature of population forecasts. For it is not simply a matter of one authoritative source changing its estimate year by year; now several authoritative sources are in competition to have their own estimate accepted as the accurate one.

The migration assumption of the Hailsham report has been discussed above. Since 1963 other migration assumptions have appeared. In 1965 for example, the National Plan[4] in so far as it related to the Northern Region, assumed the net annual losses shown in Table 3.7. To these migrants are added 52,000 'migrants-in-the-womb'—a total loss of 212,000 in the period 1964–81. The Northern Economic Planning Council (NEPC) assumes, by contrast, that the annual net loss to other places in the UK, 7,000 in 1964, will be reduced to 3,500 per annum by

61

1971 and gradually decline to zero by 1981. A final example is the Registrar General's projection[5] (Table 3.8) based on the latest revision of the national projections made by the Government Actuary's Department. The GRO 'takes into account' the views of the NEPC as expressed in *Challenge of the Changing North*,[6] but does not accept them, commenting drily:

> The views expressed by the NEPC implied a reduction in the net outflow from this region of 11,000 between 1962 and 1965 to zero by 1981.[7] This would represent a sharp change from the position of recent years; and it was not possible to incorporate the Council's suggestions fully.

The NEPC for its part rejected this projection of the GRO, which had been published in an earlier Quarterly Return, saying it did not take sufficient account of development policies.[8] All three projections accept the Government Actuary's fertility and mortality forecasts which would give a natural increase in the region of 195,000 by 1971 and 512,000 by 1981,[9] but only the figure of the GRO with it's particular migration assumptions is the 'official' estimate.[10]

The caution with which population estimates must be approached is especially great where local areas are concerned. The standard text for the methodology of local population estimates is G. R. L. Schneider's 'Local Population Projections in England and Wales', *Population Studies*, X, 1 July 1956,[11] whose first statement in this ten-year-old article is that all population estimates suffer from great disadvantages:

> Population projections are still made frequently, although it is now widely recognised that their predictive value for more than relatively few years ahead is generally low. . . .

Local population forecasts are especially limited in value. Data is much less plentiful than for the whole country. And information is scantiest and guesses at the future course of events most hazardous for migration, the element which, as he says, 'entirely dominates' the net change of local population from year to year.[12]

The Weaknesses of the Administrative Machinery

The problems connected with the rates of migration, fertility and mortality have been discussed above. It is clear that they are irremovable, for they depend upon prescience of future events. To these unavoidable hazards, however, other difficulties are added. They relate not to the opaque future, but to tardiness in incorporating existing and easily accessible data into the calculations.

Estimates of Sunderland's population are revised as new data about national and local fertility and mortality rates become available and are processed by the Government Actuary's Department. But they depend crucially also upon the application of these age-specific and sex-specific rates to the actual age and sex composition of the town. The best source of this information is the Census. Unfortunately there is a Census only once every ten years (there was an additional sample Census for the first time in 1966).

Projections in their present form were first issued in 1956 to meet the needs of LPAs in carrying out the first revision of their statutory development plans. They were based on the age-sex structure of LPA areas in 1951 and they took into account migration up to 1954. Subsequent migration loss, 'which plays the major part in the changes of local population size', was expected to be handled by the LPAs, 'those best qualified to deal with it', because they could bring more local knowledge to bear on the problem.[13] There followed a series of different estimates referred to as 'Mark 1', 'Mark 2', and so forth. Mark 7, using the 1962 mid-year estimate, gave a population in 1971 of 213,800–3,700 more than the 1956 projection–and the 1981 population as 245,000. (Diagram 2.F, p. 43.)

Mark 7 was the official estimate until well into 1965. Yet technically there would have been no difficulty for even the layman, using the data on current fertility and mortality trends and making certain assumptions about migration not inferior to those used by the LPA, to have brought Mark 7 up to date, for the 1961 Census volume for Durham County was published in 1963. The 1961 age-sex population of Sunderland was generally available to the public from that date.

Two years after the 1961 Census, the 1951-based Mark 7 played an important part in the decision to build a new township at Silksworth for a population of 20,000. The decision to build Washington New Town was also affected, for it was argued in 1963 on the basis of Mark 7 that Sunderland would have an overspill population for the new town of either 15,000 or 18,000. What is most striking, however, is that the decision to incorporate Sunderland RD into an enlarged county borough, the public enquiry into which was held in January 1965, more than a year after the Census results were published, was also taken on the basis of Mark 7.[14] It was not until March 1965 that the Northern Regional office of the MHLG received a projection based on the 1961 age-sex structure of Sunderland–the LPA itself received them somewhat later (New Series Mark 1).

The difference between Mark 7 and the New Series Mark 1 estimates of Sunderland's population in 1971 and 1981 is shown in Table 3.9. In place of a population of 214,000 in 1971 the new estimate gives a population of 207,000 and in place of a population of 245,000 by 1981 the new estimate gives a population of 231,000. As compared with Mark 7, therefore, the New Series Mark 1 gives a population in 1981 lower by an amount equivalent to 69 per cent of the population of Silksworth New Township. It is equivalent to 76 per cent of the high estimate on the Mark 7 basis of Sunderland's contribution in overspill to the New Town of Washington, and to no less than 91 per cent of the alternative low estimate.

No particular department or organisation is to blame for this. The LPA must wait upon the MHLG, the MHLG depend upon the GRO. A typical MHLG letter reads:

> As a result of the publication of the national projections and the publicity which has been given to the stepping-up of the projections . . . local planning authorities are aware that the earlier projections are inadequate. We have tried to fend off these demands . . . but we cannot go on doing this for long without incurring severe criticism from them as in some cases the new projections involve a stepping-up of twenty or more per cent.

Another MHLG letter reads:

> We take the view that . . . projections are particularly susceptible to error for individual local authority areas . . . and it seems better to call a halt to this work and await the new projections for local authority areas which the GRO will provide about the middle of next year.

The limited value of the population projection as a basis for decision-making is further illustrated by the fact that other government agencies produce population figures of their own. The Department of Economic Affairs (DEA), for example, in its revision of the national plan projections arrived at a figure of 198,000 as the population of Sunderland by 1971. This is not a calculation carried out on the data for Sunderland. It is a split of the regional total, projecting forward to 1971 the rate of the local authority's growth between 1951 and 1964, as a proportion of the region's population. Thus, if a particular local authority area had 5·0 per cent of the region's population in 1951, and 5·13 per cent thirteen years later in 1964, an increase of 0·01 per cent would be projected forward–giving 5·2 per cent growth by 1971. The Regional Demographic Unit of the GRO in Appendix B of the DEA document which dealt with these figures, comments:

> These sub-divisions are extremely rough guides. The GRO is engaged in a more thorough assessment of population statistics in counties and county boroughs. That set of projections cannot, however, be completed for several months.

Other similar cases are easy to find. The Washington New Town Working Party, in its population projection for Sunderland, assumed migration at the 1957–61 rate. Nathaniel Litchfield and Associates predicted a population of 184,000 for its zones 65, 67 and 68 (roughly Sunderland CB) by 1981.[15] The HMSO publication *Health and Welfare*[16] forecast the population of Sunderland County Borough to 1972, using a straightforward extrapolation of the 1951–61 total change in the population of the area. Neighbouring authorities calculate population projections for Sunderland in connection with their own policies. The Durham County Planning office projection made in December 1958, for example, estimated that the population of Sunderland CB by 1971 would be 177,000.

In this quandary the MHLG must step in and say which figures can be taken as the basis of decisions which lie within its jurisdiction. Of Cmnd. 1973 it is noted that 'The GRO has already told certain planning authorities to disregard Cmnd. 1973 in favour of this Department's figures', and the Durham County Planning Office projection 'as calculated by the Durham County Planning Office and amended by the B.o.T., the M.o.L. and the MHLG' is rather curtly dismissed as 'subject to a considerable margin of error. Government departments cannot be taken as committed in any way to these figures'.

NOTES TO CHAPTER 3

1 'Projecting the Population of the United Kingdom', *Economic Trends*, 139, May 1965; and the *Registrar General's Statistical Review of England and Wales*, for various years, Table A 5.
2 Royal Commission on Population, *Report*, Cmd. 7695, HMSO 1949, p. 83. (Emphasis added.)
3 Explanatory letter from the General Register Office.
4 *The National Plan*, Cmnd. 2764, HMSO 1965, Appendix A; and 'The Age Structure and Regional Distribution of the U.K. Population 1964 to 1981', *Economic Trends*, HMSO 145, November 1965.
5 General Register Office, 'Revised Projections of the Regional Distribution of the UK Population in 1971 and 1981', *Economic Trends*, 157, HMSO November 1966.
6 NEPC, *Challenge of the Changing North: A Preliminary Study*, HMSO 1966, Chap. I, Pt. I.
7 The NEPC in fact said that the reduction would be from 11,000 to 4,000 total net migrants, i.e. from 7,000 to zero net emigrants to other parts of the UK.
8 NEPC, *op. cit.* Appendix A.
9 GRO, *Quarterly Return for the Quarter Ending 31st March 1966*.
10 See e.g. *Hansard*, No. 730, 30 June–6 July 1967, Col. 1961.
11 See also 'Projecting the Population of the United Kingdom', *op. cit.*; and United Nations, Department of Economic and Social Affairs, Manuals on Methods of Estimating Population: *Manual III Methods for Population Projections by Sex and Age*, New York 1956.
12 *Op. cit.*, pp. 95, 96.
13 G. R. L. Schneider, *op. cit.*, p. 113.
14 Local Government Commission for England, North-Eastern General Review Area, Evidence of the Town Planning Officer, at the public enquiry held in Sunderland, January 1965.
15 Davies Weeks and Partners, *Washington New Town Master Plan and Report*, December 1966.
16 Cmnd. 1973, HMSO 1963.

Table 3.1
Estimated Population of Great Britain (millions) Royal Commission on Population (1949) Statistical Committee

Date	Highest Projection of Sixteen	Lowest Projection of Sixteen
By 1972	52·0	47·4
By 1982	53·5	45·7
By 1992	54·5	43·3
By 2002	55·5	40·9

Source: *Papers of the Royal Commission on Population*,
Volume II, HMSO 1950

Table 3.2
Estimated Population of Great Britain (millions) Royal Commission Report

Date	Series A	Series B	Series C
By 1977	50·2	51·8	48·6
By 2007	48·9	52·3	41·5

Source: *Royal Commission on Population, Report*,
Cmd. 7695, HMSO 1949, Table 38, 84

Table 3.3
Population of Great Britain (millions) Estimated for the Registrar General and the Registrar General for Scotland

Date	Year when estimate made: 1960	1962	1964
By 1970	53·4	56·0	55·7
By 1980	56·1	59·8	60·2

Source: *Registrar General's Statistical Review of England
and Wales* and *Annual Report of the Registrar General for
Scotland*—for years shown

Table 3.4
Population Estimates for England and Wales for the year 1971 or thereabouts (millions)

Year from which projection is made	Estimated population in 1971 (actual year in brackets)
1957	47·5 (1972)
1958	48·1 (1973)
1959	47·4 (1969)
1960	48·0 (1970)
1961	49·3 (1971)
1962	50·5 (1972)
1963	49·7 (1970)
1964	50·3 (1971)
1965	50·1 (1971)

Source: *Registrar General's Statistical Reviews* for the years 1956–64; *Economic Trends*, 157, November 1966; and *Registrar General's Quarterly Return for the Quarter ending 31st March 1966*

Table 3.5
Population Estimates for England and Wales for the year 1981 or thereabouts (millions)

Year from which projection is made	Estimated population in 1981 (actual year in brackets)
1955	46·7 (1985)
1956	48·2 (1986)
1957	48·3 (1977)
1958	49·0 (1978)
1959	49·2 (1979)
1960	50·4 (1980)
1961	52·1 (1981)
1962	54·1 (1982)
1963	53·4 (1980)
1964	54·5 (1981)
1965	54·2 (1981)

Source: *Registrar General's Statistical Reviews* for the years 1955–64 and General Register Office *Quarterly Return for the Quarter ending 31st March 1966*

Table 3.6

Births per 1,000 Women ages 15–44: England and Wales
1851–1965

Date	Per 1,000 married women age 15–44	Per 1,000 unmarried women age 15–44	Date	Per 1,000 married women age 15–44	Per 1,000 unmarried women age 15–44
1851–61	281·0	18·3	1946	128·7	13·8
1861–70	287·3	18·2	1947	139·7	12·4
1871–80	295·5	15·1	1948	121·7	11·4
1881–90	274·6	12·6	1949	114·4	10·4
1891–1900	250·3	9·6	1950	108·6	10·2
1901–05	230·5	8·4	1951	105·4	9·8
1906–10	212·9	8·1	1952	104·5	10·0
1911–15	190·7	7·9	1953	106·3	10·2
1916–1920	157·0	8·4	1954	104·8	10·2
1921–25	156·7	6·7	1955	103·7	10·3
1926–30	130·9	6·0	1956	108·2	11·4
1931	122·7	5·7	1957	111·5	12·1
1932	118·2	5·6	1958	113·9	12·8
1933	110·9	5·3	1959	114·7	13·5
1934	112·9	5·5	1960	119·2	15·1
1935	111·5	5·4	Old Series:		
1936	110·9	5·3	1961	123·2	16·5
1937	110·2	5·4	1962	125·9	18·2
1938	110·0	5·8	1963	126·5	19·0
1939	107·0	5·7	1964	128·4	20·2
1940	98·8	5·9	New Series:		
1941	94·1	7·4	1961	124·9	16·2
1942	103·8	9·0	1962	126·9	17·9
1943	107·6	10·9	1963	127·5	18·7
1944	107·4	13·8	1964	129·3	19·9
1945	103·9	16·1	1965	125·7	21·2

Source: *The Registrar General's Statistical Review of England and Wales for the Year 1964, Part II, Population*, HMSO 1966

Table 3.7

National Plan Migration Assumptions

Period	Net Annual Loss to other places in the UK	To places outside the UK
1959–64	7,000	4,000
1964–71	7,000	3,000
1971–81	7,000	2,000

Source: *The National Plan*, Cmnd. 2764, HMSO 1965

Table 3.8

General Register Office's Migration Assumptions

Period	Net Annual Loss to other places in the UK	To places outside the UK
1962–65	7,000	4,000
1965–71	4,000	4,000
1971–81	3,000	4,000

Source: *Economic Trends*, 157, November 1966

Table 3.9

Mark Seven and New Series Mark One Projection to 1971 and 1981: Sunderland CB

	Projection to 1971	Projection to 1981
Mark Seven	213,800	245,000
New Series Mark One	207,400	231,300
Difference	6,400	13,700

Source: MHLG

CHAPTER 4

POPULATION ESTIMATES AND PROFESSIONAL INTERESTS

So far the investigation has been straightforwardly demographic. It has been merely a matter of placing on one side the relevant facts, and on the other the figures which have official approval. The lesson is self-evident. It is necessary and reassuring for administrators to operate with information which is clear-cut and reliable, and which requires minimal interpretation. There is an ancient urge to discover a means of foretelling the future, a means which could then become the instrument of far-sighted practical politics. But it remains the pursuit of an *ignis fatuus*. The decision-maker who asks that a succession of new, single, reliable figures of population at a given future date should replace each erroneous prophecy is like the man who (to use Tawney's simile) when he finds that his shoddy boots wear badly, orders a pair two sizes larger, or who thinks it is satisfactory to make up for putting a bad sixpence in the plate one Sunday by putting in a bad shilling the next.[1]

What specifically is the sociological contribution to the task of relating population projections to Sunderland's housing needs? It is to elucidate more fully, and therefore to assist in controlling, the social factors which nourish the belief that, without extremely painstaking exegesis, the statement that 'the population of Sunderland will be 245,000 in 1981' is meaningful for housing policy.

Sunderland's official and semi-official projections are systematically biased in the direction of a much larger population than careful examination would allow. What is the explanation of

71

this? Clearly there are various reasons which relate merely to the realities of office existence. Local government officers as a body cannot be expected to make things difficult for themselves. They are handed down a single, simple set of figures which for the time being are settled. Which APT IV[2] would be so fool-hardy as to challenge the MHLG? The Ministry's figures have been calculated on the basis of future 'nil net migration', and to systematically work out the implications of migration is a task which is not only tedious but in the exact meaning of the word thankless also.

Were the numerous population possibilities of 1971 or 1981 to be admitted, the statutory obligations of town planners in particular would be revealed as resting on an extremely fluid and unstable foundation. The high population figure, therefore, is due partly to the every-day inertia and alienation of the ordinary office-worker–in this case, the town-planning official. On these grounds, if the MHLG figure was for some reason consistently low instead of consistently high, a consistently low future figure could be expected at the local authority level.

There are, however, more fundamental reasons for the high figures' uncritical acceptance. The first is the LPA's duty to indicate the pattern of land-use in the town for perhaps as many as twenty years ahead, together with the conspicuous commitment of the town planner to the long-term view. In land-use, clearly the 'fail safe' policy is over-allocation. If industrial land-use expands or is thought likely to expand by a given amount, then the function of the local authority's development plan is twofold. It must ensure that the additional industrial land in terms of the planning profession's criteria (as modified by local councillors and local planning officers) is favourably placed in relation to residential and other uses. Secondly, it must allocate land for associated uses such as access, car-parking, waste-disposal and, not least, housing. Similarly, if a given number of dwellings are to be built, then a calculated amount of land must be set aside for play-spaces, for civic, religious, recreational, educational and commercial purposes.

The development plan then shows whether any suggested change of land-use would distort the pattern of uses, distributed in the proportions and spatially related in the manner deemed appropriate by the local planning authority, and ideally guides the authority when it decides to allow or prohibit, or postpone as premature specific developments or changes of use. Land which in the event may not be required stores up fewer and less serious problems than would permitting development to take place on land which may prove to be essential for other purposes as a result of future changes.

Misjudgments take the form of under-use or complete sterilisation of land. Because a particular industrial enterprise might need to expand, cleared land may lie fallow and the run-down of housing in the neighbourhood may be allowed by a refusal of improvement grants or accelerated by the prospect of compulsory purchase and demolition. Householders have to improve their homes at their own expense in the knowledge that the industrial firm is backed by the local authority in claiming the land on which their homes stand for possible factory extensions.

In the same way, fewer problems are presented by over-providing rather than by under-providing land for possible housing developments, schools or parks. Expectations which indicate the need to preserve much land for dwellings in the future may result in the local housing authority (LHA) providing blocks of flats. In that case losses may be considerable for the tenants in human terms, and in financial terms to the local authority, in so far as tenants become increasingly difficult to find. So far as land-use planning is concerned, however, over-allocation for housing merely involves agricultural land on the outskirts of the town which in the meanwhile continues in productive use. Purely in terms of land-use planning the least risk policy means decisions which err on the side of generosity rather than niggardliness in land-use allocations. The planner who plays safe with his population figures leaves himself maximum flexibility in his strategy for other policies.[3]

The LPA has another reason for refraining from a critical examination of the assumptions and results of the projection which promises an increase in population. Unlike the first reason, which involves the relation between basic decision-making strategies and certain fundamental obligations placed upon the LPA by statute, this second reason is connected with the content of a specific regional policy.

Although at times (especially in the nineteen fifties) it has been

73

timidly applied, official policy ever since the nineteen thirties has aimed at stemming migration to the south of England. It was the recommendation of the reports which formed the background of wartime and early post-war thinking, and it has been the intention behind the Industrial Development Certificate system, and Development District and Development Area measures. From this point of view it is desirable that migration from Sunderland should be at a low level between now and 1981, and an estimate of the population which assumes the success of such regional policies harmonises with the wishes of the local planning authority. The population projection in this light is not so much a prophecy of what will happen, as a description of a state of affairs which the LPA hopes it will be able to bring about. It is not an unchangeable fact in the light of which it must formulate and adjust its policies. On the contrary it is itself an objective which must be reached by policies which it is the LPA's duty to devise.

More than this: to admit in public that Sunderland would have lost population by 1971 or 1981 would be to cut the ground from under the feet of those who are insisting on the survival of Sunderland as a thriving community and of the North-East as a vigorous region. Policies based on population decline and heavy net outward migration would have a serious adverse effect on the manoeuvres, the tactics and the strategies of those who hold in their hand the oriflamme of the region. ' "Stop Moaning" North East Is Told.'[4] Industrial developments, from this standpoint, are incomparably more important than statistical fastidiousness, and the population projection is quoted, amended or ignored to the extent that it can prove its utility to the town or region in negotiations with the central government or private industrialists.

To some extent the local housing authority also can accept the official population estimate as a desideratum rather than a datum. It is possible to argue that an improvement in the quality and number of dwellings will favourably affect the rate of net migration. The LHA shares other reasons with the LPA for its reluctance to question the value of the high estimate. No department has an interest in becoming smaller and less important, a consequence which would follow from evidence of declining population. A growing population, by contrast, means improved prospects of departmental growth, with the associated benefits of, for example, more rapid promotion.

Fundamentally, however, the meaning of the population estimate is quite different for the two functions of land-use planning and housing. The consequences of reserving too much land for specific uses may be expensive for the country and for individuals–but only in the sense that productive uses may be forgone and profitable enterprise stifled. Decisions about housing, however, involve expenditures not only by present consumers of housing, but also, because of the structure of interest, involve claims upon people perhaps sixty years into the future. The long life and limited alternative use of dwellings on, say, housing estates lead to additional penalties for mistaken decisions.

> Fifty-two flats that nobody wants have become a major problem for Sunderland Town Council. The flats have all stood empty for at least a month. They are in the first two 17-storey skyscraper blocks to be finished at Gilley Law, the £3,250,000 housing scheme on the southern edge of Sunderland. Three months ago the first tenants moved in, but already the area is known as 'Ghost Town'. The Housing Committee have resorted to unprecedented steps to fill the flats. 'Advertising for tenants is entirely against our principles, but it has been forced upon us.'[5]

For the land-use planner a population estimate which turns out to be extravagantly high constitutes no great problem. A too high estimate is much more damaging for the local housing authority. It may be desirable for the LHA to enquire whether the official population estimate is based upon the best evidence currently available, and to query the wisdom of tying its policies to so ramshackle a set of data. But the tradition of the LHA on the side of intelligence (in the sense of 'information gathering') is weak and the views of the planner tend therefore to predominate over those of the housing administrator.[6]

NOTES TO CHAPTER 4

1 R. H. Tawney, *The Acquisitive Society* (1920), Harvest Books, New York 1948, p. 5.
2 'Administrative, Professional and Technical, Grade IV'–a local

government officer of the rank likely to deal with population projections.

3 The chief planner at the MHLG, for example, in addressing the Royal Institute of British Architects in July 1967, forecast a population rise of six million for England and Wales by 1981: '*It is prudent* to treat this six million *as a minimum* if we are to make reasonable *provision of land* to meet housing needs.' (Emphasis added.)

4 *Sunderland Echo*, main headline, 10 July 1967, referring to a statement by the Chairman of the Northern Economic Planning Council.

5 'Modern "Ghost Town", Council flats that no one wants will now be offered to the public,' *The Journal* (Newcastle upon Tyne),12 June 1967. See also, *Sunderland Echo*, 28 June 1967 and 14 July 1967.

6 See Harold L. Wilensky, *Organizational Intelligence*, Basic Books 1967, for a general treatment of this theme.

CHAPTER 5

INDIVIDUALS AND THE HOUSEHOLD IN RELATION TO HOUSING DEMAND

It is the relation between the number of dwellings and the number of households rather than the relation between dwellings and individuals which is important for housing policy. Between 1921 and 1961 the population of Sunderland CB grew from 182,200 to 189,700, a four per cent increase. Sunderland CB/RD increased its population during the same period by slightly more than this, six per cent. A glance at the two maps (Diagram 5.A (i) and Diagram 5.A (ii)), however, shows that the expansion in its built-up area is proportionately far greater. The disparity is due partly to the development of low-density housing in peripheral council estates. It is due also to the organisation of each unit of population into more and more separate households. Between 1921 and 1961 there was a 39 per cent increase in households. This phenomenon has been evident since 1871. There were about 220 families for every thousand persons in 1871. There were about 310 families for every thousand persons by 1961. In housing terms this means a growth in need over the period of 90 dwellings per thousand population due to household fission alone. (Table 5.1.)

The first reason for this trend is the fact that parents have fewer children. Average household size in both Sunderland CB and Sunderland CB/RD has declined steadily from 4·8 in 1901 to 3·2 in 1961. The second reason is that the standard of living has risen. Individuals and families who previously would have needed to economise by sharing accommodation with another family can afford to rent or buy a separate dwelling.

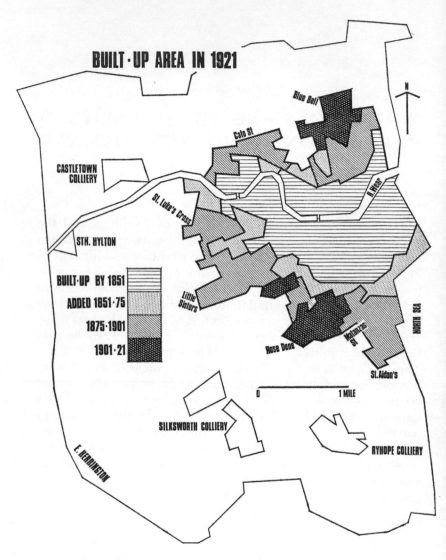

BUILT·UP AREA IN 1921

Blue Bell

Cato St

CASTLETOWN COLLIERY

St. Luke's Cross

STH. HYLTON

R. Wear

BUILT·UP BY 1851
ADDED 1851·75
1875·1901
1901·21

Little Sisters

Rose Dene

Matanzas St.

St. Aidan's

NORTH SEA

0   1 MILE

E. HERRINGTON

SILKSWORTH COLLIERY

RYHOPE COLLIERY

Diagram 5.A (i)

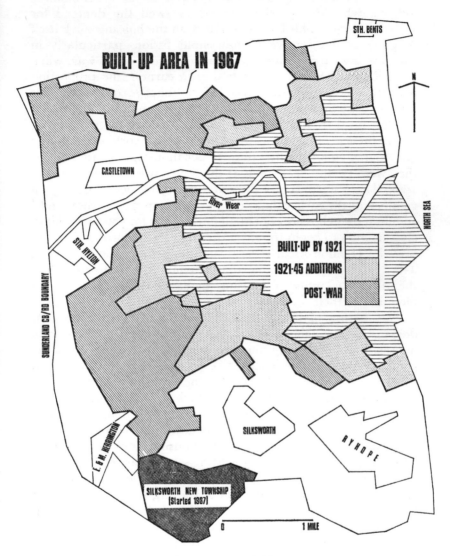

BUILT-UP AREA IN 1967

STH. BENTS

N

CASTLETOWN

River Wear

NORTH SEA

STH. HYLTON

SUNDERLAND CB/RD BOUNDARY

BUILT-UP BY 1921
1921-45 ADDITIONS
POST-WAR

SILKSWORTH

RYHOPE

E. & M. HERRINGTON

SILKSWORTH NEW TOWNSHIP
(Started 1967)

0   1 MILE

Diagram 5.A (ii)

Affluent families are reluctant to seek or to accommodate lodgers, who are therefore forced to swell the demand for separate homes. Thirdly, the increase in the housing stock itself is a powerful incentive to household fission, particularly in encouraging earlier marriages. Since the first world war, when councils first began to build houses in earnest, the proportion of bachelors getting married before the age of twenty has increased by four-and-a-half times in England and Wales as a whole, and there has been a tenfold increase in those marrying before the age of eighteen. Just after the first world war, among girls marrying for the first time 77 per thousand married before they were twenty years of age; the figure was 313 per 1,000 in 1965. There were six per thousand marrying before the age of eighteen at the earlier date; the figure is now 72 per thousand.[1] In Sunderland it is now not at all uncommon for young working-class couples to begin to rent a dwelling in the form of a flat in say, the Hendon area, several months before their marriage. The availability of housing, that is, enables them to constitute themselves as units of housing demand while they remain members of their own parental households.

The dictum of the economist that supply creates its own demand is particularly apt in this connection. On the side of household fission, young single people may increasingly seek the privacy and independence of a pied à terre in the town. Marriage at sixteen could become the norm in a society which continued to increase its housing stock to such an extent that dwellings would be available for young people living at present with their parents. On the side of the utilisation of more housing space a continuous increase in the housing stock could feed a demand for the conversion of existing semi-detached houses into detached residences, and for owners of a single terraced house to occupy the house next door also. Indeed, when the Registrar General projected forward the growth in household numbers since the Census of 1951, he was concerned primarily 'to allow for greater separation of family units *as a result of the post-censal expansion of the building programme*'.[2]

To become relevant to Sunderland's housing needs, therefore, the simple population figures for 1971 and 1981 must be converted to household units—'housing-demand units'. In housing policy the projection of household formation should indicate also, at the very least, the distribution of families by size and stage of development: the number of families composed of young couples, infants and school children, the number of families composed of older adults only, and so forth. The breakdown of the population in these terms will therefore also be discussed.

Age, Sex and Marital Condition

The methods used by the MHLG are those described in the November 1961 issue of *Population Studies*[3] by one of the former officers of the Ministry. They were evolved in consultation with the technical staff who were directly concerned with the assessment of housing requirements for development plans, and 'apart from some adjustments to take account of data derived from the 1961 Census, they still hold good'.[4] The MHLG projections are designed to show, not what the demand for housing actually will be at some future date, but to determine 'the number of units who would probably live in a separate dwelling *if financial obstacles and the housing shortage were eliminated*'.[5] The usefulness of the figure depends therefore upon the validity of these two remarkable pre-suppositions, that by 1971 and 1981 housing will be virtually free (financial obstacles would have been eliminated) and every family will have as much house-room as it wishes to consume (there will be no housing shortage).

Projections of household formation for Sunderland LPA have not been calculated by the MHLG. What are the results of applying its methods to the projected population of the town for 1971 and 1981? The first step in the calculation simplifies the age-sex-marriage structure. Twelve age-sex-marriage groups take the place of a complicated pattern formed from single-year and decennial age-groups and the marital statuses of married, single, widowed and divorced. The MHLG age-groups, however, are '15–44', 'Males 45–64', 'Females 45–59', 'Males 65 plus' and 'Females 60 plus'. These particular groups have no intrinsic advantages, they are used merely to match the breakdown of the Ministry's own projections for 1971 and 1981. They have the considerable disadvantage that an important stage in the calculation is to relate them to data from the 1951 Census where the age groups are 15–39, 40–59 and 60 plus for both

81

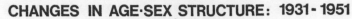

CHANGES IN AGE·SEX STRUCTURE: 1931-1951

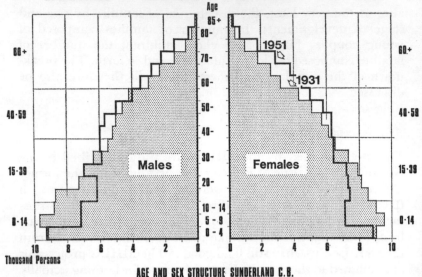

AGE AND SEX STRUCTURE SUNDERLAND C.B.

Diagram 5.B (i)

CHANGES IN AGE·SEX STRUCTURE: 1951-1961

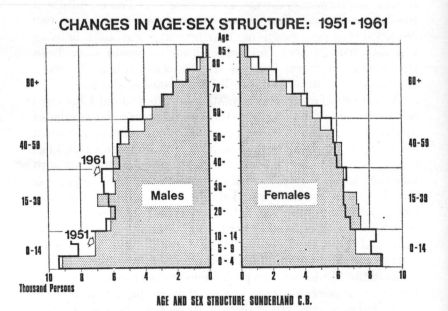

AGE AND SEX STRUCTURE SUNDERLAND C.B.

Diagram 5.B (ii)

sexes. As it is possible to derive, from the figures for Sunderland, age-groups which correspond to the 15–39, 40–59 and 60 plus breakdowns, the MHLG method will be modified to the extent that these will be preferred. (Table 5.2.)

The second step is to determine what the age and sex structure of Sunderland will be in 1971 and 1981. To the difficulties of forecasting the total population, that is, are added the difficulties of estimating how a given population will be divided into age-groups and between the sexes.

In order to stress that no one estimate of total population can be taken as a safe basis for policy, and in order to contribute an additional set of calculations to the list of possibilities, a new set of assumptions have been used to arrive at the total population of Sunderland for 1971 and 1981. Mortality rates have been assumed to be those of the Northern Region, and to decline over the whole period to 1981 and for all age-groups.[6] Net migration is assumed to run at half the percentage (not number as in previous calculations) which each five-year age cohort experienced in the ten years 1951–61. Fertility is assumed to remain at its 1963 level in the Northern Region (excluding Tyneside).[7] The population of Sunderland CB would be 200,400 in 1971 and 213,200 in 1981. (Table 5.3.) (Diagrams 5.B (i) and 5.B (ii) show the actual change in age-sex structure 1931–61, and Diagrams 5.B (iii) and 5.B (iv) show the pattern of change 1961–81 on the present assumptions.)

Marital status is the main determinant of household formation and the third step therefore is to estimate the numbers in each of the 1971 and 1981 age-groups who will be married, single, widowed and divorced in those years. Although there is a tendency in England and Wales as a whole towards still younger marriages and a higher proportion of the population ever marrying–from the present point of view more housing-demand units being formed–no such definite trend is discernible in the figures for Sunderland CB. In so far as a trend has been visible between 1946 and 1956, there has been a decline in the marriage rate from a normal 19 or 20 persons marrying per thousand home population each year to 15 or 16 (and in 1963 as few as 14) persons marrying per thousand home population. (Table 5.4.) It will therefore be assumed that there will be no change in the age-specific marriage rate for Sunderland CB

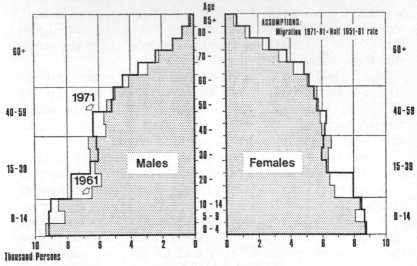

A POSSIBLE PATTERN OF CHANGE: 1961-1971

Age

ASSUMPTIONS:
Migration 1971-81 = Half 1951-61 rate

Males Females

AGE AND SEX STRUCTURE SUNDERLAND C. B.

Diagram 5.B (iii)

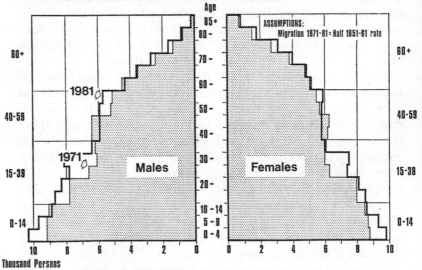

A POSSIBLE PATTERN OF CHANGE: 1971-1981

Age

ASSUMPTIONS:
Migration 1971-81 = Half 1951-61 rate

Males Females

AGE AND SEX STRUCTURE SUNDERLAND C. B.

Diagram 5.B (iv)

between 1961 and 1981. To the extent that marriage rates may be declining this assumption follows the usual pattern of these analyses and overestimates rather than underestimates housing demand in 1971 and 1981. The various marital-condition rates for age-sex groups are shown in Table 5.5.

An age-sex-marital status table can now be derived by applying these marital-condition factors (MCFs) to the age-sex groups of Sunderland's population in 1971 and 1981. (Table 5.6 and Table 5.7.)

Household Formation

The fourth step is to calculate how many households—i.e. how many housing-demand units—will be formed from populations so constituted. The only guidance on this point is provided by Table Fifteen of the County volumes of the 1951 Census. This shows how many separate households were formed in 1951 from each of the twelve age-sex-marital status groups. The ratio between the number of heads of households in each age-sex-marital condition (A/S/MC) group is its household formation factor (HFF). (Table 5.8.)

If the 1951 HFFs had been applicable in 1961, Sunderland's population of 189,700 would have formed itself into 56,400 households. (Table 5.9.) Actually there were 58,600 households. Fission between 1951 and 1961 therefore created 2,200 households additional to those which would have been created if the HFFs of 1951 still obtained.

Unfortunately the 1961 Census did not follow the Census of 1951 in producing HFF figures and there is no direct evidence on the distribution of these extra households between the age-sex-marital condition groups. If it is assumed that all groups experienced the same rate of fission, the pattern of households in Sunderland CB in 1961 would have been as shown in Table 5.10.

Each household, the head of which is below the age of forty, may be regarded as likely to add to its numbers—by births in the case of married heads, by marriage in the case of the single, widowed and divorced. These are the 'expanding households'. The households where the heads are married but between the ages of 40 and 59 are the 'declining households'; the children are growing up, marrying and leaving to form households of their own. All other households may be regarded as 'stationary'. In 1961, therefore, among Sunderland's 58,600 households there were 16,800 expanding households, 19,800 declining households and 22,000 stationary households. (Table 5.11.)

The Walkden-MHLG method refines these HFFs. It has been assumed so far that the household is synonymous with a housing-demand unit. But it is argued on the one hand that some households will not require separate accommodation. This applies particularly to single persons who are 'willing sharers' of existing dwellings. Walkden estimates that three-quarters of all single-person households who are sharing their accommodation will wish to do so in the future. These households must therefore be subtracted from the total number of households if household numbers and dwelling requirements are to be equated. Sunderland had 3,600 single persons in shared households in 1951. These are assumed to be distributed proportionately throughout the A/S/MC groups 4–12.[8] (Table 5.12.)

There are, on the other hand, a number of family groups which have not yet constituted themselves as separate households, but would do so if they could get a house—e.g. married couples living with parents. An estimate of these 'concealed households' by A/S/MC group is provided in the One Per Cent Sample of the 1951 Census, but the figures provided come no closer to Sunderland than the Northern Region as a whole. The approach for smaller areas is therefore necessarily different. The problem is to estimate the number of these concealed households and allocate them to A/S/MC groups. It is assumed that the number of concealed households will be equivalent to the number of married couples (with or without children) who live in a household of which neither spouse is head. Those which will be content with their subordinate status are thought to be broadly balanced by other elements not involving married couples who would nevertheless be expected to want separate housing. The figure for concealed households is thus given by the difference between the number of heads of primary family units (PFUs) and concealed households in each age, sex and marital condition group in 1951.[9] The Sample Census does not differentiate into age-groups the marital statuses of single, widowed and divorced, and the ratios of Walkden's own example are therefore those which are used here. (Table 5.13 and Table 5.14.)

The HFF for each age, sex and marital condition group can now be calculated. It is the number of 'true' households (in the Walkden/MHLG sense) divided by the number of persons in the corresponding A/S/MC group. The number of true households is arrived at by adding the concealed households to the enumerated households, and subtracting three-quarters of the households composed of single persons who are sharing a dwelling. (Table 5.15.)

By applying these hypothetical factors to the hypothetical population and A/S/MC structure of Sunderland in 1971 an estimate is obtained of 63,300 households. (Table 5.16.) This is 4,700 more than the households enumerated in the 1961 Census. Of these, 21,700 would be expanding households, 20,200 would be declining and 21,400 would be stationary. By 1981 there would be 67,800 households, an increase of 9,100 on 1961. (Table 5.17.) Of the 67,800 households in 1981, 24,300 would be expanding households, 20,200 would be declining and 23,300 would be stationary. A need for 455 new houses per annum thus results, on these assumptions, from population growth and household fission.

Household Formation within the Population which is Estimated on the Assumption of 'One-and-a-half times the 1951–61 Numbers of Migrants'

If households form in the pattern which has been assumed in the previous section, then the average household size will be 3·2 in both 1971 and 1981. Using the population estimates which (it has been argued) ought to be regarded as maximum rather than expected numbers, namely those which assume that migration in 1961–81 will run at a rate half as high again as it did between 1951 and 1961, then the population of 193,200 in 1971 will form 60,400 households, i.e. an increase of 1,700 on the enumerated households of 1961. By 1981 there would be 62,300 households, an increase of 3,700 on enumerated households of 1961. In total, there would be 20,700 expanding households in 1971, 19,200 would be declining and 20,400 would be stationary. In 1981 there would be 22,300 expanding

87

households, 18,600 declining households and 21,400 stationary households.

To meet the housing shortage which would be occasioned over the twenty years 1961–81 by population growth and household fission alone, therefore, Sunderland CB would need to build an additional 185 dwellings a year, and the parallel demographic development of the rural district would require a pro rata allowance of 28 dwellings. The housing need of Sunderland CB/RD in the sense of shortages which may arise from an increased population and the growth in the number of households to 1981 is therefore an expected maximum of 213 dwellings per annum.

Alternative Methods of Forecasting the Type and Number of Households

The projection of household numbers is simpler on a national or regional than on a local scale. In order to arrive at a conclusion about the use to which local forecasts can be put in framing local housing policies, it is therefore instructive to look at some national and regional examples.

The General Register Office used three methods of forecasting the trend of household fission between 1931 and 1941.[10] The first was simply to equate the expected number of households with the expected number of married women. When this assumption was applied to the actual age-sex-marriage pattern of England and Wales in 1951, the expected number of households would have been 11·1 million, with an average size of 3·8 persons per family. These are the results which are arrived at when the method is applied to the actual, known 1951 population statistics. In so far as the forecast from 1931 could not say what the 1951 structure would be, the forecast would have been additionally unreliable to a corresponding degree. The second method was to equate the number of future households with the total of married women in 1931, plus the number of widows and widowers under 65 years of age. When applied to the actual 1951 population structure this gives a figure of 12·3 million households. The third method added 10 per cent of the single persons aged 20–44 to the two groups of the second method. This results in an estimate of 12·4 million households when applied to the actual 1951 population figures. The actual number of households was 13·1 million and the actual average size was 3·2.

The use of Cullingworth's well-known projections of household numbers in England and Wales for the twenty years up to 1978 is recommended to town planners in at least one course of training in these words:

> As far as quantitative needs are concerned, the age-specific headship concept provides an *invaluable and reliable* means of estimating future requirements. (Emphasis added.)

They are based on the GRO's methods. The GRO's 1958 assumption was that the pattern of household formation in 1978 would be approximately the same as in 1951. The exception would be in the group of married males aged 15–39. Of these 79 per cent were household heads in 1951. The GRO assumed that this would have increased to 85 per cent by 1965 and to 90 per cent by 1975. The validity of his calculations depends upon the GRO's population projections for England and Wales from 1958 to 1978. Cullingworth notes that 'it is possible to calculate the number of households that can reasonably be expected *if these projections prove accurate*'.[11]

He makes four sets of assumptions. The first is that by 1978 each of the twelve age-sex-marriage groups will be forming households at the same rate as in 1951. The second is that the GRO's 1958 hypothesis will be borne out–that the only change will be among the married males 15–39, 90 per cent of whom will form households in 1978 instead of the 71 per cent of 1951. The highest number of households by 1978 is given by his fourth set of assumptions, that by 1978 all married males will be heads of households. His lowest estimate predicted 14·9 million households in England and Wales by 1978 (a figure which was actually reached in 1961–the year following the publication of *Housing Needs and Planning Policy*).[12] His highest gives a figure of 16·0 million households by 1978.[13]

Between the highest and lowest of these four estimates, therefore, there is a difference of over one million dwelling units, even when the 1958 population figure for 1978 is assumed to be reliable. But by 1964 the 1958 figure for the 1978 population had itself been altered by the GRO from 49·0 million to 54·5 million (a difference of 5·5 million). Revisions of this magnitude must undermine confidence in the value for present housing decisions of predictions of future household growth over the periods of time discussed here. This conclusion is supported by the finding of the Commons Estimates Committee in its report on the Government statistical services.[14]

A method much more elaborate in conception has been developed by Eversley, Jackson and Lomas.[15] They seek to predict future household size (therefore, if the population is known, the future number of households) from various demographic and socio-economic factors.

The data from the Census of 1961 showed that for the areas for which the calculations were carried out, those of the Birmingham conurbation, household size was related to age-structure, education and social class.

The two models which showed the highest degree of fit gave the following regression equations:

(1) $Ye = 2 \cdot 827 + 0 \cdot 653X_1 - 0 \cdot 51X_2 - 0 \cdot 027X_3$

(2) $Ye = 2 \cdot 905 + 0 \cdot 608X_1 - 0 \cdot 0088X_4 - 0 \cdot 028X_3.$[16]

In 1961 the average values for the four variables for the whole of the Birmingham conurbation were:

$$X_1 = 1 \cdot 285 \quad X_2 = 2 \cdot 067 \quad X_3 = 14 \cdot 048 \quad X_4 = 12 \cdot 385$$

The 1986 values for variables X_1 and X_3 are derived from the population projections calculated by the authors themselves. The value for X_2 is derived from an assumption that by 1971, and in 1986, 10 per cent of all young persons over 18 will be enjoying the benefit of some form of higher education. The value for X_4 is based on the assumption that there will be twice as many people by 1986 who on present living standards would be included in socio-economic groups I or II.

The future pattern of households is therefore predicted on the basis of many large assumptions: that the projection of population numbers is accurate; that the four variables of the equations will bear the same functional relationship to one another in 1986 as they did in 1961; and that a future rise in the material living standards of one class will mean that its behaviour will assimilate to the present behaviour of the class which is at present above it. In spite of the possession of the highest statistical skills, in spite of the availability of current information in the greatest detail, it is not unfair to suggest that this impressive attempt to see into the year 1986 amounts after all to another argument *obscurum per obscurius*.

NOTES TO CHAPTER 5

1 *The Registrar General's Statistical Reviews of England and Wales*, Table K.
2 *The Registrar General's Statistical Review of England and Wales for the year 1958*, HMSO 1960. (Emphasis added.)
3 A. H. Walkden, 'The Estimation of Future Numbers of Private Households', *op. cit.*, Volume 15, No. 2, November 1961, pp. 174–86.
4 Explanatory letter from MHLG, December 1966.
5 Walkden, *op. cit.*, p. 176. (Emphasis added.)
6 The age-specific survival rates for the Northern Region and the trend to 1981 are those supplied by the Northern Region Office of the MHLG.
7 Live births per thousand women by age-groups for 'Remainder of Northern Region', *The Registrar General's Statistical Review of England and Wales for 1963*, Part II, Table GG, p. 138.
8 Walkden considered that 'one-person households', whether sharing accommodation or not, were sufficiently alike to justify the use of the data included in Table 12A of the *Housing Report* of the Census to represent one-person 'sharing' households. *Op. cit.*, p. 184.
9 Walkden, *op. cit.*, p. 184.
10 GRO, Census of England and Wales 1931, *Housing Report*, Chapters V and XII.
11 J. B. Cullingworth, *Housing Needs and Planning Policy*, Routledge and Kegan Paul 1960, p. 43. (Emphasis added.) His calculations are also based partly on the estimate by the GAD (Government Actuary's Department) of the distribution of the population of Great Britain by marital condition in 1979.
   GAD, *Report of the First Quinquennial Review of the National Insurance Act 1946*, House of Commons Papers No. 1, HMSO 1954.
12 *Census* 1961: Total households in England and Wales $=14,889,805$.
13 *Ibid*. Table 18.
14 House of Commons Estimates Committee, *Fourth Report: Government Statistical Services*, HMSO 1966. The Report recommends that urgent steps be taken to increase research into methods of forecasting.
15 D. E. C. Eversley, Valerie J. Jackson and G. M. Lomas, *Population Growth and Planning Policy*, WMSPRU, University of Birmingham 1965, Appendix IV.
16 Where: Y_e = the predicted household size;
   X_1 = the ratio of persons under 15 years of age to females 15–49 years of age;

X_2 = the percentage of persons 15 or older whose terminal educational was 20 or older;

X_3 = the percentage of the total population that is 60+ years of age or older;

X_4 = the percentage of occupied and retired males registered in the Registrar General's socio-economic groups I and II.

Table 5.1

Families per Thousand Persons
Sunderland CB and Sunderland CB/RD 1871-1961

Date	Sunderland CB	Sunderland CB/RD
1871	218	217
1881	214	211
1891	210	202
1901	210	208
1911	216	213
1921	223	220
1931	249	246
1951	294	292
1961	309	308

Source: Census of England and Wales

Table 5.2

Household-projection Age-Sex-Marriage Groups

Groups	Sex	Age (MHLG age-groups in brackets)		Marital Status
1	Persons	15–39	(15–44)	Married
2	Persons	40–59	(Males 45–64 Females 45–59)	Married
3	Persons	60+	(Males 65+ Females 60+)	Married
4	Persons	15–39	(15–44)	S/W/D
5	Males	40–59	(45–64)	Single
6	Males	60+	(65+)	Single
7	Females	40–59	(45–59)	Single
8	Females	60+	(60+)	Single
9	Males	40–59	(45–64)	W/D
10	Males	60+	(65+)	W/D
11	Females	40–59	(45–59)	W/D
12	Females	60+	(60+)	W/D

Table 5.3

Age and Sex Structure of Sunderland CB in 1961, 1971 and 1981

Age-Group	1961 Census Males	1961 Census Females	1971 Calculated Males	1971 Calculated Females	1981 Calculated Males	1981 Calculated Females
0–4	9,448	8,708	9,235	8,788	10,345	9,836
5–9	8,180	8,148	9,160	8,717	9,740	9,264
10–14	8,601	8,437	9,103	8,483	8,904	8,568
15–19	6,534	6,800	7,790	7,979	8,731	8,540
20–24	5,896	6,473	7,819	8,046	8,277	8,095
25–29	6,326	6,375	6,566	6,332	7,838	7,434
30–34	6,606	6,370	6,076	6,035	8,067	7,509
35–39	6,714	6,576	6,183	6,066	6,429	6,033
40–44	5,622	5,999	6,386	6,152	5,888	5,840
45–49	5,734	5,943	6,434	6,282	5,944	5,810
50–54	5,498	5,780	5,214	5,667	5,949	5,833
55–59	4,970	5,718	5,057	5,521	5,713	5,866
60–64	4,074	5,057	4,472	5,166	4,278	5,101
65–69	2,910	4,234	3,531	4,875	3,633	4,755
70–74	2,180	3,312	2,375	3,836	2,650	3,976
75–79	1,299	2,320	1,301	2,666	1,608	3,133
80–84	745	1,247	689	1,517	762	1,806
85+	300	542	223	663	234	784

Source: Census 1961 and special calculations

94

Table 5.4

Number of Marriages Solemnised each Year in Sunderland CB 1946–65

Date	Persons marrying per 1,000 home population	Date	Persons marrying per 1,000 home population
1946	19	1956	19
1947	19	1957	18
1948	19	1958	17
1949	20	1959	17
1950	19	1960	17
1951	19	1961	15
1952	20	1962	15
1953	19	1963	14
1954	18	1964	15
1955	19	1965	16

Source: *The Registrar General's Statistical Reviews of England and Wales*, Table F

Table 5.5

Rates for Various Marital Statuses (Age Specific): Sunderland CB 1961

Group 1	Sex 2	Age 3	Marital Status 4	Number in marital status 5	Total in age and sex group 6	Marital status rate (percentage 5 is of 6) 7
1	Persons	15–39	Married	38,532	64,670	59·6
2	Persons	40–59	Married	37,390	45,264	82·6
3	Persons	60+	Married	15,367	28,220	54·5
4	Persons	15–39	S/W/D	26,138	64,670	40·4
5	Males	40–59	Single	2,126	21,824	9·7
6	Males	60+	Single	843	11,508	7·3
7	Females	40–59	Single	2,543	23,440	10·8
8	Females	60+	Single	2,112	16,712	12·6
9	Males	40–59	W/D	456	21,824	2·1
10	Males	60+	W/D	1,445	11,508	12·6
11	Females	40–59	W/D	2,500	23,440	10·7
12	Females	60+	W/D	7,697	16,712	46·1

Source: Census 1961

96

Table 5.6
The Age-sex-marital condition Structure of Sunderland CB in 1971

Group	Sex	Age	Total in age-sex group 1971	Marital Condition	MCF	Total in age-sex-marital status group in 1971
1	Persons	15–39	68,892	Married	60	41,335
2	Persons	40–59	46,713	Married	83	38,772
3	Persons	60+	33,314	Married	55	18,323
4	Persons	15–39	68,892	S/W/D	40	27,557
5	Males	40–59	23,091	Single	10	2,309
6	Males	60+	12,591	Single	7	881
7	Females	40–59	23,622	Single	11	2,598
8	Females	60+	18,723	Single	13	2,434
9	Males	40–59	23,091	W/D	2	462
10	Males	60+	12,591	W/D	13	1,639
11	Females	40–59	23,622	W/D	11	2,598
12	Females	60+	18,723	W/D	46	8,613

Source: Special calculations

Table 5.7
The Age-sex-marital condition Structure of Sunderland CB in 1981

Group	Sex	Age	Total in age-sex group 1981	Marital Condition	MCF	Total in age-sex-marital status group in 1981
1	Persons	15–39	76,953	Married	60	46,172
2	Persons	40–59	46,843	Married	83	38,880
3	Persons	60+	32,720	Married	55	17,996
4	Persons	15–39	76,953	S/W/D	40	30,781
5	Males	40–59	23,494	Single	10	2,349
6	Males	60+	13,165	Single	7	922
7	Females	40–59	23,349	Single	11	2,568
8	Females	60+	19,555	Single	13	2,542
9	Males	40–59	23,494	W/D	2	469
10	Males	60+	13,165	W/D	13	1,711
11	Females	40–59	23,349	W/D	11	2,568
12	Females	60+	19,555	W/D	46	11,733

Source: Special calculations

Table 5.8

Household Formation Factor: Sunderland CB 1951

Group 1	Sex 2	Age 3	Marital Status 4	Household Heads in 1951 5	Total in age-sex-marital status group in 1951 6	HFF (percentage 5 is of 6) 7
1	Persons	15–39	Married	14,270	35,828	40
2	Persons	40–59	Married	18,223	35,683	51
3	Persons	60+	Married	7,203	12,928	56
4	Persons	15–39	S/W/D	859	30,205	3
5	Males	40–59	Single	583	1,812	32
6	Males	60+	Single	465	930	50
7	Females	40–59	Single	945	3,003	31
8	Females	60+	Single	965	1,757	55
9	Males	40–59	W/D	591	827	71
10	Males	60+	W/D	1,733	2,556	68
11	Females	40–59	W/D	2,420	2,829	86
12	Females	60+	W/D	5,134	6,554	78

Source: Census 1951

Table 5.9

Household Formation on the Hypothesis of the 1951 HFF: Sunderland CB 1961

Age-sex-marriage Group	Number in group 1961	1951 HFF	Number of households on 1951 HFF hypothesis
1	38,532	40	15,413
2	37,390	51	19,069
3	15,367	56	8,605
4	26,138	3	784
5	2,126	32	690
6	843	50	421
7	2,543	31	788
8	2,112	55	1,162
9	456	71	324
10	1,445	68	983
11	2,500	86	2,150
12	7,697	78	6,004

Source: Special calculations

Table 5.10
Estimated Distribution of Households Sunderland CB 1961

Group	Distribution of 1961 Population if HFF of 1951		Estimated distribution of households 1961
	Number	Per cent	
1	15,413	27·34	16,035
2	19,069	33·82	19,835
3	8,605	15·26	8,950
4	784	1·39	815
5	680	1·21	710
6	421	0·75	440
7	788	1·40	821
8	1,162	2·06	1,208
9	324	0·57	334
10	983	1·74	1,021
11	2,150	3·81	2,235
12	6,004	10·65	6,246

Source: Special calculations

Table 5.11
Expanding, Declining and Stationary Households
Sunderland CB 1961

Group	Household type	Number of households
1	Growing	16,000
4	Growing	800
	Total growing	16,800
2	Declining	19,800
	Total declining	19,800
3	Stationary	9,000
5	Stationary	700
6	Stationary	400
7	Stationary	800
8	Stationary	1,200
9	Stationary	300
10	Stationary	1,000
11	Stationary	2,200
12	Stationary	6,200
	Total stationary	22,000

Source: Special calculations

Table 5.12
Single-person Households in Shared Dwellings
Sunderland CB 1951

A/S/MC group	Households 1951		Three-quarters of single persons sharing households 1951
	Number	Per cent	
4	859	6·27	170
5	583	4·26	115
6	465	3·40	92
7	945	6·90	186
8	965	7·05	190
9	591	4·32	117
10	1,733	12·65	342
11	2,420	17·67	478
12	5,134	37·49	1,015

Source: Census 1951

Table 5.13

Concealed-Household Factor (CHF): Walkden's Example

Group	Enumerated Households 1951	Married couples living in households of this group neither of whom is head	Concealed-Household Factor
1	23,649	5,934	25
2	36,969	659	2
3	11,761	87	1
4	1,101	580	53
5	593	13	2
6	257	6	2
7	829	23	2
8	821	16	2
9	906	4	0
10	1,765	13	1
11	3,012	15	0
12	5,635	43	1

Source: Walkden, *op. cit.*, p. 185

Table 5.14
Concealed Households: Sunderland CB

Group	Enumerated Households 1951	CHF	Concealed Households
1	14,270	25	3,580
2	18,223	2	342
3	7,203	1	53
4	859	53	453
5	583	2	13
6	465	2	11
7	945	2	26
8	965	2	19
9	591	0	3
10	1,733	1	13
11	2,420	0	12
12	5,134	1	39

Source: Census 1951 and Walkden, *op. cit.*

Table 5.15

'True Household Formation Factor (HFF)' Sunderland CB

Group 1	Enumerated Households 1951 2	Three-quarters of 'single-person sharing' households 3	Concealed Households 4	2-3+4 5	Persons 6	True HFF 7
1	14,270	—	3,580	17,850	35,828	50
2	18,223	—	342	18,565	35,683	52
3	7,203	—	53	7,256	12,928	56
4	859	170	453	1,142	30,205	4
5	583	115	13	481	1,182	27
6	465	92	11	384	930	41
7	945	186	26	785	3,003	26
8	965	190	19	794	1,757	45
9	591	117	3	477	827	58
10	1,733	342	13	1,404	2,556	55
11	2,420	478	12	1,954	2,829	69
12	5,134	1,015	39	4,158	6,554	63

Source: Special calculations

Table 5.16

Households in 1971: Sunderland CB

A/S/MC Group	Persons	'True HFF'	Households 1971
1	41,335	50	20,700
2	38,772	52	20,200
3	18,323	56	10,300
4	27,557	4	1,100
5	2,309	27	600
6	881	41	400
7	2,598	26	700
8	2,434	45	1,100
9	462	58	300
10	1,639	55	900
11	2,598	69	1,800
12	8,613	63	5,400

Source: Special calculations

Table 5.17

Households in 1981: Sunderland CB

A/S/MC Group	Persons	'True HFF'	Households 1981
1	46,172	50	23,100
2	38,880	52	20,200
3	17,996	56	10,100
4	30,781	4	1,200
5	2,349	27	600
6	922	41	400
7	2,568	26	700
8	2,542	45	1,100
9	469	58	300
10	1,711	55	900
11	2,568	69	1,800
12	11,733	63	7,400

Source: Special calculations

CHAPTER 6

CONCLUSIONS ON POPULATION GROWTH AND HOUSEHOLD FISSION

Conclusions on Population

For the factors it incorporates up to the base year and in its assumptions about national rates and trends the population projection which the Ministry of Housing and Local Government issues to LPAs is demographically somewhat sophisticated. But beyond the base the LPA must fend for itself. It has to analyse the history, current experience and future prospects of the town's fertility, nuptiality, employment and migration. The 'official' figure is only the beginning of a prognosis, not the definitive population.

Such an analysis when carried out for Sunderland in the mid-sixties makes any figure above 193,000 for 1971 and 199,000 by 1981 (the figure given by the assumptions of 'one-and-a-half the 1951–61 migration numbers' and 'two per cent rise in fertility per quinquennium') look artificial and out of accord with current knowledge. Nor is there anything to indicate that the population of the rural district has expanded, or will expand to make up for the deficiencies in the estimates for the county borough. The rural district is composed of Ryhope, where the colliery has recently closed, Castletown and Silksworth, where the future of the collieries is at best uncertain,[1] and of the stagnant village of Hylton. The small residential suburb of East Herrington is the only area where growth has taken place. It may therefore fairly be assumed that the rural district's rate of growth is unlikely to significantly exceed that

107

of the borough. This gives a maximum figure for Sunderland CB/RD of 222,000 by 1971 and 229,100 by 1981.

The LPA's version of Mark 7 (266,800) therefore over-estimates the 1981 population of Sunderland CB/RD by a population equivalent to the whole population of the rural district in 1961, plus a third again. Its version of New Series Mark 1 (251,500) overestimates the population of Sunderland CB/RD in 1981 by a figure equivalent to 79 per cent of the population of the rural district in 1961. The MHLG official figures over-estimate Sunderland's population by much more than this, of course, as they do not take migration into account at all.

There is ample indication on the other hand that these figures of 193,000 and 199,000 are likely to be the ceiling of prospective population growth, for in recent years the population of Sunderland has not been climbing towards these figures but has shown an absolute decline. Between mid-1962 and mid-1966 the rural district gained 1,700 and the county borough lost 2,900. The net decline in the population of the county borough and the rural district taken together was 1,200. (Table 6.1.)

The second conclusion is that, with regard to population, Sunderland's housing need is not the chimerical ability to foretell the future. The character of the information means that the decision-maker who wants to use population projections must unavoidably live with uncertainty. The need with regard to housing policies is rather that councillors and citizens, as well as technical officers should be in a position to assess in an informed way the plans which are advocated on the grounds of future population growth or decline.

Schneider observes that ' "The single best guess" of what will happen, *however fallible* is often preferred by the user, to several alternative sets of assumptions which leave him the problem of selection',[2] and from this point of view, he adds, the single best guess best meets 'administrative needs'. But it is also the approach which invites a spurious simplification of the issues involved.[3] As Popper says, a prediction of details which is inexact in details is a poor foundation for policy,[4] and the indispensable intellectual equipment of citizen, councillor and technical officer ought therefore to be a well-based scepticism about any proposals which are predicated upon population forecasts, the elements of which have not been most carefully and critically scrutinised.

Conclusions on Household Fission

Allowing for the fact that a population of any given size is tending to split into more housing-demand units than in the past, the highest expected number of households by 1971 is 60,000 and by 1981 62,000. These figures represent an annual demand for 185 extra dwellings plus 28 dwellings per annum for population growth in the rural district.

It has also been demonstrated that household-formation forecasting and population predictions are of limited value. The search is vain, as R. M. Titmuss has said, for 'the master forecaster of a technocratic society'. Calculations may be able to show on the basis of existing trends that a particular set of expectations do not follow from the given premises. This is the case with the official figures. But they cannot produce a specific quantity and maintain that, in so far as the housing problem is a problem of producing new dwellings to meet shortages due to population growth, it represents the magnitude of the housing problem throughout some future period.

This investigation has shown two things. The first is that no method has been devised the reliability of which is anything but extremely low, if it is possible to speak of reliability at all; and it is difficult to envisage either the logical or existential basis for the expectation that such methods may become available. The Italian sociologist Pareto in talking of social prediction used the analogy of map and compass. A man who wants to reach a certain destination will have no difficulty if he can read a map, if his map is accurate and if he can orient it in relation to the actual territory by landmarks. If he has no map or a map and no compass but experience has made him sensitive to a large number of signs, no one of which is reliable in itself but which in accumulation provide some guidance, he may reach his destination by what is called intuition. The one thing which is certain to take him to the wrong place is faith in a false map or a faulty compass.

Unfortunately it has also been demonstrated that these

predictions are used, not as ceilings or as lower limits, but as confident projections which deck out policy with the trappings of scientific impartiality and professional dignity. Carmichael has said outright that posterity will look upon them as 'a gigantic confidence trick'.[5] However that may be, it is clear that for Sunderland's housing needs, household projections no less than population estimates are complicated, hazardous, yet crucially important, especially in their mis-use, and the councillor and citizen are right to look for caution, realism and rationality in the analysis of problems and policies which are formulated on their assumptions.

The boldest and most imaginative housing decision in the history of Sunderland was to create a self-contained community at Silksworth, a new township of 20,000 to supplement the overspill of 15,000 or 18,000 which would be accommodated at Washington New Town. The most important political event for eighty years was the extension of the borough boundaries, which increased its area by one-half from 9,000 acres to 13,000 acres. The public arguments for both of these changes was the need for more houses. A number of factors, not population alone, influence the supply of new dwellings. The case was centred, however, on the expected increase in the population of the borough from 190,000 in 1961 to 230,000 by 1981. The expectation that many thousands of *additional* dwellings were to be provided was one of the principal reasons which led the Corporation to finance the Sunderland's Housing Needs study.

The evidence does not indicate that such growth can be expected. Instead of the expansion of population requiring more than 13,000 dwellings between 1961 and 1981, the maximum is likely to be less than one-third of this; the borough and the added areas of the rural district taken together need fewer than 215 houses a year to meet population growth.

What is presented, therefore, is the interesting phenomenon of a professional group which adopts a decision-making strategy of minimizing maximum losses (a strategy known as 'mini-maxing')[6] as far as its own members are concerned ('plenty of land to play with') but which can only justify its own freedom of action by presenting 'technical facts' which require 'maximizing' (high-risk) policies from other groups. In this case, the planners 'minimax' on their land-use claims but they can do this only by showing that the local housing authority must provide the 'maximum' number of new dwellings.

Let us turn now to another set of decisions in Sunderland, 'the decision to demolish'. To what extent do the planners again adopt 'minimaxing' policies for themselves–policies which cannot possibly do themselves very much harm–but which are at the same time 'maximizing' decisions imposed on other groups, which, had they been left to themselves, would have been much more cautious and realistic?

NOTES TO CHAPTER 6

1 *Hansard*, No. 731, 7–13 July, Col. 975.
2 Schneider, *op. cit.*, p. 95. (Emphasis added.)
3 See the remarks by Ruth Glass on the report of the South-east England Economic Planning Council (Cmnd. 2308, 1964). 'The authors of the Study, though well aware that national projections are precarious, and local projections even more so, *present only one set of assumptions–the most facile one.*' *The Times*, 6 April 1964. (Emphasis added.)
4 Karl Popper, *The Poverty of Historicism*, Routledge Paperback 1961, p. 38.
5 John Carmichael, 'Housing "Needs" ', *Vacant Possession*. Hobart Papers No. 28, 1964, p. 29.
6 See Herbert A. Simon, *Administrative Behaviour* (1945), Second Edition, New York 1960.

Table 6.1

**The Population of Sunderland CB and Sunderland RD
1962–66**

Mid-year	Sunderland CB	Sunderland RD	Sunderland CB/RD
1962	190,600	28,400	219,000
1963	190,500	28,900	219,400
1964	189,600	29,300	218,900
1965	188,300	29,800	218,100
1966	187,600	30,200	217,800

Source: The Registrar General's estimates of home
population of local authority areas at 30 June each year

PART TWO
THE DECISION TO DEMOLISH

SECTION I
Introduction

CHAPTER 7

THE REPLACEMENT OF EXISTING DWELLINGS: A PROBLEM OF SOCIAL VALUES

Population predictions and forecasts of household fission are problems of some difficulty. They are made more difficult by the fact that there is a conflict between an impartial assessment of the data and the consequences of making public such an impartial assessment, for prediction of population growth can help to stimulate growth and a prediction of decline may accelerate decline. There is also the possibility of submerged conflicts between objectivity on the one hand and, on the other, personal or professional well-being or a required commitment to a particular school of official thought.

Nevertheless, the problems are mainly of a technical kind. There is little dispute about the social values involved. In modern Britain it is uncontroversial that each elementary or 'nuclear' family (husband, wife and their dependent children) is entitled to a separate dwelling–'a separate dwelling for every family that desires to have one'.[1] More than that: it would be regarded as peculiar if two nuclear families when given the chance of separate accommodation chose to continue to live together in the same dwelling. There would be the feeling in the neighbourhood, among relatives and among workmates that something was wrong, that a moral code was being violated. The emphasis on the isolation of the nuclear family, which makes it not only a right but also a duty for spouses and offspring to form a clearly separate housekeeping unit, is one of our principal *mores*, i.e. one of the fundamental unquestioned rules which govern the way in which our society will be organised.

To what extent is the replacement of existing dwellings also a technical matter? The clearest case of replacement need is the traditional slum. The existence of slum property and the decline towards slumdom of houses reaching the end of their useful lives are facts that arouse shock and indignation. Here, too, there appears at first sight to be unanimity of value, leaving open only the question of the best technical means of realising the valued end. Slums are attacked as evils, and in much the same terms, in both official publications and popular journals. 'When the slum clearance programme began about 1925', the Housing Management Sub-committee of the MHLG wrote in 1956,

> and reached its full force with the Housing Act of 1930, many people realised with pained surprise the fact that there were still slums that would have been regarded as a disgrace in the middle of the nineteenth century. A generation has now passed and there remain a mass of ugly and venomous slums. In the mass type of construction dating back a hundred years or more there is neither order nor decency. Indoor sanitation and water do not exist, but worse still is the stagnant air, the mixing-up of dwellings with other buildings, the shared water-closets in tiny airless yards and the unspeakable decay of the houses themselves. No family can be expected to live happily or bring up children under such conditions. There is generally overcrowding, but what makes the slum is the dilapidation and ruin in these dwellings which frustrate any attempt at home-making.[2]

The *Daily Mirror* writes of the dwellings 'that are half-a-million smears across the face of the North in the winter of 1965'. In the North-west alone, a DEA survey showed that one in every 25 houses in the area was unfit to live in, or would be in sixteen years. That adds up to 440,000 houses.[3]

For some, the demolition of outworn dwellings, and not the provision of additional houses to meet population growth, is the key issue. 'The crucial problem of the future [is] the replacement of old houses. If in the next ten years we can go on building at an average rate of 350,000 houses we can get rid of at least two million old houses. Are we prepared to pull down two million houses, not all classifiable as slums?'[4] Ashworth thus envisaged that 3·5 million houses would have been built between 1954 and 1964, 1·5 million for shortages and population growth, two million to replace old houses. Six years later these figures were echoed by J. B. Cullingworth: 'A desirable rate of demolition would probably be of the order of 200,000 houses a year. This would enable all pre-1877 houses to be demolished by 1978.'[5] Cullingworth did add, however, that it was fairly obvious from indications at the time that the desirable rate of demolition would be unattainable. He therefore recommended, as second best, an extensive programme of modernisation.

At the end of 1966 the view of the Principal Architect of the MHLG Development Group was that 'we have about three million dwellings which must be cleared as soon as possible'.[6] One million of these were 'unfit' in the sense of the Housing Act and 'there are probably two million which are unlikely to be worth improving'. Audrey Harvey takes an even more extreme view: 'It is estimated that we need half a million new houses a year simply to keep pace with the housing "death rate". That estimate may sound exaggerated, but it may be too low. It is not disputed that literally millions of people, particularly in northern industrial cities are living in homes which ought to have been swept into oblivion years ago.'[7]

The peculiar feature of population projections which needed to be explained was the LPA's systematic tendency to take account of factors which indicated a high future population figure, and to devote less care to facts which indicated a low future figure. The peculiar feature of replacement estimates is their extreme disparity, the one compared with another. In 1960 Cullingworth, for example, had envisaged the demolition of 200,000 houses a year, exactly the same rate as that advocated by Ashworth, a principal exponent of the view that 'the core of the housing problem is the slum'.[8] In 1963, after he had examined the problem in the context of a particular town, he had turned (not necessarily inconsistently) from the advocacy of large-scale demolition nationally towards a policy of conservation in Lancaster.

It needs to be stressed that the problem of old housing in Lancaster is not one of slums. The problem is no longer one of old insanitary courts, of back-to-back houses, of dangers to public health or of abject poverty. The nineteenth-century concept of 'slum clearance' is becoming increasingly outmoded. The majority of the remaining old houses in Lancaster are basically sound, and with adequate maintenance and improvement could usefully provide for local needs for at least another generation.[9]

In contrast to the view of the MHLG Development Group's Principal Architect that three million dwellings ought to be demolished, one of his colleagues at the Ministry believes that 'probably no other country possesses so large an inheritance of basically sound older houses'.

> While in the past many of the houses we have been clearing have been obvious slums by any standards, rotten, damp, ruinous, verminous, the houses towards which health inspectors are now beginning to turn their attention are increasingly of a much better kind, and although in one or more respects they may be substandard it is often a simple matter to put them right.[10]

The randomness of replacement estimates can be seen clearly in the returns made by local authorities under Section I of the Housing Repairs and Rents Act 1954, which relate not to the difficult problem of replacement in general, but to the comparatively straightforward problem of public health slums. The returns have been rightly described as grotesque. There are grotesque similarities. 'Slums remaining' form the same percentage of the houses of Middlesbrough and Reigate (both 1·9 per cent). Rotherham and Tring are the same (3·1 per cent). The percentage for both Consett and Sunbury-on-Thames is 2·7. There are grotesque differences. According to the returns, Liverpool's slum-clearance problem is proportionately 107 times worse than that of Newport. The proportions of 'slums remaining' in neighbouring and prima facie similar towns are widely discrepant: Sheffield 9 per cent, Rotherham 3 per cent; Batley 34 per cent, Dewsbury 10 per cent.

The returns for the largest towns of England and Wales give percentages which range from 44 per cent of the total number of permanent houses in the area (Liverpool) to 0·2 per cent in the case of Cardiff. (Table 7.1.)

The discrepancy between what local authorities decided were slums in 1955 and what they had decided were slums by 1965 (which is also, partly at least, a matter of the discrepancy between the local authority's judgment and that of the MHLG) is shown by the fact that in Cardiff, for example, the number of slum dwellings in orders actually confirmed by the MHLG between 1 January 1955 and 31 December 1966 was 552 per cent of the number classified as 'remaining slums' in 1955. In Middlesbrough the percentage is 402. For Sunderland CB/RD the figure is 128 per cent – i.e. by 1966 one third as many again as the number of 'remaining slums' in 1955 had been condemned as slums in actual fact. The 1955 return for Sunderland CB had shown 3,500 dwellings as slums; between 1955 and 1966 4,527 orders were confirmed. The rural district showed 352 dwellings as slums in 1955; 407 orders were confirmed between 1955 and 1966. (Table 7.2 and Diagram 7.A.) These adjustments, however, had not evened out puzzling differences in 1966. (Table 7.3.)

Before the Housing Repairs and Rent Act, 1954, slum clearance standards were explicitly variable from locality to locality. In determining whether a house was fit for human habitation the local authority had to have regard to the extent to which 'by reason of disrepair or sanitary defects the house fell short of the provision of any bye-law or Local Act, or of the general standard of housing accommodation of the working classes in the district'.

The 1954 Act, however, largely following the recommendations of the 1946 report of the Mitchell sub-committee of the Central Housing Advisory Committee, laid down a standard (indeed what the Milner Holland report calls 'a uniform and comprehensive standard'),[11] for determining a dwelling's fitness:

> In determining for any of the purposes of this Act whether a house is unfit for human habitation regard shall be had to its condition in respect of the following matters, that is to say (a) repair; (b) stability; (c) freedom from damp; (d) natural lighting; (e) ventilation; (f) water supply; (g) drainage and sanitary conveniences; (h) facilities for the storage, preparation and cooking of food and the disposal of waste water and the house shall be deemed to be unfit for human habitation if and only if it is so far defective in one or more of the said matters that it is not reasonably suitable for occupation in that condition.[12]

Clearly, however, this is not a standard. It is merely a list of items the standards of which are to be regarded as relevant to a

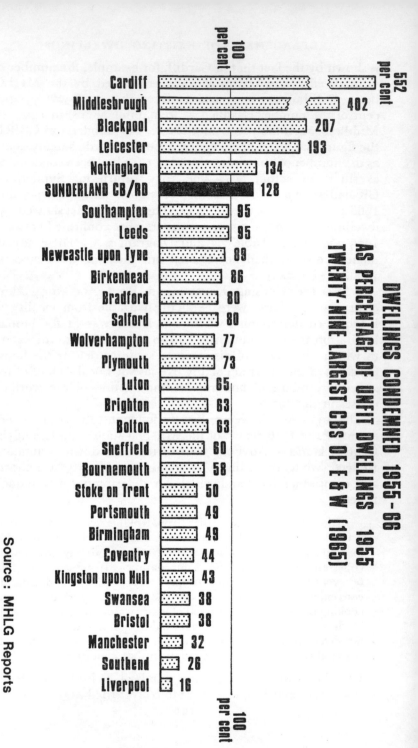

DWELLINGS CONDEMNED 1955-66 AS PERCENTAGE OF UNFIT DWELLINGS 1955 TWENTY-NINE LARGEST CBS OF E & W (1965)

City	per cent
Cardiff	552
Middlesbrough	402
Blackpool	207
Leicester	193
Nottingham	134
SUNDERLAND CB/RD	128
Southampton	95
Leeds	95
Newcastle upon Tyne	89
Birkenhead	86
Bradford	80
Salford	80
Wolverhampton	77
Plymouth	73
Luton	65
Brighton	63
Bolton	63
Sheffield	60
Bournemouth	58
Stoke on Trent	50
Portsmouth	49
Birmingham	49
Coventry	44
Kingston upon Hull	43
Swansea	38
Bristol	38
Manchester	32
Southend	26
Liverpool	16

Diagram 7.A

Source : MHLG Reports

judgment of a dwelling's fitness. The degree of dampness and the extent of disrepair and so forth—the standards of the items—are matters with which the Act does not deal. The courts merely repeat the statement about 'reasonable' standards. The standard of fitness is that of 'the reasonable man', a dwelling is unfit if the state of repair is such that damage may naturally be caused to the ordinary user in respect of personal injury to life or limb or injury to health.[13] It is therefore equally possible to be extremely cautious and hesitant in replacement policies, or to think in terms of 'a sea of slumdom' and entertain the vision of 'sweeping it all away in one operation'.[14]

The oscillations and wide variety in judgments of the need for replacement, and the absence of unambiguous statutory rules both stem from the dwelling's fundamental characteristics. First: it is immensely important to each family *given all its circumstances* that it finds the home most suitable to it in all those circumstances. Second: the dwelling is only one of the claimants to the family's income; it has to compete with educational expenses, with the working-man's club or the motor-car, with food, bets, clothing, holidays, furniture and fares. Third: the dwelling itself is exceedingly complex as a source of benefits. It provides not only shelter but also prestige. A private tenancy differs from owner-occupation in terms of security, stability, and the opportunity offered for self-expression as well as in terms of financial cost. One family may prefer space to equipment, another equipment to space. Proximity to work must be weighed against the amenity of the neighbourhood, congenial neighbours against distance from relatives, access to schools against access to shops.

The decision to retain or replace dwellings and relocate residents whether temporarily or permanently depends essentially on the way in which these various elements are given a weight and ranked in order of priority. Replacement, that is, is essentially a matter of the valuation placed upon the advantages and drawbacks of a given housing situation by the different parties involved in the replacement decision.

The value placed by various groups on the importance of the families whose houses may be demolished and their endorsement or rejection of the decision is one such element. A profession with a strong tradition of technocratic attitudes may stress the inefficiency of the delays which result from an 'over-emphasis on the judicial as distinct from the administrative nature of appeals and other planning procedures'.[15] Other groups may place more emphasis on the 'rights and dignity of the poor' in replacement decisions and take the view that 'nothing should be done for people that is not also done with them'.[16]

The value judgments of groups and individuals differ also on the question of the limits of justifiable public intervention. The sanitary policy of Chadwick, Disraeli and Joseph Chamberlain was legitimated not at all in terms of distributive social justice. It was intended simply to ensure that the community as a whole did not suffer from the ill-health of the poor, and it was applied to them whether they were unable or merely unwilling to house themselves in such a manner that the health of *other people* was not threatened. Dwellings may be regarded as appropriate objects of compulsory replacement if they constitute a danger to individual health even though contagion may not be an issue (just as cigarette smoking is an individual but not a public health hazard). Statements which link social disorganisation to inferior housing may encourage public agencies to replace existing dwellings. 'Crime, drug addiction, drunkenness and delinquency affect us all. They are the by-products of overcrowded slums.'[17] 'Family break-ups, truanting children, physical and mental illness are attributed by doctors and teachers to generally bad housing.'[18]

At a further remove, 'slum clearance' of dwellings which, as Thomas Sharp says, are not actually slummy but which are to be found in the 'infinitely dreary and unworthy quarters of last century's standardised streets', may be advocated. 'The actual slums must go first. But the aesthetic slums should follow quickly.'[19] Town planning for some 'is, curiously enough, largely a matter of skyline'.[20] The great importance Sharp and Dale attach to the visual impact of urban structures is characteristic of 'a powerful segment' of the planning profession.[21]

A replacement decision may depend less on the intrinsic merits of the dwelling than on, for example, protecting the monetary value of houses not likely to be affected directly by slum clearance:

> Some experts now feel that unless slum clearance is speeded up there may be an embarrassing surplus of empty property before

long. Charles Goodhart, the economist, stated 'Any attempt to push up rates of house-building to the target level without a simultaneous rapid increase in slum clearance would cause a very rapid rise in voids and would shortly precipitate a collapse in the housing-market'. Such a collapse would mean a serious drop in the value of second-hand houses, and many of us might wake up onc of these days to find the nest-egg we've been living in has suddenly lost its yolk.[22]

The supporters of each of these particular value orientations have counterparts upholding the contrary view. Rapid replacement in the interests of a healthy building industry and a buoyant housing market may be publicized as the 'cynical expropriation' of the poor in the interests of business and real estate.[23] Similarly, the view that replacement may be justified if it serves the local authority's interests as landlord has its opponents. 'In some of our towns there is no shortage of housing and in some of these the local authorities are now turning to the twilight areas with clearance in mind. It has been said that the clearance of such areas was in part a device for finding tenants for their splendid new blocks.'[24] Those who see special value in light and airy dwellings may be contradicted, rightly or wrongly, by those who see virtues in the gloomy and archaic. Modern dwellings are hygienic, practical and well equipped, but for the child there is 'no small place which belongs to it and it alone. Shadows and twilight are as necessary to a child as sun and fresh air'.[25] Gustav Doré's 'Over London by Rail' is an artist's expression of the visual horror of urban life for the working classes. The pictures of the artist L. S. Lowry, whose summers are spent savouring the atmosphere of Sunderland, are much more ambiguous.[26]

The choice between the replacement or retention of an existing dwelling depends upon an assessment of expected benefits. In any particular case the essential questions to be answered are:

1. What weight should be given to the various advantages and disadvantages, the specification array, of living in a particular house in a particular area—the effectiveness of the dwelling as a protection from the weather, how much fresh air and sunlight it admits, how easy it is to keep it clean, how

private it is, how costly, the accessibility of friends and relatives and so forth?

2. What weight should be given to the interests of the different groups involved in a replacement programme. How may one rate the welfare of the children in the family against the selfish or merely mistaken desires of their parents? What weight should be given to the interests of the landlord as against those of the tenant, to the interests of the owner-occupier, the interests of the family whose home will be demolished as against the interests of others who may benefit from the demolition, the interests of the building industry, the interests of housing officials, and in general the interests of those who gain from demolition as against those who lose?

3. Who should weigh these various losses and gains, the beneficiaries and victims, one against the other? How much power should lie with the private landlord, with the tenant, with the local authority, with the councillors, with technical officers, with any particular government department? When a man has a choice between on the one hand making an autonomous decision and yet risking material hardship for himself and his children, and on the other hand of having a better chance of material prosperity by allowing someone else to decide for him, under what circumstances should he choose the one or the other? How much improvement in public health may be regarded as adequate compensation for how much distress on the part of how many families rehoused against their will?

A set of data on the structural condition of given dwellings, on infantile mortality rates, rates of morbid conditions among children and adults, road accidents to young and old, rents, tenure, expressed preferences and so forth, may be regarded by all as fully validated by the evidence. But depending on the society's culture or his membership of a sub-group within the society, one person's answer will be to demolish, another person's answer will be to preserve, while a third person will say, 'I haven't the right to wield any power one way or the other, it is for each family to make the best or the worst of its chances'.

The number of new houses to meet Sunderland's replacement needs cannot be given, therefore, by applying any set of technical criteria or by following blindfold the confident step of a particular profession. What is the minimum standard of housing that must be insisted upon by public authorities? An answer to that deceptively simple request can be found only when its meaning is fully understood. As recently as 1966 the Ministry of Housing clearly recognised the severe problems connected with this issue. Its sub-committee on standards of housing fitness was asked to consider 'the *practicability* of specifying objective criteria for the purposes of slum-clearance, rectification of disrepair and other minimum tolerable standards of housing accommodation'.[27] The sub-committee was asked 'to go ahead with devising new standards without undertaking major research projects'.[28] Even if full research had been recommended and carried out, the search for standards would have been fruitless so long as it continued to be misconceived as a question of technology. In Weber's terms, the crucial issues are those which are primarily oriented to the ends to which replacement decisions must refer.[29]

The task of analysis is to clarify the elements in the present and possible future situation upon which the ultimate judgments of value depend. Such a clarification will be aided by knowledge of past replacement decisions, and the discussion of the current replacement problem will be preceded, therefore, by an examination of the issue as it presented itself to Sunderland in the nineteen thirties, in the fifties and in the early nineteen sixties.

NOTES TO CHAPTER 7

1 Ministry of Reconstruction, *Housing*, Cmd. 6609, 1945.
2 MHLG Housing Management Sub-committee, *Moving from the Slums*, HMSO 1956, pp. 1, 2.
3 'The Heartbreak of a Statistic Like Cathy', *Daily Mirror*, 9 November 1965.
4 Herbert Ashworth, 'Economics of Finance of Twentieth Century Housing', *The British Housing and Planning Year Book 1954*, p. 53.
5 J. B. Cullingworth, *Housing Needs and Planning Policy*, London 1960, pp. 53-54.
6 Housing Symposium, University of Newcastle upon Tyne, 1966.
7 Audrey Harvey, *Tenants in Danger*, Penguin 1964, p. 67.
8 Ashworth, *op. cit.*
9 J. B. Cullingworth, *Housing in Transition: A Case Study in the City of Lancaster 1958–62*, London 1963.

10 Colin Jones, 'The Renewal of Areas of Twilight Housing', RIBA Conference, *Living in Britain*, July 1967, p. 4.

11 *Op. cit.*, p. 235.

12 Housing Act 1957, Part II, 4 (1). See also MHLG, *Circular 69/67*.

13 Hall *v.* Manchester Corporation.

14 Cr. Frank Price, 'Making a Clean Sweep to the City of the Future', *Birmingham Mail*, 10 March 1958.

15 *Planning Delays*, a memorandum submitted by the Town Planning Institute to the MHLG on 5 June 1967.

16 Peter Marris and Martin Rein, *Dilemmas of Social Reform*, London 1967, pp. 9, 15 and *passim*.

17 Notting Hill Housing Trust advertisement, *The Guardian*, 30 June 1964.

18 Jean Stead, 'Oldham Renewed', *The Guardian*, 25 March 1964.

19 Thomas Sharp, *Town Planning*, Harmondsworth, revised edition, 1942.

20 L. Dale, *Towards a Plan for Oxford*, London 1944, Note to Plate III.

21 John N. Jackson, *Surveys for Town and Country Planning*, Hutchison's University Library 1963, p. 12.

22 Robert Troop, *Sunday Times*, 30 July 1967.

23 Marris and Rein, *op. cit.*, p. 14. They are referring to urban renewal in the United States.

24 The device is disapproved of by the MHLG architect who made this statement. Colin Jones, *op. cit.*, p. 13.

25 Lady Allen of Hurtwood, Talk to the Annual Meeting of the Housing Centre, 7 October 1958.

26 See, for example, Lowry's 'Stockport Viaduct', a canvas similar in theme to Doré's 'Over London by Rail'. Other canvasses by Lowry of particular interest here are 'Going to the Match' (1928), 'Old Houses' (1945), 'Oldham Road' (1948) and 'Ferry at Blyth' (1963).

27 MHLG Welsh Office, Central Housing Advisory Committee, Sub-Committee on Standards of Housing Fitness, *Our Older Homes*, HMSO 1966, p. 1. Emphasis added.

28 *Ibid.*, p. 1.

29 Max Weber, *The Theory of Social and Economic Organisation*, Talcott Parsons editor, OUP 1947, p. 162.

Table 7.1

The Percentage of the Total Number of Permanent Houses in the Area Estimated as 'Slums Remaining'

	Total number of permanent houses in area	Estimated as 'slums remaining'	Percentage 'slums remaining'
Liverpool	204,486	88,233	44
Manchester	208,144	68,000	33
Salford	50,881	12,026	24
Birmingham	311,805	50,250	16
Stoke on Trent	82,393	12,000	15
Kingston upon Hull	101,616	14,768	15
Leeds	164,478	22,500	14
Wolverhampton	44,065	5,600	13
Bradford	94,983	11,148	12
Portsmouth	64,068	7,000	11
Bolton	56,400	5,500	10
Sheffield	156,614	13,500	9
Bristol	120,000	10,000	8
Birkenhead	37,500	3,000	8
SUNDERLAND CB/RD	55,316	3,852	7
Swansea	42,972	2,402	6
Newcastle upon Tyne	88,216	4,645	5
Leicester	87,339	4,000	5
Southampton	53,577	2,151	4
Brighton	47,791	1,650	3
Plymouth	49,525	1,500	3
Nottingham	93,109	2,651	3
Coventry	76,159	1,678	2
Luton	32,000	683	2
Middlesbrough	42,130	813	2
Southend on Sea	47,455	228	0·5
Bournemouth	40,491	106	0·3
Cardiff	63,641	141	0·2
Blackpool	45,300	70	0·2

Source: MHLG, *Slum Clearance: Summary of Returns Including Proposals under Section 1 of the Housing Repairs and Rents Act 1954*, HMSO 1955, Cmd. 9593

Table 7.2

Unfit Dwellings in Orders Confirmed January 1955– 31 December 1966 as a Percentage of the Estimate of Unfit Houses in the 1955 Return

	Percentage Number of Orders Confirmed is of 1955 Return		Percentage Number of Orders Confirmed is of 1955 Return
Cardiff	552	Brighton	63
Middlesbrough	402	Bolton	63
Blackpool	207	Sheffield	60
Leicester	193	Bournemouth	58
Nottingham	134	Stoke on Trent	50
SUNDERLAND CB/RD	128	Portsmouth	49
Southampton	95	Birmingham	49
Leeds	95	Coventry	44
Newcastle upon Tyne	89	Kingston upon Hull	43
Birkenhead	86	Swansea	38
Bradford	80	Bristol	38
Salford	80	Manchester	32
Wolverhampton	77	Southend on Sea	26
Plymouth	73	Liverpool	16
Luton	65		

Source: MHLG, *Slum Clearance*, HMSO 1955; MHLG, *Housing Return* (Appendix); and MHLG, *Local Housing Statistics*

Table 7.3

Unfit Dwellings Included in Orders Confirmed 1 January 1955–31 December 1966, per 1,000 of the estimated mid-1966 Population

	Unfit dwellings per 1,000 population		Unfit dwellings per 1,000 population
Salford	66	Portsmouth	16
Leeds	42	Nottingham	11
Manchester	35	Southampton	10
Bradford	30	Bristol	9
Leicester	27	Brighton	6
SUNDERLAND CB/RD	23	Swansea	5
Birmingham	22	Plymouth	5
Bolton	22	Cardiff	3
Stoke on Trent	21	Luton	3
Kingston upon Hull	21	Coventry	2
Middlesbrough	21	Blackpool	1
Liverpool	20	Bournemouth	0·4
Birkenhead	18	Southend on Sea	0·4
Sheffield	17		
Newcastle upon Tyne	16		
Wolverhampton	16		

Source: MHLG, *Housing Return* (Appendix); and
MHLG, *Local Housing Statistics*

CHAPTER 8

THE GROWTH OF SUNDERLAND

The Growth of Sunderland before 1850

Sunderland as an economic and social entity is essentially the creation of nineteenth-century industrialism. At the end of the sixteenth century it was a settlement of thirty households. The town was 'in great decay and little frequented', and its economy consisted only of seven fishing cobles, some shallow coal workings and a few salt pans.[1] Its early development was hindered by the Charter (1606) which gave the Trinity House of Newcastle upon Tyne the right to levy primage due on all goods handled by Sunderland.[2] During the Civil War, however, Newcastle took the Royalist side and refused to send coal to the rebel city of London. This gave the 'upstart artificial harbour' of Sunderland its chance as a coal exporting town. By 1717 Sunderland was important enough to have a River Wear Commission set up by Act of Parliament. The town continued to grow slowly with the port in its primitive state, namely, coal being taken by small keels to colliers standing out in the river. It was not until the 1820s, however, that the town embarked upon its modern career. In 1822 the first coal measures were reached at Hetton. In 1829 564,900 Newcastle chaldrons of this coal (1,498,000 tons) were shipped from the river.[3] The population of the township of Bishopwearmouth, where the coal staithes were located, rose from 9,500 in 1821 to 14,500 in 1831 (an intercensal increase of 53 per cent), and to 24,200 in 1841 (an intercensal increase of 64 per cent).[4]

Growth north of the river was retarded by the fact that the easy gradients of the Team and Derwent directed the early

132

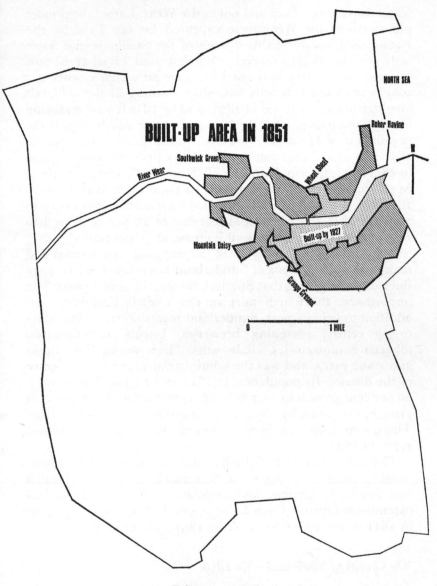

BUILT-UP AREA IN 1851

NORTH SEA

Roker Ravine

N

Southwick Green

Wheat Sheaf

River Wear

Mountain Daisy

Built-up by 1827

Grange Crescent

0   1 MILE

Diagram 8.A

wagonways to the Tyne and not to the Wear. Later (1834) more pits north of the Wear were captured for the Tyne by the Pontop and South Shields branch of the Stanhope and Tyne railway.[5] In 1834, however, the first coal of what is now Wearmouth colliery was reached. The pit's high quality gas coals were loaded directly into ships waiting at the colliery's own staithes, constructed in 1835, and by 1842 it was producing over 55,000 tons of coal. As a result of these developments the population of Monkwearmouth township grew from 1,500 in 1831 to 2,200 in 1841 (an increase of 44 per cent) and to 3,400 in 1851 (an intercensal increase of 56 per cent). The township of Monkwearmouth Shore increased its population from 4,900 in 1821 to 6,100 in 1831 (an intercensal increase of 23 per cent), to 7,700 in 1841 (an intercensal increase of 28 per cent) and to 10,100 in 1851 (an intercensal increase of 31 per cent).[6]

These developments favoured the shipping, commercial and manufacturing interests of Sunderland township itself. In 1831 Burnett was boasting that Sunderland was 'in point of maritime importance, the fourth port in the United Kingdom'.[7] In addition to being a port, Sunderland township was a manufacturing centre, possessing breweries, biscuit manufactories, tobacco manufactories, chain works, iron works, lime works and stone yards, and was the administrative and leisure centre of the district. Its population in 1811 was 12,300. There was a 20 per cent growth to 14,700 in 1821, and a further 16 per cent growth, to 17,100, by 1831. Its population in 1851 was 19,100. There were 1,620 inhabited houses in 1821, 1,720 in 1841 and 1,780 in 1851.

The only other part of the borough involved in the replacement problem of the 1930s was Southwick, the growth of which was due to its quarries and associated lime kilns, as well as extensive shipyards. From being a small village of 600 persons in 1811 it had grown to 2,700 by 1851. (Diagram 8.A.)

The Growth of Sunderland after 1850

After 1850 Sunderland's economy continued to be based partly on shipping,[8] on the export of coal 'for which Sunderland has gained such celebrity',[9] upon coal mined from Monkwearmouth colliery, 'the deepest mine in the world, being 381 fathoms deep'[10] and upon iron forging, the manufacture of iron, paper, pottery, glass and chemicals, and the quarrying and burning of lime.

But after 1850 Sunderland became increasingly important, too, as a shipbuilding centre. In 1801 there had been nine shipyards, in 1814 twenty-four, in 1833 thirty-four and in 1840 sixty-five yards employing 1,600 men.[11] By 1834, according to the annals of Lloyd's Register, Sunderland was 'the most important shipbuilding centre in the country, nearly equalling, as regards number and tonnage of ships built, all the other ports together',[12] and by 1852 most of its main shipyards had come into existence.

But so long as the hull was made of wood and propulsion depended upon sail, Sunderland and the shipbuilding industry of Great Britain suffered keen competition from, for example, the United States, where forests grew freely.[13] In 1787, however, the iron hull of John Wilkinson's canal barge *Trial* began a process which was to culminate in Sunderland's pre-eminence as a shipbuilding centre.[14] The first iron ship to be launched on the Wear was the *Loftus*, in 1852; but 1863, the year in which Doxford's launched their last wooden ship, is generally regarded as the pivotal year for Sunderland when the age of iron really began.[15] Still more important for Sunderland was the replacement of iron by steel. First the Bessemer converter (1856), then the Siemens Open Hearth (1866) and finally the Gilchrist-Thomas basic process (1878) made steel progressively cheaper as a material for the hull.

Sunderland was also a celebrated centre for the construction of sailing ships. For example, the ship described by Joseph Conrad as 'the wonderful *Torrens*' when he was its first mate in 1891–3, and which broke the record for the run to Australia, was built at Laing's yard in 1875. 'That steel grey lovely barque' as Masefield called the *Chepica* was another Wear ship. But Sunderland owes less to sail than to steam. William Symington took out his patent for a marine steam engine in 1786 and sailed his *Charlotte Dundas* under steam on the Forth and Clyde canal in 1803. In 1819 the *Savannah* used steam for eighty hours during her twenty-nine-day crossing of the Atlantic, and in 1833 the *Royal William* crossed the Atlantic entirely under steam. Again, however, it was not until mid-century that innovations had

135

accumulated to such an extent that this mode of propulsion became economically competitive on a large scale. In 1854 John Elder of Govan enabled steamships to effect great savings in fuel with his compound engine. Later came triple and quadruple expansion engines.[16]

Sunderland's growth was hastened by other developments. The repeal of the Corn Laws and the financial reforms that followed, the discovery of the Australian and Californian goldfields, the conquest of India by the products of the Lancashire power loom, the opening up of China, the astounding development of the United States, all meant the dawn of a new industrial epoch and, especially important for Sunderland, a 'colossal and unparalleled' expansion in world trade.[17] The opening of the Suez Canal in 1869 strongly reinforced the position of powered ships on one of the great trade routes of the world. After 1880 shipbuilding was greatly stimulated when the cable, the railway and a multitude of other forces expanded trade between nations, and resulted in a huge expansion of Britain's own imports and exports.[18]

Sunderland's shipbuilding industry produced only 8,000 tons in the peak year of 1804, 64,400 tons in the peak year of 1840. 68,500 tons in the peak year of 1853, and 73,100 tons in the peak year of 1865. The next peak, however, 1872, showed production to have almost doubled to 134,800 tons. In 1883 212,300 tons were produced, in 1901 295,500 tons, and in 1906 366,000 tons. (Table 8.1.)[19]

At the time of the Census of 1901 out of the 48,968 occupied males 9,982 (20 per cent) were engaged in the construction of ships. Around shipbuilding grew a complex of metal producing and metal working industries, and a further 7,222 men were employed in engineering and machine making (15 per cent).

After 1850, therefore, Sunderland became the Luton, the Slough, the Coventry or the Cape Kennedy of the nineteenth century, playing a leading part in the development of the most advanced technology of the time. It was a boom town with high wages. The secretary of the Amalgamated Society of Engineers (Walter Allen) told the 1867 commission on the Trade Unions that 'away in the North of England wages have improved vastly within these few years—year after year almost, but this has arisen from the fact of the large amount of shipbuilding going on at Newcastle and the different parts round there'.[20]

In March 1882, the Sunderland engineers are reported to have for 'years past' had 3s. od. or 4s. od. higher rates than their neighbours in Newcastle, and that in January 1881 had an increase of 2s. od. and now had received 2s. od. more. . . . In 1883 Sunderland engineers, then receiving the highest rate they ever had, asked for another rise, and received an increase of 2s. od. to those of 35s. od. or under, and 1s. od. to those at over 35s. od. This would indicate that they then received 37s. od., which is not only higher than they ever had before, but higher than they ever had since.[21]

In the late 1840s, the time-rates for Sunderland shipwrights had been 18s. od. a week; the rate rose gradually to about £2 os. od. a week at the end of the century, although in exceptional early years (for example, 1853) it was already as high as 39s. od. a week.[22] The wages in various engineering trades were even higher than rates in shipbuilding. In boiler-shops, anglesmiths had time-rates of 41s. od. a week in 1891 and 42s. od. a week in 1899–1901.[23]

Engineers and shipyard workers were better paid than other occupational groups. In 1886 the average earnings in a full week of all male workers in engineering and shipbuilding was 23 shillings, in coalmining it was 21·2 shillings and in textiles only 19·4 shillings. In 1906 the average earnings for males in a full week was 31·5 shillings for coalminers, 28·1 shillings for engineering workers and shipbuilders and only 22·9 shillings for textile workers.[24] Not only were wages high and rising; the cost of living was falling. The cost of living index, as calculated by Bowley, stood at 105 in 1880 (1914 = 100), and it fell throughout the period to 1896, when it stood at 83. It then showed a secular rise to the time of the first world war.[25]

At the period of its most rapid growth, therefore, Sunderland did not have the problem of accommodating pauper apprentices or newly urbanised peasants. On the contrary, it was attracting and housing an elite from the class of skilled artisans.

In the second half of the nineteenth century, too, the business class seemed to take its urban responsibilities more seriously.[26] During this period local industrialists, whatever their motives, were more active in their concern for the well-being of the towns in which they made their money than before or since, whether it was Bolckow who 'stood by the side of the iron cradle in which Middlesbrough was rocked and had watched over the child with care as it grew',[27] the Wills family and the Thomases at Bristol, Joseph Chamberlain at Birmingham or the Partingtons and Woods at Glossop.[28] Sunderland's local business men engaged in a variety of public activities, as J.P.s, town councillors, River Wear commissioners, and members of other bodies.[29]

In 1851 there were 8,600 houses within the pre-1967 boundaries of the county borough. During the period of its Victorian growth and prosperity 1851–1911, it added a further 18,100 houses. The parishes which were added to Sunderland in 1967, Offerton, Tunstall, Ryhope, Silksworth, Ford, Hylton and Herrington, had a stock of 600 houses in 1851; by 1921 (the figure for 1911 is not given in the Census) this stock had increased to 4,600.[30]

After the first world war local industrialists as the providers of civic amenities were gradually superseded by a democratised local government and a more active bureaucracy. The depression of 1907–08 brought to a close Sunderland's growth. 'It is literally true that streets of houses in Pallion were empty and boarded up. Many people left the district to seek work elsewhere. Men broke stones in the grounds of the workhouse for 2s. 0d. a day.'[31] On Friday mornings a band of young men would go out with washing baskets into the colliery districts. 'They were never refused a loaf of bread.'[32] Sunderland shipbuilders have filled their order books over the past twenty years, but the town, except under wartime or immediate postwar conditions (333,300 tons in 1920; 374,800 tons in 1942), never again showed the same dominance of the shipbuilding market. In 1923 production was at a lower level than it had been since 1875, in 1926 it was lower than it had been since 1844, and in 1932 it was lower than it had been in 1790. Marine engineering had to meet similar difficulties.

> We regret that the position forecast last December—that unless more orders for engines were obtained, there would be heavy redundancies in our engine works—has occurred. We have only booked one engine in the last twelve months and the prospects of

booking any more for a reasonably early delivery appear unlikely.[33]

The nineteen twenties and thirties, therefore, gave Sunderland the reputation of a depressed, poor town—a northern relic of some old forgotten, far-off time. But between 1851 and 1914, houses were being built predominantly for the workers in industries which, though subject to cyclical slumps, were in a phase of secular growth. The coalminers, the shipyard workers and the engineering workers were particularly well-paid in comparison with workers in other occupations. The majority of these dwellings were in the form of the terraced bungalow—the single-storied Sunderland cottage. They were built of locally-produced clay brick (in contrast to, for example, the poor shale brick of the working-class houses of Oldham produced in the same period), they were mortared by the high quality lime of the local quarries and, after 1875, the indigenous economic and social forces which were producing these cottage streets were supplemented by new by-laws which controlled the construction of all new dwellings.

NOTES TO CHAPTER 8

1 Report of the Commissioners sent by Queen Elizabeth to Sunderland 1588–89 to inquire why no customs dues were forthcoming.

2 Taylor Potts, *Sunderland: A History of the Town, Port, Trade and Commerce*, Sunderland 1892, p. 219.

3 James Burnett, *Directory of the Parishes of Sunderland, Bishopwearmouth, Monkwearmouth and Monkwearmouth Shore*, Bishopwearmouth 1831.

4 *Census of Great Britain, 1851*, Volume II, Division X, p. 21.

5 James Bird, *The Major Sea Ports of the United Kingdom*, London 1963.

6 *Census of Great Britain, 1851*, Volume II, Division X, p. 23.

7 James Burnett, *op. cit.*

8 It was still claimed in 1855 that Sunderland was the fourth port after London, Liverpool and Newcastle in respect of the number and tonnage of ships registered. William Whellan, *The History, Topography and Directory of the County Palatine of Durham*, 1856.

9 Barnes, *Directory of Sunderland*, 1865, p. 5.

10 *Ibid.*, p. 5.

11 W. C. Mitchell, *History of Sunderland*, Sunderland 1919.

12 J. W. Smith and T. S. Holden, *Where Ships are Born*, Sunderland 1946, p. 1.

13 W. H. B. Court, *A Concise Economic History of Britain from 1750 to Recent Times*, Cambridge 1954.

14 C. R. Fay, *Great Britain from Adam Smith to the present day* (1928), Fifth edition, 1950.

15 Mitchell, *op. cit.*

16 Later developments—turbines, the change to oil-burning in order to raise steam, and subsequently the change to the marine internal-combustion engine, the development of specialised ships such as the Doxford Turret steamer or the highly specialised refrigerator ships produced by Bartram's—have been important in keeping Sunderland firms viable, but they have not had the same importance in the growth of the town as had earlier developments. See C. R. Fay, *op. cit.*, and R. S. Cogdon, 'Civil Engineering in the Development of Shipyards . . . in the Port of Sunderland', Institution of Civil Engineers' Northern Counties Association, *Chairman's Address 1960–61.*

17 Friedrich Engels, Preface to *The Condition of the Working Class in England in 1844*, English Edition 1892, p. vi.

18 Court, *op. cit.*

19 Smith and Holden, *op. cit.*, p. 93.

20 A. L. Bowley and George H. Wood, 'Wages in Shipbuilding: Non-Trade Union Sources', *Journal of the Royal Statistical Society*, September 1905, p. 593.

21 *Ibid.*, p. 594.

22 Bowley and Wood, *op. cit.*, March 1905, pp. 104–37; and Bowley and Wood, *op. cit.*, September 1905.

23 Bowley and Wood, *op. cit.*, March 1905.

24 A. L. Bowley, *Wages and Income in the United Kingdom since 1860*, Cambridge 1937, pp. 50, 51.

25 Bowley, *op. cit.*, p. 30.

26 Edward Shils, 'The Intellectuals—Great Britain', *Encounter*, April 1955, p. 11.

27 Asa Briggs, *Victorian Cities*, London 1963, p. 259.

28 See, e.g. A. H. Birch, *Small-Town Politics: A Study of Political Life in Glossop*, London 1959, esp. pp. 8–33.

29 *Seaports on the N.E. Railway: Sunderland*, Edinburgh 1898.

30 The source of these figures are the successive Censuses of England and Wales. 'Houses' means inhabited houses.

31 C. H. G. Hopkins, *Pallion 1874–1954*, Sunderland 1954, p. 58.

32 *Ibid.*, p. 51.

33 *Sunderland Echo*, 20 April 1967. The report refers to the decision to pay off 400 of the 640 men employed at the George Clark Engine Works.

Table 8.1

Annual Tonnage of Ships Launched:
Sunderland 1836–1966

Year	Gross Tonnage (Thousands)	Year	Gross Tonnage (Thousands)	Year	Gross Tonnage (Thousands)
1836	27	1866	63	1896	216
1837	32	1867	52	1897	181
1838	43	1868	70	1898	259
1839	60	1869	72	1899	258
1840	64	1870	70	1900	267
1841	40	1871	82	1901	296
1842	26	1872	135	1902	251
1843	20	1873	99	1903	206
1844	27	1874	88	1904	247
1845	38	1875	80	1905	343
1846	42	1876	54	1906	366
1847	48	1877	88	1907	314
1848	38	1878	113	1908	92
1849	44	1879	87	1909	142
1850	50	1880	109	1910	185
1851	52	1881	131	1911	321
1852	57	1882	183	1912	346
1853	68	1883	212	1913	342
1854	67	1884	100	1914	319
1855	61	1885	62	1915	111
1856	63	1886	57	1916	160
1857	55	1887	84	1917	210
1858	42	1888	143	1918	268
1859	37	1889	217	1919	289
1860	40	1890	194	1920	333
1861	47	1891	189	1921	154
1862	57	1892	191	1922	131
1863	70	1893	118	1923	57
1864	72	1894	166	1924	208
1865	73	1895	126	1925	103

Table 8.1—*Contd.*

Year	Gross Tonnage (Thousands)	Year	Gross Tonnage (Thousands)	Year	Gross Tonnage (Thousands)
1926	37	1941	352	1956	217
1927	161	1942	375	1957	213
1928	208	1943	300	1958	270
1929	244	1944	258	1959	249
1930	176	1945	218	1960	210
1931	9	1946	192	1961	269
1932	3	1947	194	1962	218
1933	12	1948	178	1963	209
1934	19	1949	182	1964	234
1935	31	1950	192	1965	258
1936	139	1951	198	1966	269
1937	156	1952	242		
1938	170	1953	194		
1939	123	1954	190		
1940	206	1955	223		

Source: Smith and Holden, *op. cit.*, and
Sunderland Echo

SECTION II
Replacement in the Nineteen Thirties

CHAPTER 9

SLUM CLEARANCE IN THE NINETEEN THIRTIES

Sunderland's pre-1850 Dwellings

Many of the working-class dwellings built in Sunderland before 1850 were in the form of single-storied cottages. 'What is a house, is it the single-storied cottage of Sunderland, the double-storied pair of flats in Newcastle or the six-storied, twelve-flatted tenements of Edinburgh?'[1]

The single-storied cottage is to be found in other towns but nowhere in such numbers as in Sunderland. With the exception of the tenements of Sunderland township itself, a few Tyneside flats scattered across the town and even fewer back-to-backs it was the almost universal solution in Sunderland to the problem of the working-class family which could afford to buy only a small amount of dwelling space. They were praised by the commissioners who examined the state of the large towns and populous districts in the 1840s. They refer to Sunderland's 'single-storied cottages, occupied by one or at most two families; comfortable and cleanly, and furnished with small yards and other conveniences'.[2] With its own paved and walled yard, with front street and back lane, with no shared passages, landings or other shared amenities, the single-storied Sunderland cottage avoided many of the drawbacks of the courts, back-to-backs, tenements, two-storied flats and shared dwellings of other towns.

But every great city had one or more slums and in general a separate territory had been assigned to it. Ventilation was impeded by the confused method of building the whole quarter. The long rows of irregularly built dwellings bordered streets which were generally unpaved, dirty and filled with animal and vegetable matter, without sewers or gutters. Thus Engels generalised from the early studies of urban development.[3] Many of these dwellings had survived into the twentieth century. In his first study of York, Rowntree describes its slums, back-to-back, 'not-through' and court dwellings, which were poor from the day they were built, and were old and decrepit by 1899.[4] They were still there thirty-five years later when he conducted his second survey of York.[5]

Most of the houses which Sunderland replaced in the 1930s, certainly, were built as slums and nearly a hundred years previously had been publicly recognised as places of 'filth and tottering ruin'. After reading reports of the slums of Sunderland in 1832, Charles Greville, clerk of the Privy Council, recorded that conditions there were 'more suitable to the barbarism of the interior of Africa. We who float on the surface of society know but little of the privations and sufferings which pervade the masses'.[6]

Much of the housing in Sunderland parish consisted of back-to-back dwellings 'leaving no intervening space for ventilation or necessary conveniences'.[7] Of the thirty-seven streets in the parish, thirteen were 10 feet or narrower. Bull Lane, for example, was 5 ft. 3 ins. in width, Spencer Lane 6 feet, Moor Lane and Watson Lane 6 ft. 6 ins. Union Lane, some of which is still standing, complete with evidence of a former slaughter house, is 10 ft. wide. An investigation into housing in various towns in the 1880s condemned the absence of backyards and bad ventilation as 'among the most mischievous evils attaching to poor dwellings in populous neighbourhoods'.[8]

The houses of Sunderland parish consisted characteristically of three or more storeys and dark cellars.[9] The original structural deficiencies of ventilation and natural lighting were exacerbated by the operation of the window tax. In order to avoid it owners blocked up windows. As the commissioners said, the effect of this was to 'greatly aggravate' and in some cases to constitute 'the primary cause of' much sickness and mortality.[10]

Most of the cottages which were being built in Bishopwearmouth in the 1840s had privies in their backyards, and in some of the 'principal houses' there were water closets emptying into a cesspool.[11] In the tenements of the East End, however, the position was quite different. The parish of Sunderland housed 17,000 people (3,700 families), and only 13 per cent of the 1,700 dwellings had a privy attached.

> There are several hundreds of houses let into tenements, inhabited by six or seven families without the slightest convenience of this description, producing necessarily much uncleanliness, causing offensive smells, and operating in many respects detrimentally to the health and general comfort of the inhabitants.[12]

The soil of those families without privies was removed by night-carts, 'or suffered to remain in boxes', which were occasionally emptied into the river, some public ashpit or onto the public middensteads.[13]

The conflict between housing needs and the disposal of the dead also caused the commissioners great concern. The churchyards were 'all crowded with the remains of the dead, and scarcely a day passes over but that in preparing a place of sepulture all decency and propriety are outraged by the exposure to the public gaze of the mouldering remains of some fellow mortal'.[14]

Water was laid on to fewer than seven hundred of the municipal borough's 6,000 houses;[15] and north of the river, wells were the only source of water and 'questions of extreme importance' had been raised by the fact that the sinking of Monkwearmouth pit had at one period drained them all dry.

Bathrooms were, of course, unknown in working-class houses, and the prices at the public bath houses were 'manifestly too high for the means of the labouring class'.

Clothes washing was also of interest to the commissioners. One 'not very cleanly custom' received their particular attention.

> We copied from the lips of a female of the labouring classes a description of this odoriferous process. The following is the good dame's description of this specimen of North Country cleanliness. 'The urine is kept in stone bottles until very strong, and then added to the soapsuds.' This is certainly a roundabout and filthy mode of obtaining carbonate of ammonia.[16]

With the exception of clearances for the construction of railways, railway termini, docks and so forth (as part of old

Sunderland was cleared to make way for the Hudson Dock), the slums—built as slums in the first half of the nineteenth century and before—found successive generations of occupiers. The mid-century slum which had been used for scores of years in the manner described above was still physically present, with the difference that it was more aged and more decrepit.

The Growth of Local Authority Power

The desirability of giving public agencies the right to remove nuisances (such as offensive middensteads) and to improve the environment (by the provision of water supplies, cemeteries and sewerage systems) was fully recognised by 1848. A Nuisance Removal Act was passed in 1846, a Town Improvement Clauses Act in 1847, and the 1848 Public Health Act empowered the Central Board of Health to set up local boards on the petition of rate-payers or compulsorily when mortality reached a certain figure. These Boards of Health were expected to deal with problems of sewerage, water supply and offensive trades. In Sunderland itself some of these powers had been obtained much earlier. Under the Sunderland Improvement Act of 1809 commissioners were appointed with powers to levy assessment and to pave, light and cleanse the streets, to build a market hall and town hall, and to establish a river watch; in 1824 the commissioners 'lighted the town brilliantly with gas'.[17] In 1826 another Sunderland Improvement Act enlarged the powers of the commissioners.

By 1864 Disraeli was pressing upon the Tories his policy of (as he said) *sanitas sanitatum, omnia sanitas*, a phrase later seized upon by Randolph Churchill as expressing 'the scheme of social progress and reform' of Tory democracy.[18] It was under Richard Cross, Disraeli's Home Secretary, that the first slum clearance legislation was passed, the Artisans' and Labourers' Dwellings Improvement Act of 1875. The 'clearance schemes' of this and the other Cross Acts (1879 and 1882) gave local authorities the power to pull down whole areas and have them reconstructed with new buildings devoted to the use of the workers, where the houses to be demolished were 'so structurally defective as to be incapable of repair, and so ill-placed with reference to each other as to require to bring them up to proper sanitary conditions nothing short of demolition and reconstruction'.[19] The Housing of the Working Classes Act of 1890 consolidated these measures, and other housing legislation of the previous forty years.

The Housing, Town Planning etc. Act of 1919 required local authorities to complete a 'Form of Survey of Housing Needs'. Section II of this form asked for an estimate of the number of houses needed during the following three years to rehouse persons to be displaced by clearance of unhealthy areas, replace other houses which were unfit for human habitation and could not be made fit and to replace other houses which, although they could not at that time be regarded as unfit for human habitation, 'fell definitely below a reasonable standard'. Under Section V of the survey the Medical Officer of Health was asked to indicate on a six-inch Ordnance Survey map the extent of four different types of area where replacement needs existed, the fourth group of which was 'any considerable areas which, although in fair sanitary condition, nevertheless for one reason or another fall definitely below the ultimate standard at which it is reasonable to aim, or contain a large proportion of houses which fall below such a standard'.

Very little was accomplished in Sunderland under these provisions. Before the first world war some dwellings were demolished. They were replaced by Sunderland's earliest council houses, eighty-four tenements, which were first occupied in 1903. 'As a result of a progressive housing policy the old insanitary tenements have been practically swept away and replaced by model artisans' dwellings.'[20] An equally modest view was taken of the local authority's powers after the 1919 Act. 'The council are at present building 94 houses on Pallion Estate—beyond this nothing is contemplated owing to the exceedingly unsatisfactory financial conditions.'[21]

The Chamberlain Act of 1923 made grants available to local authorities to meet half the loss incurred in slum clearance and rehousing, but the impact of this too was slight. The first effective slum clearance measure was the Greenwood Act of 1930. This made it compulsory for local authorities to carry out a survey and to prepare a plan to abolish in five years—by demolition or improvement—all those found to be slums.

Slum clearance in the 1930s

In the early 1930s building costs fell and it became national policy to withdraw local authorities from the provision of dwellings to meet the housing shortage and general needs. Normal working class demands could now be left to private enterprise, without subsidy. The Greenwood Act was therefore followed in 1933 by legislation which limited the local authority to the task of housing replacement. Exchequer grants ceased for ordinary rehousing, and slum clearance became the only category to qualify for subsidy. Local authorities were asked to prepare programmes for slum clearance 'on the basis of clearing all areas that required clearance not later than 1938'.[22]

Six hundred and fifty-three dwellings were initially included in Sunderland's 1930–35 programme. In 1931 the programme was increased to 709, and the new five-year programme required by the 1933 Act more than doubled this to 1,455.[23] Before 1930 replacement for all purposes took place at the rate of about 25 or 30 dwellings a year; by contrast, 549 dwellings were demolished in 1939, mainly under the impulse of slum-clearance legislation. (Table 9.1.)

The result of these replacement policies, therefore, was a massive de-population of the slum areas. In 1931 East ward, Central ward and Sunderland ward (the East End) had a population of 26,300. These three wards, together with a part of Bridge ward, had been amalgamated to form a new Central ward by the time of the 1951 Census. This new Central ward had a population of 13,200 – a population decrease of 50 per cent since 1931. Monkwearmouth ward (1951 boundaries) declined in population from 11,700 in 1931 to 6,700 in 1951, a decrease of 43 per cent. Monkwearmouth Shore ward had a population of 12,000 in 1931, and this had fallen to 7,700 by 1951, a decrease of 36 per cent. Colliery ward lost 21 per cent of its population in the same period.

Benefits

Who benefited from these measures and in what identifiable ways? Slum-clearance decisions depended on structure and lay-out, not on over-crowding.[24] Because of the population pattern of the slum areas, however, these measures tended to make densities lower, and in particular affected large numbers of children (especially after 1936 when the obligation to abate over-crowding was laid upon local authorities). On average there were 5·06 persons in each of the families rehoused in the four years 1933–6,[25] as compared with 4·02 in the town as a whole. Slum clearance, therefore, attacked directly the problem of 'the boy on the mildewed bed'.[26] The way in which slum-clearance in the 1930s affected children is shown in studies in other towns too. 'These families are not an ordinary sample of the working-class community in Bristol. They consist largely of families in which the number of dependent children is abnormally high.'[27]

The first and obvious benefit aimed at was an improvement in the health of the population. Statistical studies had for long shown an association between slum conditions and high death and morbidity rates. It was taken for granted by many people (though by no means everybody) that the association was one of cause and effect.

Sunderland was especially important in the development of views about the connection between the slum and public health for the first victim[28] of asiatic cholera in England was claimed in the town. In 1848 Sunderland was again the first town to be affected. Deaths from cholera and other infectious diseases were concentrated in the pre-1850 tenements of Sunderland parish.[29]

Other obvious benefits were higher space standards, better amenities and greater value for money. The remedy for the slum was a slightly modified form of the Tudor Walters' standard–the three-bedroom dwelling in the surburban estate, with adequate sunlight and ventilation assured by low density development.[30] The 445 families which were rehoused in Sunderland in 1933, 1934, 1935 and 1936 had occupied 881 rooms in the slums. They occupied 1,671 rooms in their new homes. They had in addition a bath, a scullery, a w.c., a garden and other amenities. The average rent was higher by 3s. 8d. per family, but the rent per room had fallen from 2s. 10d. to 2s. 5d.[31]

In details, too, there were unequivocal benefits. 'One persistent evil of slum property is the presence of bugs, for although bugs have not been definitely connected with carrying disease, yet there is sufficient evidence that a bug-ridden house has ill effects upon health.' Tenants of infested slum houses were required to call at the health office for soap, paraffin and Izal. On the day of their rehousing their bedding was removed for steam disinfestation, and they themselves scrubbed all their furniture and bedsteads under the supervision of a health inspector. 'I believe the object lesson of making the tenants carry out the disinfestation is a good one.'[32] Out of the 179 families rehoused in 1934, the bedding and furniture of 103 (57 per cent) had to be disinfested.[33]

The Sunderland MOH, through the visitors of the Guild of Health, tried in 1936 to assess the effects of slum-clearance upon the families rehoused. Most of these families were at Ford Estate or Marley Potts (64 per cent) and the majority had been in their new homes for about a year (56 per cent). (Table 9.2 and Table 9.3.) Over 90 per cent of the families expressed overall satisfaction with their council dwelling as compared with their former homes. (Table 9.4.) These findings are supported by the fact that throughout the period of clearance letters to the local newspaper on the subject almost exclusively expressed the hope that clearance would be accelerated.

> I live in a slum area which will not be dealt with for twelve months. The house is in too bad a condition to repair. Eight people sleep in one room, as the rain pours in the others. The ceilings are down, and the w.c. is not a flush. Outside there is a rubbish heap which the Corporation won't move, and the flies come in in hundreds.[34]

Early studies elsewhere, such as that by the MOH for Edinburgh, which compared families removed to new cottages in 1912 with a control-group still under bad conditions in old tenement houses, had shown that families benefited not only in terms of their feeling of satisfaction, but also in terms of health and longevity.[35]

Losses

Early studies had suggested also, however, that there may be a need to mitigate certain drawbacks for all slum-cleared groups and that some groups of persons might find themselves actually worse off in new dwellings. The first cause of such drawbacks was the poverty of the slum dwellers. The 1885 commissioners gave detailed accounts of the earnings of the various employment groups most likely to be affected by the replacement schemes, for example, costermongers, hawkers, and 'the large class of dock-labourers', such as were to be found in Sunderland's East End. The commissioners insisted that 'sight must never be lost' of the precarious condition of their earnings. 'Even if employment were regular, the wages are so low that existence must be a struggle at the best of times.'[36] The commissioners mention two associated drawbacks: 'In the remoter suburbs food is much dearer than in the centre of the town. There is moreover to be considered the difficulty many of the poor have in moving from a neighbourhood on account of the credit they have built up with the little shopkeepers of the district.'[37]

The MOH for Stockton-on-Tees, G. C. M. McGonigle, studied families rehoused in 1927, and compared them with families still in the slums. He was disconcerted to find that unlike the earlier experience in Edinburgh, the death-rate had risen among the rehoused families and fallen among the slum families, and at all ages was higher for the former than for the latter. He attributed the high rates to inadequate diet resulting from insufficient money.[38]

The study by the Sunderland MOH in 1936 had the same objective, 'to determine whether the removed families pay increased rents at the expense of vital foodstuffs'.[39] The average weekly income per family from all sources was £2 3s. 4d. and the average income per person per day was 1s. 2½d. Nearly one half of the families (44 per cent) derived their income solely from public sources, the Unemployment Insurance Board, the Unemployment Assistance Board, the Public Assistance Committee or solely from a combination of these three agencies. A further 33 per cent derived part of their income from these agencies. This gives a total of 77 per cent who derived practically all their income from public relief. (Table 9.5.) Sixty per cent of the families said that the cost of food was higher in the new neighbourhood. Twenty-three per cent said that at least one person in the family was short of food. Some of the families which said they were not short of food said that they were nevertheless 'better fed in town', or that there was 'shortage in the case of illness' or that under other special circumstances they did not have enough to eat. While respondents nevertheless took the view, on the whole, that the extra amenities and the improvement in their health outweighed the extra cost of the new homes (84 per cent), the conclusion of the MOH was that his survey had 'definitely proved' that there were large numbers of families removed from slum areas to new housing estates 'who have difficulty in obtaining essential food values'.[40]

Another hazard which faced some slum-cleared families was the loss of accessibility.

> A large class of labourers hear of casual work to be had at six o'clock next morning, so they must choose a central position from which no part of the town is inaccessible. The dock labourers are a class that must be on the spot, because they have always to wait for calls that may arise at any moment. Then there is the extensive and hard-working population of coster-mongers. The only choice a coster-monger seems to have in settling his residence is either to live near the locality where he obtains a market for his goods or else near the place where he lays in his stock. This precarious element in the struggle for employment is thus a most powerful cause of the pressure upon habitable space. If regular work was to be had the poor might pick and choose the locality for their dwellings.[41]

In the 1930s, as in the 1880s, the subsidiary employment of the wife had to be taken into consideration. 'There is no doubt that the work of charwomen and seampstresses attract great numbers to the densely populated districts which provides such employment and away from the suburbs where such work would be out of reach.'[42] The Sunderland MOH's conclusion was the same, that it would be beneficial if accommodation could be found in the East End for those who worked in the docks.[43]

Finally there was the loss to be considered which resulted from the mere fact of disturbance itself, 'the reluctance that is found among the poor to leave their old neighbours',[44] and again the findings and sentiments of the 1885 Commission are echoed by the Sunderland MOH. He concludes that elderly couples would have benefited if accommodation could have been found for them 'near their old homes'.[45]

Objectors came forward at the five public inquiries–9 May

1933, 15 May 1934, 29 January 1936, 7 September 1937 and 15 February 1938.

The owner of a house in Covent Garden Street, for example, complained that the Corporation's case against the property was of a 'very trifling nature'. A builder and contractor called as a witness said that the dwelling was well-built, safe, strong and well lighted and ventilated, with a water-tight roof and a large yard. In reply the Town Clerk argued that there was no indoor water, the sanitary accommodation was insufficient, and there was no sink, wash-house or ventilated food cupboard. 'That, to my mind, is the essence of the matter–the house is not provided with the essentials for the health of the people living in it.'[46] In an attempt to retain what they regarded as superior conditions, some families placed themselves under siege.

> Three elderly Sunderland spinster sisters, who love their old home more than anything in life, are holding up one of the greatest improvement schemes undertaken in the East End for many years. For many weeks Corporation workmen have been engaged in demolishing the slum area bounded by High Street East, George Street, Spring Garden Lane and Coronation Street. 'They are very respectable and rather eccentric women', a neighbour told me. 'Although every other tenant has been persuaded to leave– and some of them not without some difficulty–the Misses Coleman seem determined to remain.'
>
> The Corporation, of course, have very wide powers to secure eviction, and the sisters' gallant fight for what they consider their rights must soon come to an end.[47]

Thirty-seven of the 445 rehoused families found that after several months or years they still felt, on the whole, worse off in their new homes: the schools, the shops, or the town were too far away, the grandmother was confined to the house, the house was too expensive or draughty, they were lonely and so forth.[48]

The Balance of Gains and Losses

But the issues raised by the removal of these century-old slums in the 1930s were relatively straightforward. No survey prior to rehousing sought to elicit the views of families about the impending move, but it might be supposed that many of them lived in wretched accommodation for the sole reason that they were unable to afford anything better. The Misses Coleman, for example, became the victims of hostile demonstrations as a result of their obduracy. 'Certain people have shown a hooligan spirit by demonstrating outside the house and throwing stones. We urge them to refrain from repeating such conduct.' The local newspaper found it necessary to explain that the sisters were not refusing to leave. They merely harboured the quaint idea that as they were living rent free in their own house, they were right in waiting until the Corporation was able to offer them alternative rent-free accommodation.[49] In any case, the interests of the children could largely justify the use of compulsion; with certain exceptions, such as the Town Clerk's arguments in the Covent Garden Street case, public health was stressed rather than matters of individual health and hygiene which did not affect other people; it could be argued that the welfare of other people in the town ought to override the interests of those who no doubt would lose in the transaction; and in the event the wishes of the local authority were vindicated by the satisfaction of the great majority of rehoused families.

NOTES TO CHAPTER 9

1 Harry Barnes, *Housing: The Facts and the Future*, London 1923, p. 27.
2 The Commissioners for Inquiring into the State of Large Towns and Populous Districts, *Second Report*, Appendix, HMSO 1845, p. 192.
3 Friedrich Engels, 'The Great Towns', *The Condition of the Working Classes in England in 1844* (German Edition 1845), London 1892, p. 26.
4 B. Seebohm Rowntree, *Poverty, a Study of Town Life*, London 1901.
5 *Poverty and Progress*, London 1941.
6 Quoted David Roberts, *Victorian Origins of the British Welfare State*, New Haven 1960, p. 4.
7 The Commissioners for Inquiring into the State of Large Towns and Populous Districts, *Second Report*, Appendix, HMSO 1845, p. 191.
8 Royal Commission on the Housing of the Working Classes, *First Report*, HMSO 1885, p. 11.
9 Large Towns Commission, *Op. cit.*, p. 192.
10 *Ibid.*, p. 201.
11 *Ibid.*, p. 202.
12 *Ibid.*, p. 202.
13 *Ibid.*, p. 202.

14 *Ibid.*, p. 200.
15 *Ibid.*, p. 197.
16 *Ibid.*, p. 197.
17 James Burnett, *History of Sunderland*, Sunderland 1830, p. 45.
18 Samuel H. Beer, *Modern British Politics*, London 1965, p. 265.
19 Royal Commission on the Housing of the Working Classes, *First Report*, HMSO 1885, p. 6.
20 *The Borough Guide to Sunderland for 1913.*
21 County Borough of Sunderland, *The Annual Report on the Health and Sanitary Conditions of Sunderland for the Year 1920*, p. 25.
22 Ministry of Health Circular, 1933.
23 County Borough of Sunderland, *Annual Report of the MOH for the year 1938.*
24 County Borough of Sunderland, *Annual Report of the MOH for the year 1937*, pp. 141–42.
25 County Borough of Sunderland, *Annual Report of the MOH for the year 1936.*
26 Robert Sinclair, *Metropolitan Man* (1938 Ed.) London, p. 58.
27 Rosamund Jevons and John Madge, *Housing Estates*, Bristol 1946, p. 9.
28 William Sproat, was the first, officially. He died at noon on 26 October 1831 in his first-floor room at the Fish Quay. Cholera, which had been kindled in India and which had swept through Persia and hence to Europe, reached the unprepared towns of England through Sunderland. Norman Longmate, *King Cholera*, London 1966. See also W. Reid Clanny, *The Cholera of Sunderland*, 1832.
29 In the cholera epidemic of July–December 1866 there were sixty-four deaths in the area bounded by High Street on the north, Coronation Street on the south, Villiers Street on the west and the Town Moor on the east; in all the rest of the town there were fifteen deaths. The rate of deaths from infectious diseases per thousand population in 1890 was 20 for the parish of Saint John in the East End, while for the well-to-do parish of Christ Church the rate was four per thousand. Data taken from six-inch map in Sunderland museum archives 'Infectious Diseases in Sunderland in 1890'.
30 The Local Government Board, *Report of the Committee on Building Construction in Connection with the Provision of Dwellings for the Working Classes* (The Tudor Walters Committee), HMSO 1918.
31 County Borough of Sunderland, *Annual Report of the MOH for the year 1936.*
32 County Borough of Sunderland, *Annual Report of the MOH for the year 1934*, pp. 125, 126.
33 County Borough of Sunderland, *Annual Report of the MOH for the year 1934.*
34 Letter to the *Sunderland Echo*, 25 August 1936.
35 A. E. Martin, 'Environment, Housing and Health', *Urban Studies*, Volume IV, No. 1, pp. 1–21, February 1967.
36 Royal Commission on the Housing of the Working Classes, *First Report*, HMSO 1885, p. 16.

37 *Ibid.*, p. 18.
38 G. C. M. McGonigle and J. Kirby, *Poverty and Public Health*, London 1936. For comments on this and subsequent discussions see A. E. Martin, *op. cit.*
39 *Op. cit.*, p. 132.
40 *Ibid.*, p. 142.
41 Royal Commission on the Housing of the Working Classes, *op. cit.*, p. 18.
42 *Ibid.*, p. 18.
43 *Op. cit.*, p. 143.
44 Royal Commission on the Housing of the Working Classes, *op. cit.*, p. 18.
45 *Op. cit.*, p. 143.
46 *Sunderland Echo*, 9 May 1933, p. 6.
47 *Sunderland Echo*, 3 April 1934, p. 3.
48 *Op. cit.*, p. 134.
49 *Sunderland Echo*, 5 April 1934.

Table 9.1

Wastage, Slum-clearance and MOH Demolition Orders 1930–40: Sunderland CB

Date	Number of demolitions	Date	Number of demolitions
1930	44	1936	159
1931	12	1937	312
1932	0	1938	393
1933	2	1939	549
1934	87	1940	38
1935	181		

Source: Sunderland CB Engineer's Department

Table 9.2

Location of Rehoused Families: Sunderland CB 1933–36

Place	Number of Families	Percentage
Ford Estate	98	44
Marley Potts	90	20
High Southwick	64	14
Grangetown	83	19
East End (Drury Lane and Harrison's Buildings)	10	3
Total	445	100

Source: Sunderland MOH Report for 1936

Table 9.3

Date of Removal of Slum-Clearance Families: Sunderland CB 1933–36

Date of Removal	Number of Families	Percentage
1933	62	14
1934	98	22
1935	251	56
1936	34	8
1933–36	445	100

Source: Sunderland MOH Report for 1936

Table 9.4

Answers to the Question 'Is the Family satisfied with the change?' Rehoused Families Sunderland CB 1933–36

Answer	Number of Families	Percentage
Yes	405	91
No	37	8
Not ascertained	3	1
Total	445	100

Source: Sunderland MOH Report for 1936

Table 9.5

Source of Income Rehoused Families 1933–36, Sunderland CB

Source of Income	Number of Families	Percentage of Families
Solely from UIB	19	4
Solely from UAB	105	24
Solely from the PAC	39	9
Solely from a combination UIB, UAB, PAC	34	8
Partly from UIB, UAB, PAC	146	33
Wages or other	85	19
Not ascertained	17	4
Total	445	100

Source: Sunderland MOH Report for 1936

SECTION III
Replacement 1956–60 and 1960–65

1. 'The houses of Sunderland parish consisted characteristically of three or more storeys and dark cellars.' (p. 146)

2.
'The interests of
children could largely
justify compulsion.'
(p. 156)

2 'Dwellings which
were originally sound
but in which decay
had been preceded
by a change in the
. . . character of
their use.' (p. 167)

CHAPTER 10

SLUM CLEARANCE IN THE NINETEEN FIFTIES

Sunderland's second five-year programme, the programme for the years 1938–43, aimed at demolishing a further 1,918 dwellings and rehousing five thousand families,[1] but the outbreak of the second world war prevented any action being taken. By 1945, out of the country's stock of twelve million houses half a million had been destroyed or were too seriously damaged for re-occupation; and no new houses had been built for five years. The Ministry of Reconstruction, therefore, recommended that priority should be given to the provision of new houses to meet the housing shortage.

Not only was slum clearance held in abeyance, all existing property was neglected. The rent restriction acts, whatever other benefits they brought, continued to blight the repair and maintenance activities of landlords. In the post-war period the neglect of older property was accepted as an unfortunate consequence of the housing shortage. The Ridley Committee in 1945 recommended that war-time controls should continue until there was an adequate supply of houses throughout the country, which they estimated would take ten years. The Ministry of Health told local authorities that 'because of the need to concentrate on the erection of new houses for families without a separate home of their own it will not be practicable to require the execution of works to existing houses'.[2] This neglect was not stemmed until 1954, when local authorities were urged to resume the full exercise of their powers under the Housing Act of 1936.[3]

The housing White Paper of 1953 signalled the government's intention that local authorities should revert to slum clearance.[4] 'Normal' housing demands were to be met by private enterprise, which had been freed from rent and price controls over new and converted houses in 1952 and was soon to be freed of Defence Regulation 56A, which controlled the supply of building materials. 'Local authorities alone can clear and rehouse the slums, while general housing needs can be met by private enterprise.'[5]

Section I of the Housing Repairs and Rents Act of 1954 required local authorities to assess the extent of their slums and estimate the time required to eliminate them, and especially to provide a close estimate of the slum-clearance programme for the years 1955–60. Under the Housing Subsidies Act of 1956 the general needs subsidy was reduced from £22 1s. od. to £10 0s. od. a year for 60 years, and the rate subsidy was no longer obligatory. The Housing Subsidies Order later in the year abolished general needs subsidies altogether except for those available for one-bedroom dwellings. Exchequer subsidies were to be available only to replace slums and for certain other specialised housing purposes.

The nineteen fifties therefore saw the resumption of slum clearance in Sunderland. (Table 10.1.) By 1961 Central ward had lost 7,086 of its 1951 population (54 per cent). Bridge ward had lost 38 per cent, Hendon 27 per cent, Monkwearmouth 26 per cent and Deptford 25 per cent. (Table 10.2.) Central ward lost 30 per cent of its dwellings, Bridge ward 18 per cent and Hendon 12 per cent. (Table 10.3.)

What sort of dwelling was demolished in the 1950s, who benefited and in what ways? The East End, cleared in the 1930s, was composed of dwellings which were insanitary from their inception. To the west and south, by contrast, were wide streets of substantial two-storied houses and of the single-storied cottages of artisans, with private yards and back lanes. There were also several mansions which were reminders of the former popularity of Hendon 'as a place of residence for the wealthy'.[6]

The advantages of the area as a place of residence had been reduced, however, by the opening of the Hudson Dock in 1850 and by the construction through the area of the Londonderry railway a few years later—a line built to transport coal from

Seaham to Sunderland.[7] With the loss of 'the chalybeate waters of the spa'[8] and the development of industry the larger houses were abandoned by the well-to-do. By 1900 a single-family dwelling was 'more or less a rarity', and 'two, three, four or even five families, consisting in extreme cases of 25 to 30 individuals' were to be found in its eight-roomed houses.[9]

The 1930s' clearances, therefore, meant the removal of 'structural slums', dwellings which were built as slums and which no family could have made into an attractive or healthy home. The 1950s' clearances dealt in large part with dwellings which were originally sound but in which decay had been preceded by a change in the occupancy of the buildings and in the essential character of their use. From being the residences of families financially capable of maintaining and improving the property and strongly motivated to do so, the houses became the tenement homes of families unable to afford even the simplest and most essential works even where they were eager to carry them out.

> Could not something be done to brighten up our dismal house-fronts around the locality of Woodbine Street, Hendon? The tenants are sick to death of asking the landlord to furnish the paint, the application of which they would gladly do themselves. The landlord declares the expenses are too high for him. In that case, who makes the slums, the landlord or the tenants?[10]

The area skirting the town centre deteriorated for similar reasons. The extension of Sunderland's commercial and shopping functions turned it into the typical interstitial slum in an area of marginal urban use, where homes become increasingly interspersed with offices, shops, public houses, garages and small industries, and therefore lose their attractiveness to families which can afford surroundings where land-use is geared to residential purposes.[11]

Thus in the Lawrence Street area, which was cleared in 1955–6, 61 per cent of the rehoused families had been living in the same dwelling as at least two other families, and 15 per cent had been living in the same dwelling as at least four other families. (Table 10.4.) In the Wear Street (Hendon) area, cleared 1957–8, 54 per cent of the families lived at three or more families per dwelling, and 21 per cent at four or more families per dwelling. In the Central Area clearances, late in 1959, 62 per cent of the families shared a dwelling with at least two other families, and 24 per cent shared their dwelling with at least three other families. In the Howick Street clearances of 1957 27 per cent of the families came from dwellings containing three families or more. In the Railway Street clearances of mid-1959 19 per cent of the families came from dwellings containing three families or more.

The dilapidation of this property was, then, largely a matter of multi-occupation, accelerated by the peculiar conditions of war-time and of the post-war period. However respectable, conscientious or socially sensitive the occupants may have been they would have found it more difficult to prevent deterioration than would have been the case if they had been tenants of single-family houses.

The 'slumminess' of people in areas of deteriorated property is frequently a matter of gross exaggeration. It is nevertheless true that such property attracts more than its share of people who for one reason or another lack the ability—financial, managerial or psychological—to prevent the further deterioration of the property, and behave in other ways which are condemned by the respectable majority.

> A friend of mine is sick in Henry Street, Hendon, and I have been looking after her at nights. What nights! Really, I think it is disgusting the way the women down that street behave. They shout and bawl after self-respecting people have retired for the night. I have never felt so disgusted with my sex in all my life. Someone ought to turn a hose on them.[12]

The dwellings cleared in the 1950s, therefore, were slums in that they suffered from structural and environmental defects. Some of them were slums also in the sense, not that only 'slummy' families lived there, but that they were the areas inhabited by various undesirable elements, human derelicts, criminals and drunkards, and the heterogeneous mass of the unsuccessful from the ranks of unskilled labour.[13]

NOTES TO CHAPTER 10

1 County Borough of Sunderland, *Annual Report of the MOH for 1938.*
2 Ministry of Health, *Standards of Fitness*, Circular 61/47, HMSO 1947.
3 MHLG, Circular 30/54.
4 MHLG, *Housing, The Next Step*, Cmd. 8996, HMSO 1953.
5 Harold Macmillan, in a speech at the annual conference of the Urban District Councils Association, June 1954.
6 R. A. Waters, *Hendon: Past and Present*, Sunderland 1900, p. 6.
7 W. W. Tomlinson, *The North Eastern Railway*, Newcastle 1914, pp. 548–49.
8 R. A. Waters, *op. cit.*
9 R. A. Waters, *op. cit.*, p. 8.
10 *Sunderland Echo*, 1 September 1934.
11 Walter Firey, 'Ecological Considerations in Planning', in Paul K. Hatt and Albert J. Reiss Jr., *Cities and Society*, Second Edition, Glencoe 1957, pp. 791–804.
12 *Sunderland Echo*, 30 August 1933, p. 5.
13 Harvey W. Zorbaugh, *The Gold Coast and the Slum*, Chicago 1929, Chapter 7.

Table 10.1

**Wastage, Slum Clearance and MOH Demolition Orders
Sunderland CB 1945–60**

Date	Number of Houses	Date	Number of Houses
1945	6	1953	134
1946	9	1954	316
1947	27	1955	103
1948	35	1956	233
1949	46	1957	385
1950	77	1958	428
1951	74	1959	379
1952	79	1960	561

Source: Sunderland Engineer's Department

Table 10.2

**Population Change: Sunderland CB Wards 1951–61
(1961 Boundaries)**

Ward	Population 1951	Change 1951–61	Percentage change
Central	13,133	−7,086	−54
Bridge	10,247	−3,874	−38
Hendon	10,808	−2,920	−27
Monkwearmouth	15,501	−3,996	−26
Deptford	11,779	−2,900	−25
Bishopwearmouth	9,429	−1,529	−16
Park	12,610	−1,697	−13
Roker	9,952	−1,226	−12
Colliery	11,038	−1,249	−11
Pallion	11,579	−1,055	− 9
Humbledon	11,113	− 732	− 7
Thornhill	8,682	− 59	− 1
Fulwell	8,495	1,339	16
Southwick	7,545	1,727	23
St. Michael	8,972	2,112	24
Pennywell	12,828	3,802	30
Thorney Close	7,807	12,892	165
Hylton Castle	47	14,616	31,097

Source: Census 1961

Table 10.3

Structurally Separate Dwellings Occupied: Sunderland CB Wards 1951–61 (1961 Boundaries)

Ward	Dwellings 1951	Difference 1951–61	Percentage Difference
Central	2,449	—744	—30
Bridge	2,650	—482	—18
Hendon	2,908	—342	—12
Southwick	2,651	19	1
Roker	2,819	138	5
Pallion	2,979	204	7
Colliery	2,741	290	11
Thornhill	2,592	408	16
Humbledon	2,612	465	18
Park	2,275	460	20
Fulwell	2,700	684	25
Bishopwearmouth	1,815	583	32
St. Michael	2,415	1,074	44
Pennywell	2,539	1,193	47
Monkwearmouth	1,553	1,821	117
Thorney Close	1,775	3,552	200
Hylton Castle	not available	3,826	—

Source: Census 1961

Table 10.4

Percentage of Households Rehoused from Dwellings Containing Three or More Households: Sunderland CB 1955-60 Slum Clearance Programmes

Clearance Area	Households per cent	100 per cent=
Central Area	62	320
Lawrence Street	61	483
Wear Street	54	263
Howick Street	27	367
Railway Street	19	296

Source: Sunderland CB Housing Department

CHAPTER II

BENEFITS FROM THE 1960–65 CLEARANCES

The Housing Act 1961, which altered the basis of subsidies in order particularly to assist those local authorities unable to balance their housing revenue account, also relaxed the emphasis upon slum clearance. Exchequer subsidies were to be paid on all new houses built with the Minister's approval whether for rehousing from cleared slums, rehousing from over-crowded houses, for old people's dwellings or for some other purpose. But it was not until 1965 that the direction of policy was definitely altered.

> Since 1956 attention has been concentrated almost exclusively on building for specific objects, slum clearance, overcrowding relief and old people's dwellings. Each must retain a high priority. But it is now essential to tackle the overall shortage of houses at moderate rents. The Minister is prepared to consider proposals from authorities to meet this general need.[1]

With the completion or near completion of the once-and-for-all programme of the late 1950s, therefore, a programme was designed to accomplish the demolition of further areas.

The 1960–5 programme was predominantly the work of the Health Department of the local authority. The new areas for clearance were selected on the basis of the knowledge of unfit properties in the town derived from the day-by-day work of the various District Inspectors: complaints coming to the public health authorities from tenants dissatisfied with their accommodation and anxious to bring statutory pressure to bear

4. 'Those parts of the town with the least attractive environments.' (p. 173)

5. 'Areas of low-lying, damp, poorly equipped cottages.' (p. 174)

6. 'We have to sit with the electric light on all day.' (p. 176)

on their landlords was one such source; requests for sanitary inspection in order to gain housing points in connection with application for council dwellings was another; a third was the statutory investigation of the local authority area made from time to time to ascertain whether any house in the area was unfit for human habitation.[2] The districts with the largest numbers of unfit houses and those parts of the town with the least attractive environments–the noise, dirt and traffic of the shipyards, the smoke and water spray from the power station or paperworks, the grit and dust from the coal-mine, the ugliness of scrapyards, fumes from paint factories or smells from the gasworks–were thus well known in a general way to the town's public health inspectors.

All dwellings in prospective slum-clearance areas were then examined to enable particular decisions to be made about their fitness for human habitation. According to a public health inspector the investigation of each dwelling during this exercise took about two minutes. Notes were taken on the size of family and on stability and sanitary condition. An application for a compulsory purchase order was made for those areas for which slum-clearance was considered the appropriate measure, or, in exceptional cases, directly for a clearance order. According to this same informant an MHLG inspector then visited every house. After the public inquiry, at which objections came mainly from owner-occupiers dissatisfied with the amount of compensation, the house of each objector was again visited, on this occasion by the inspector directing the inquiry.

The largest schemes in the 1960–5 period (some of which represented uncompleted portions of the 1956–60 programme) were those to rehouse over eleven hundred families from Dock Street (Monkwearmouth), over six hundred families from The Parade (Hendon) and nearly four hundred families from the Bramwell Street area (Hendon). (Table 11.1.)

Several of the clearance areas dealt with the rehousing of children, and in that respect resembled the clearances of the 1930s. In Sunderland CB 39 per cent of the households present at the time of the 1961 Census (57,800) were couples or persons living alone. The remaining 61 per cent were households composed of three or more people–a figure which (it may be supposed) would vary directly with the number of families with children. By comparison 68 per cent of the 296 families in The Sheepfolds area contained three persons or more. In both The Parade clearance area (644 households) and the Bramwell Street (Phase I) clearance area (363 households) the figure was 65 per cent. In both the Carley Road area (222 households) and the Dock Street area the figure was the same as that for the town as a whole, 61 per cent. For the Hendon Road area (256 households) it was only slightly below this, 60 per cent.

The 1960–5 clearances left over from 1956–60 and the 1960–5 programme itself dealt with a variety of areas and an assortment of problems of dwelling and environment. Some were built up before 1850–areas of low-lying, damp, poorly equipped cottages surrounded by industrial plants. Other areas were composed mainly of two-storied dwellings, structurally defective, lacking in amenities and with little prospect of either landlord or tenant repairing, maintaining or improving them.

At the time that the SHN fieldwork was undertaken in autumn 1965 some of the 1960–5 slum-clearance areas had not been dealt with and it is therefore possible to examine in more than usual detail this part of the programme. These remaining areas may be taken as indicative of the type of clearance which took place throughout the 1960–5 period, with the proviso that it is likely that the dwellings of the survey were of a somewhat higher standard than those demolished earlier.

A list was prepared of dwellings included in the 1960–5 programme but not dealt with by July 1965 (the '1960–5 remainder') and a 1:10 sample was drawn from it (119 cases). In thirteen cases the family or families were already rehoused and the dwelling was either demolished or standing vacant. In two cases the addresses listed were business premises. Eighty-one interviews were obtained–a response rate of 78 per cent.

Structural Condition

The families of the 1960–5 remainder were asked about the structural condition of their dwellings. 'What about the condition of the building now (dryness, ventilation, lightness, etc.)?' 'Would you say it was satisfactory or not satisfactory? Would you say it was very satisfactory, somewhat satisfactory, somewhat unsatisfactory or very unsatisfactory?' Those informants who described the structural condition of their dwelling as unsatisfactory were then asked, 'What is the matter with it?'

Sixty-five per cent of the families reported defects of structure. Thirty-one per cent described the structural condition as very unsatisfactory. Sixty-two of the informants were tenants (the remainder were owner-occupiers) and of these 35 per cent said that the standard of maintenance by the landlord was very low; a further 13 per cent said that the standard of maintenance was somewhat low. Informants were asked about the maintenance undertaken by the landlord in the last five years or since the tenant came to the house if he had not been there for as long as five years. Thirty per cent said that no maintenance had been carried out in the past five years.

Those householders who were tenants of private landlords had little incentive, of course, to repair the dwelling. But both tenants and owner-occupiers tended to lack the economic resources to engage in major works of maintenance. Twenty-four per cent of the heads of households were housewives; a further 16 per cent of heads of households were retired; 24 per cent were in unskilled occupations; 12 per cent were in semi-skilled occupations; only 22 per cent were in skilled manual occupations. No heads of households were in professional or managerial occupations and in only two cases were the occupations in the clerical grades. Over half of the total sample of eighty-one families (51 per cent) said that they had done no maintenance in the past 5 years or since they came into the house.

Some idea of the state of the worst property may be gathered from examples. The following is a description of a tenemented house.

George Street is dingy, dirty and roughly cobbled. The house is next to the Castletown to Wearmouth colliery railway, which still uses steam engines. The atmosphere is therefore one of noise, smoke, steam and coal dust. There is no paint at all on the outside of the house. The passage is dark. There is still no electricity supply to the house, which is lit by gas. It is in a deplorable condition, filthy and dropping to pieces. The informant says that the area is infested with rats. It is very noisy especially when a ship's engine is being tested day and night. On those occasions it is impossible to sleep. There is nowhere for the children to play except for a patch of dirty waste ground nearby, the site of a former clearance scheme.

Of a young couple in an adjoining street the interviewer notes:

It is a very dark living room; the tenants need the electric light on all day. There are no facilities for washing; the wash-house is broken down. The couple upstairs will not let the informant keep her pram in the passage so she has to struggle through the living room with it to get it out of the way in the bedroom. 'Little things like that eat away at you worse than the big things.' It is noisy and dirty and they have not much room. The couple dislike it very much and the house cannot be pulled down quickly enough for them.

Here are two more examples:

The dwelling is in very poor condition generally and it is especially damp. There is no door on the outside toilet. She does her washing in a pail on the gas-ring.

This dwelling is one of three which were formed from a former shop. It is very damp and plaster is falling from the walls. Coal is kept in a cupboard. Three families share the yard. The informant is an old man living alone and maintenance is of a very low standard.

Forty-three of the informants complained of dampness. 'The rain pours in.' 'The bedroom is very damp.' 'It is very damp, fungus grows out of the skirting boards.' 'The house is soaking wet.' 'It is below the level of the back street and is often flooded.' 'It is very damp and the walls of the living room and the carpet went green-mouldy in the bedroom.' 'Terrible damp on the outside walls especially the front, water is held between the plaster and the bricks.' 'Very, very damp all over the house, including the ceilings.'

Six informants specifically complained of inadequate daylighting. 'The kitchen is very dark.' 'It's dark in the kitchen, we have the light on all day nearly.' 'We have to sit with the electric light on all day.' Six families mentioned the decayed condition of the structure. 'The plaster is falling off the walls.' 'The outside wall bulges.' 'The plaster in the rooms at the back of the house is flaking.' 'We can use only two rooms out of the three because the floor has collapsed in the front bedroom.'

Internal Facilities

The dwellings of the sample also lacked amenities. Eighty-six per cent were without a fixed bath. Of those without a fixed bath, 78 per cent felt that this was a great drawback, and another 10 per cent felt it was something of a drawback. Only 6 out of the 12 households who had a fixed bath had a separate bathroom. Eighty per cent of the households in the sample had no piped hot water. Only 2 per cent had an indoor toilet. Seventy-two per cent of those with outdoor water closets felt this to be a disadvantage; on the other hand 23 per cent considered it advantageous to have the water closet outdoors rather than in the house. Twenty-seven per cent of the households shared the w.c. with one other family and 10 per cent shared it with two other families. Fifty-six per cent of the families lacked an indoor supply of cold water. Twenty-two per cent shared with one other family and 14 per cent shared with two other families. The dwellings were felt to be deficient in various other respects too: for example, 42 per cent of the respondents thought that the arrangements for washing dishes were unsatisfactory. The main complaint additional to the specific questions about w.c.s, baths etc. was the shortage of electricity outlets (seventeen complaints), and the next most frequent complaint was about old or broken fireplaces— (thirteen cases).

The prospect of improvement was not promising. 'What modernisation has the landlord carried out while you have been tenant here?' Eighty-seven per cent of the sample said that no modernisation had been carried out and only 5 per cent described any major modernisation, such as the provision of a fixed bath, the provision of an indoor w.c., the provision of a new electricity circuit or the provision of a bathroom. Taking the whole sample of tenants and owner-occupiers together, no modernisation had been carried out in 54 per cent of the cases.

Overcrowding

Many of the dwellings were small. Fifty-two per cent of the households had only one bedroom, and a further 31 per cent had only two bedrooms. Nearly half of the families (43 per cent) were dissatisfied with the amount of space available in their dwelling–17 per cent were very dissatisfied. Of the 81 families of the sample nearly one quarter complained of lack of space, and 16 per cent said the dwelling was much too small.

Environmental Amenity

In the majority of cases (86 per cent) there was no private outdoor space in front of the dwelling. In only seven cases was there a garden at the front. In only 8 per cent of the cases was there a back garden. Twenty-nine per cent were dissatisfied with the private space at the front of the dwelling, or lack of it; 10 per cent were very dissatisfied. Twenty-seven per cent were dissatisfied with their back yards and 12 per cent were very dissatisfied. Nearly half (47 per cent) were dissatisfied and 27 per cent were very dissatisfied because they had no garden.

The largest areas of dwellings included in the 1960–5 remainder were all insalubrious, close to the power station, to a paper mill and piggeries, to railway sidings, scrap yards, and so forth. Fifty-nine per cent of the respondents said that the amenity of the locality was unsatisfactory, and 54 per cent said it was very unsatisfactory.

A young couple with four children under the age of six were unhappy about the danger from the heavy traffic. They also disliked the noise from the nightclub across the road, which, according to them, continued until three or four o'clock in the morning. Tramps had taken to sleeping in the basement. Another informant described the locality as 'very noisy, dirty and dangerous; there are no good points in living here; most of the shops have been pulled down; I cannot hang my clothes because of the dirt from the colliery'.

> The electricity power station is right behind the house, practically in the back yard. It makes the house very dark inside and causes a lot of dirt. The street is very dangerous and very noisy because of the amount of traffic passing up and down it.

> It is very noisy and dirty living here. There is a bus stop outside the bedroom window. The Power Plant is at the end of the street and clothes get marked by it when the washing is put out to dry.

A housewife living in a dwelling attached to an off-licence

shop in Hylton Road said that she was very dissatisfied and would like to be out into a council house to lead a quiet life. 'There is quite a bit of noise from the children round about. It is very dirty as well.'

> It is very dirty here. The Monkwearmouth colliery to Hylton colliery railway line passes the bottom of the street. There is a scrapyard just beyond the railway. Her little boy gets filthy. The family upstairs has five children; when they walk across the floor the ceiling light dances. She would love to have a council house.

> The lorries from Tyzacks start at 5 o'clock in the morning and go on until one o'clock the next morning.

Twenty of the respondents complained of the dirtiness of their locality; sixteen complained of industrial or commercial noise; seven complained of danger from traffic; three complained of animals such as dogs and pigeons; two complained that the streets were not swept frequently enough; two complained of vandalism; and there were various other complaints arising only once in the course of the interviews, such as rat infestation, the congestion of the buildings and lack of fresh air.

Neighbours

Thirteen informants complained more about their neighbours than about any other feature of the area. Six referred to the bad behaviour of children in the neighbourhood. 'A lot of new neighbours are moving into the street with their very cheeky kids. If the wife goes to bed early she can't get to sleep for the noise they kick up in the streets till very late at night.' 'A lot of kids—a bad lot—the other day they tried to take money from my five-year-old daughter.' In nine instances there was reference to adult neighbours who were dirty, who were 'letting the place degrade', standing about the doors or drinking at night. 'The people on my side of the street are very friendly but the people opposite have been rehoused from The Avenue and are awful. They won't wash themselves.'

Attitudes to Rehousing

The main advantage of a council dwelling for the majority of respondents was that they would enjoy better internal amenities. Out of the 142 responses[3] on this subject, fifty gave the main advantage of a council house as a fixed bath. Piped hot water was given as the main advantage in twenty-eight of the responses. Twelve of the responses mentioned an inside w.c. or an unshared w.c. as the main advantage. Eight responses gave as the main advantage the state of repair or general newness of a council dwelling. Six responses mentioned more space as the main advantage and a further six mentioned the possession of a garden as the main advantage.

Many fewer respondents had thought specifically about the advantages of a council district. Only 23 responses were offered when this question was asked. Eighteen referred to the superior standards of amenity on housing estates: eight of the responses mentioned cleanliness; three mentioned quietness; two mentioned the fresher air. Three of the responses dealt with neighbours: 'We'd have one or two neighbours who'd do something for you'; 'We'd be on our own away from neighbours'; 'We'd be nearer friends'. Other respondents mentioned the proximity of relatives: 'If I got to Baltic Terrace I would be nearer my mother-in-law.'

Just over half of the families in the sample were already on the council's housing list (41 cases). Nearly everyone expected the property to be demolished in the near future (97 per cent). Eighty-three per cent of the respondents expected that the house would be demolished in under five years. Nearly three-quarters of the families considered they would be better off in a council dwelling; one half believed that they would be much better off. However, only 42 per cent considered that they would be better off in a council district and as a result not every family which was in favour of a council dwelling was in favour of demolition and rehousing. Even so, over half of the families were in favour of demolition (57 per cent) and 42 per cent were very much in favour of demolition.

NOTES TO CHAPTER 11

1 MHLG, *Circular 21/65*, HMSO 1965.
2 Housing Act, 1957.
3 The analysis is of 142 responses from the 81 informants. Where an informant gave more than one 'main' advantage, that is, all were included in the analysis.

Table 11.1

Slum-Clearance Areas: Sunderland CB 1960–65

Area	Number of Households	Area	Number of Households
Dock Street (1)	1,143	Lucknow Street (4)	70
The Parade (1)	644	Dundas Street (2)	67
Bramwell Street	363	Gosforth Street (3)	65
Beach Street (4)	311	Morgan Street	50
Deptford (1)	297	Camden Street (3)	49
The Sheepfolds (1)	296	Biss Street (4)	45
Hendon Road	256	Bennett Street (2)	38
Stoney Lane (3)	249	Garden Place (2)	36
Peacock Street West (2)	242	Spelterworks Road (4)	34
Carley Road	222	Holly Terrace (5)	32
Rothsay Street (3)	137	Wharncliffe Street (4)	30
Hahnemann Street	100	Albany Street (5)	30
Brandling Street (3)	91	Cambridge Terrace (5)	25
Fulwell Road (3)	82	Ogden Street (5)	15
Stanley Street (2)	81		

Source: Sunderland CB Housing Department,
Planning Department, Health Department

Notes:
(1) Areas from the 1956–60 programme dealt with 1960–65.
(2) Areas covered by orders approved by the Minister of Housing and Local Government, but not rehoused within the period of the 1960–65 programme.
(3) Areas covered by orders approved by the local authority but awaiting submission to or approval by the Minister at the end of the 1960–65 period.
(4) Areas from the 1960–65 programme not dealt with during that period.
(5) Areas included in the original 1960–65 programme, but subsequently reallocated to the 1965–70 programme.

CHAPTER 12

THE EMERGING PROBLEMS OF REPLACEMENT 1960-65

A large proportion of the families from the 1960–5 remainder were dissatisfied with their dwellings and environment and were looking forward to slum clearance and to a council tenancy. These families can be regarded as differing from those dealt with earlier in the programme only in that they probably enjoyed somewhat better conditions. It can be supposed, therefore, that such majority support by the residents of the statutory definition of unfitness applied to the whole of the 1960–5 programme. Each figure in the previous chapter, however, has as its complement the responses of those people who feared that in one way or another they would find that they had suffered rather than gained by rehousing.

Accessibility

A substantial proportion of the families valued the favourable location of the districts of the 1960–5 remainder as compared with council districts. Of the 26 families who were concerned with the proximity of schools, 81 per cent thought that access was very satisfactory. Access to shops was important for all the sample families, and 80 per cent found that access was very satisfactory. Out of 107 spontaneous responses relating to access, 33 of them mentioned shops. Their remarks were frequently accompanied by the observation that there was no unnecessary travelling by bus and no travelling expenses. Ninety-four per cent of the total sample regarded the house as satisfactory from the point of view of access to the town centre and 77 per cent found the location very satisfactory. Nineteen of the spontaneous responses referred to the centrality of the dwelling as one of its main advantages. Of the 58 respondents who had someone in the family for whom work access was relevant, 81 per cent regarded the location of the dwelling as satisfactory for that purpose and 62 per cent thought it was very satisfactory; only 3 per cent thought the dwelling was very unsatisfactory from this point of view. Seventy-nine per cent of the 81 respondents regarded access to those places of entertainment used by the family as satisfactory and 60 per cent regarded such access as very satisfactory. On the question of access to medical services the figures were 84 per cent answering that access was satisfactory, 59 per cent that it was very satisfactory.

There were eleven critical statements about communal facilities on council estates directed against lack of shops and to a lesser extent distance from work, entertainment and the town centre.

Neighbours

The location of the dwelling is regarded by some respondents as important in a second respect: they weigh in their total housing experience the behaviour and character of their neighbours. Some like their neighbours because they are friendly; others because their neighbours are reserved and 'keep themselves to themselves'. Some like their neighbours because they are helpful and outgoing; others like their neighbours because they do not interfere in one another's affairs. Some like them because they take an interest in one another; others like their neighbours because they mind their own business. The 1960–5 remainder showed a mosaic of different practices and the informants who liked their neighbours were those who found them behaving in the preferred manner.

One half of the informants said their neighbours were very friendly; an additional third said that they were somewhat friendly. Fifty-five per cent said their neighbours would be ready to help without being asked and a further 13 per cent said that they would willingly help but only when help was asked for. Nearly one half said that they liked their neighbours very much (47 per cent) and a further third (34 per cent) said that they liked them but they would not say it was very much. In ten instances the neighbours were mentioned as one of the best points about living in the present area. 'Nice respectable people live here.' 'There are not a lot of children.' 'I know everyone, I have my own neighbours.' 'The neighbours are friendly.' 'When I was ill the neighbours phoned for a doctor and went for my relatives. They helped in every way they could.'

Conversely the type of neighbour with whom they might be willy nilly rehoused was a matter of concern to some families. 'It depends on who you get beside.' 'It's just if the neighbours weren't all right.' 'You don't know who your neighbours are.' 'They don't consider where they put their tenants.' 'You don't know who you'll get put beside.' 'Some council people don't get on together.' 'Kids on council estates are always fighting.' 'You might get a place with children.'

In other instances the proximity of relatives was mentioned as either one of the best points about living in the present area or one of the main disadvantages of a council district.

Overall 54 per cent of the 1960–5 remainder were very satisfied with their locality and a further quarter were somewhat satisfied. Thirty-five per cent thought that they would be worse off in a council district and 24 per cent thought that they would be much worse off.

Cost

After accessibility, cost was the most frequently mentioned factor in the assessment of preferences. Eighty-three per cent of the tenants in the 1960–5 remainder paid less than 25 shillings weekly in rent and rates and 32 per cent paid less than 15 shillings. All the owner-occupiers had paid off their mortgages and their only housing cost, apart from maintenance and renovation, was rates. Twelve statements were made which related to cost as the main disadvantage of a council dwelling. 'The rent is very dear. I would have to go on the P.A.C.' 'Bigger rents. I couldn't afford it on my pension.' 'The rents are fabulous.' 'The rent. I would have to see the N.A.B.'

Privacy

Nearly one half (49 per cent) of the dwellings in the 1960–5 remainder were single-storied cottages. Fourteen per cent were houses. Only one in five (21 per cent) were flats and a further 16 per cent were 'rooms'. A highly valued characteristic of the house and the cottage was the privacy it afforded the residents. Eighty-six per cent of the 1960–5 remainder were satisfied with their dwelling from the point of view of privacy and 69 per cent were very satisfied. Ninety-five per cent thought that flats were the worst type of council dwelling, mainly because of the loss of privacy.

Internal Space

Many families feared a loss of internal space if they were re-housed by the council. The policy of Sunderland Corporation has been so-called 'tailor-made' housing and from this point of view many of the families of the 1960–5 remainder were 'over housed'.

> I like this house and don't want to leave it, but I know it has to come down on account of the others. When I get a council house I won't have the room I have here. There is room for family gatherings. But there is nothing else for it but slum clearance.

> Two cottages have been converted into one. The informant likes living here very much and does not want to move. When she was slum cleared she was offered a top-floor council flat. She did not want it so she took one of these cottages. This informant has a mentally-handicapped child and she 'dreads' being given a flat as her daughter would not be able to play outside at all. At the moment she can play quite safely in the back yard.

Thirty per cent of the sample lived at an occupancy rate of half a person per room or below; a further 48 per cent lived at an occupancy rate of over half to one person per room. The proportion of the population which has at least one room per person was almost identical with that of the town as a whole (77·9 per cent in 1961).

The households in the 1960–5 remainder were smaller on the average than those of the town as a whole. Forty-eight per cent of the households in the 1960–5 remainder contained only one or two persons; the figure for the town as a whole was 43 per cent.[1] Thirty-eight per cent of the households in the town as a whole were composed of four persons or more; in the 1960–5 remainder the figure was 32 per cent.

Basic Amenities and Structural Condition

In some cases what most people would perhaps regard as defects were considered by those concerned as advantages. Although very few of the dwellings had gardens, for example, over half (52 per cent) of the informants said they were satisfied with this state of affairs, and 40 per cent said they were very satisfied. Similarly nearly one quarter (23 per cent) of the informants with an outdoor w.c. said that an outdoor w.c. was better than an indoor w.c. Of the 69 informants without baths over one in ten (12 per cent) said they did not regard this as a significant drawback. 'You can always keep yourself clean if you want to.'

A surprising feature of the dwellings of the 1960–5 remainder was the amount of modernisation which had taken place in the last five years in spite of the imminence of slum clearance. Although 56 of the 64 tenants in the sample reported no modernisation by the landlord, nearly half (46 per cent) of all the informants, tenants and owner-occupiers taken together, had affected some improvements to the property. Of the 37 families reporting improvements nearly half of these (49 per cent) were classified as major—meaning by 'major' the provision of piped hot water, fireplace replacement, the installation or replacement of an electricity circuit and jobs of similar magnitude. The improvements which were classified as 'minor' were such things as putting railings round the garden, flushing the doors with hardboard, or lowering the staircase ceiling.

In the same way, it was perhaps surprising that so much maintenance work was reported by the informants. Such work reflects not only the decayed condition of the structure; it is also a function of the tenants' positive attitudes towards their homes.

The Balance of Advantages and Disadvantages

Nearly one-third of the sample (31 per cent) had lived in the present dwelling for twenty years or more; 42 per cent had

186

lived there for fifteen years or more; 53 per cent had lived there for ten years or more. Only five per cent of the sample had lived in the present dwelling for less than one year. In one-third of the cases (34 per cent) the head of the household was aged 65 or older. One of the bases of the attitudes of those families which objected to being rehoused was the sense that their present dwelling and neighbourhood had proved itself over a long period of time to be capable of providing a sufficient balance of satisfactions over dissatisfactions. When asked about the best points about the present area twelve of the responses were phrased in terms of familiarity and a long experience of adjustment. 'I've always lived here and I dread leaving.' 'I was bred and born down here.' 'I've been here a long time and I'm used to it.' 'I've lived here all my life.' 'It's home. I wouldn't like to live anywhere else. It's my life.' 'I'm used to it. I've been in the area for sixty-odd years.'

> The old lady living here is partially blind. She likes living here because the cottage has no stairs and she knows her way around the district. People know her and help her when she is out. She does not want to leave the area but if she has to she would want accommodation in a bungalow.

> Seventy-three-year-old Miss Forster was born at No. 9 Rothsay Street and apart from a short spell in domestic service has lived there most of her life. 'I love it here', she said today. 'I never feel lonely; somehow I can feel the presence of both my mother and sister, both of whom lived here until they died.'[2]

A majority of the families of the 1960–5 remainder took a favourable view of the policy of the local authority; the statistics and verbal responses also indicate, however, that a substantial minority were opposed to it. Half the families were not on the council's housing list – they had shown no spontaneous desire to be rehoused. Forty-three per cent were not in favour of demolition and 19 per cent were very much against. Thirty-one per cent considered they would not be better off in a council dwelling and 16 per cent considered they would be very much worse off. Nearly a quarter of the families (23 per cent) considered they would be very much worse off in a council district as compared with their present area. Sixty-one per cent were satisfied with where they were then living–the dwelling and the area taken together–and 35 per cent were very satisfied.

The programmes of the 1930s and 1950s had dealt with problems in relation to which the term 'slum' still retained its conventional meaning: a district of a squalid and wretched character inhabited by people of a low class or by the very poor.[3] Districts of this character remained or were in the making; but, increasingly, decay and rising standards of living were bringing into the purview of policy districts which had never before been thought of as 'slums' and were not so considered either by the people who lived in them or by the public at large. In some cases the primacy of certain criteria, such as public health and individual hygiene, could still be taken for granted. To cope with the now ageing dwellings which had been constructed in the most notable period of Sunderland's growth, however, it was becoming necessary in other cases to introduce new considerations in order to justify clearance and maintain the pace of urban renewal in the sixties.

The replacement of dwellings in Sunderland was losing its early simplicity. Compulsory powers and state subsidies were no longer means only to overcome obstacles between oppressed and powerless tenants and better housing conditions–obstacles in the form of private landlords and the prohibitively high cost of new construction. It had always been necessary to some extent to use compulsory legal powers against the beneficiaries from replacement schemes; by 1965 there were signs that this was becoming their main purpose. More and more the Corporation was having to use the words of Don Carlos' hangman: 'I assassinate thee–for thine own good'.

NOTES TO CHAPTER 12

1 General Register Office, *Sample Census 1966, County Report, Durham*, HMSO 1967.
2 *Sunderland Echo*, 16 January 1967.
3 *The Oxford Universal Dictionary on Historical Principles*, Revised Edition (C. T. Onions), 1955.

SECTION IV
Replacement Proposals 1965–70

CHAPTER 13

BENEFITS FROM THE 1965–70
PROPOSALS

STRUCTURAL CONDITIONS

The 1960–5 clearance had dealt with sound property and with
many reluctant movers. However, when the local authority
was required to submit a further programme of slum clearance
to cover the five years up to 31 December 1970, deteriorated
property with which the residents were currently discontented
could be included. Such property had been built shortly before
or at about the time of the building by-laws of the late 1870s
and was therefore approximately one hundred years old. Some
of it had been continuously neglected. The greed and in-
competence of private landlords was partly to blame. But (as
Wendt points out in his study of post-1945 housing in the
United Kingdom, Sweden, Western Germany and the United
States) the United Kingdom has pursued policies which have
fixed rents below the level necessary for adequate maintenance.[1]
Cullingworth shows that while the local authority spent an
average of 5s. 0d. a week on maintaining its post-1918 dwellings,
11 per cent of private landlords in Lancaster received a total
weekly rent of only 5s. 0d. a week or less and the average of all
private rents was 8s. 3d.[2] There was government encouragement
of maintenance and improvement after 1949, but few landlords
'had the heart to invest money in their property in the face of
rent controls and rising building costs'.[3] Improvement legislation was administered through the local authorities. In
Sunderland, as in other areas, the council did not want competition for scarce labour and materials and some local

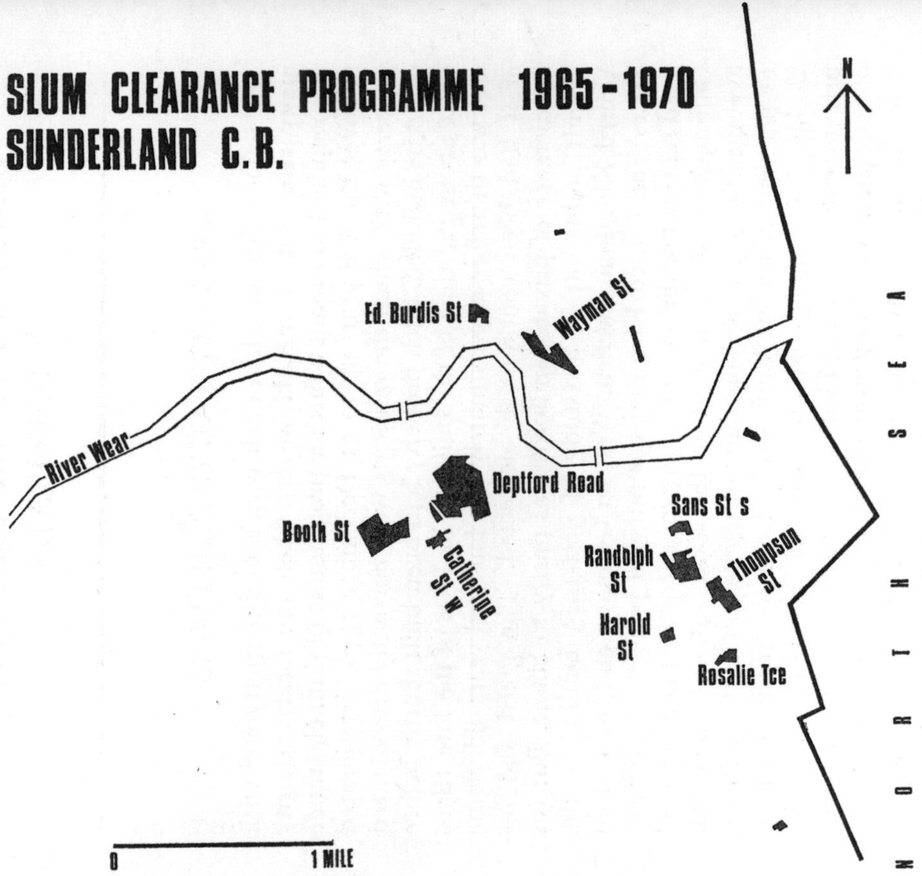

SLUM CLEARANCE PROGRAMME 1965-1970
SUNDERLAND C.B.

River Wear

Booth St
Catherine St W
Deptford Road
Ed. Burdis St
Wayman St
Randolph St
Harold St
Sans St S
Thompson St
Rosalie Tce

NORTH SEA

N

0   1 MILE

Diagram 13.A

7. 'The Power Plant is at the end of the street and clothes get marked when the washing is put out to dry.' (p. 178)

8. 'Many families feared a loss of internal space if they were rehoused by the Council.' (p. 185)

9. 'Some of the areas included small slum enclaves of many years' standing.' (p. 193)

authorities 'opposed in principle any scheme that would put public money into the hands of private landlords'.[4] As a result some types of dwelling were subject to a process of unremitting decay.

An estimated 2,056 dwellings were included in the new areas of demolition approved by the council in May 1965. (Diagram 13.A.) A random sample of one in every fifteen of the addresses programmed for slum-clearance was drawn and 126 families were interviewed.

Small Enclaves of Slum Property

Some of the areas included small slum enclaves of many years' standing. Rutland Street, for example, complete with pawn shop, Salvation Army Citadel and, until recently, billiard saloon, formed such an enclave among the generally staid cottages of the proposed Millfield clearance area. Letters to the local newspaper pleading for a new house, if they originated in the proposed Millfield slum-clearance area, came only from Bell Street and a short section of Rutland Street.

> May I, through the medium of your paper, inquire when we in Rutland Street will be rehoused. My husband and I and four children are living in a one-bedroomed cottage which is soaking wet and overrun with blacklocks . . . they are even in the chairs we are sitting in, and in the drawers. They say they are harmless, but you can't tell the children that when they wake up through the night and find them crawling across the pillows. We are not the only ones living in these conditions. My neighbour has the same family as myself and her house is the same. How others can get houses with one child I do not know. Maybe this will open the eyes of those concerned.[5]

Brandling Street was a decayed area of Tyneside flats, markedly below the standards of the cottage streets to the west and the terraces running down to the sea-front in the east. Albany Street in the Wayman Street clearance area was also a deviant group of tenemented, privately-rented properties among single-family cottages and houses mainly owned by the National Coal Board.

> This is an old lady (80) living in two rooms upstairs in poor circumstances. She has no cooking facilities apart from the fire

in her old-fashioned black grate. She has to go downstairs into the yard for her cold water. The w.c. is also in the yard and is shared by two other families. At the time of the interview the cistern was not working, and according to the informant the landlord would not repair it. All the families in the building were using a neighbour's w.c. She finds the stairs too much for her and would like a bungalow or a cottage.

The east end of Ocean Road at Grangetown was also a deviant area of Tyneside flats in an area of Sunderland cottages. 'The toilet door has been off for months. When we scraped the bedroom wall all the plaster fell off. One of the rooms is only a rough wash house; we can't eat in it, but we have to cook there.'

There were enclaves of decayed property in the other slum-clearance areas also. In the Deptford Road district such dwellings were particularly common in the old streets on the east of the area.

There is dampness throughout the house. There are no electricity outlets except for the light sockets which must provide the power for all electrical appliances. 'The house next door is knocked to bits and we can't keep this place clean. It's not a good cottage, it's a wreck.'

'Every wall is damp—not just one. The rain comes in: it's penetrating damp, there is no cement left at all between the bricks. The downcomers are all cracked and leaking. The place is deteriorating at the back—the cement, the brick, the wood, it is all a bit musky now. My husband has had two heart attacks, yet he has got to use the stairs; we have no option but to be up and down stairs for water all the time.'

'The front-room joists have all gone, but the Health Inspector says it's too expensive for the price of the house to get the landlord to repair them. It is soaking all along the living-room wall when it rains and you can't put in a d.p.c. because the back yard is above the level of the living-room floor. Three houses were knocked down in the first war. We were bombed again in the second war and we had no roofs or doors for six months. The whole place has been undermined by the blasting and the lifting of the air raids.'

Another group of cottages in the Deptford Road area were among the oldest properties in Sunderland.

'When you have been out of the house a couple of days it is all foisty when you come back in. You can't kill the smell with Dettol or anything. The floor is all rotten with woodworm. I would gan out tomorrow. It's been unlucky to me this house! I'd only been here two years. We blamed the house when we lost the bairn—we lost a bairn y'knaa. Three months. Pneumonia. Dampness. I wish they'd pull it all down this week. The daughter is full of caad— she gets a cold once every month. We had a few floor boards replaced, but only after we've had the Health Inspector in four or five times. Which estate would we prefer? Just put "Any"!'

In all areas there were isolated examples of decrepit and neglected property. An interviewer's report describes the conditions of a woman living alone in a ground-floor flat in the Booth Street area. 'It is very damp. The wallpaper is coming off the front bedroom wall. The informant complains that the landlord will do no repairs at all. She would love another place to have more comfort but wouldn't like to move far away.' A letter from this area to the editor of the local newspaper reads: 'I have three children, and my husband and myself live in two rooms. We, too, are overrun with blacklocks and have had mice as well. We had the Health people to spray the room for blacklocks and I agree with Hopeful they are twice as bad as before. We have had two medical notes from my doctor, but to no avail.'[6]

The Hendon Slum-Clearance Area

On a much larger scale, however, Hendon (for reasons which have been discussed in Chapter Ten) has presented problems of tenancy as contrasted with owner-occupation and of sub-divided houses as compared with single-family cottages for many years.[7]

Only 5 per cent of the Hendon families reported 'no structural defects' as compared with 31 per cent of the general sample. Over half (55 per cent) of the Hendon families reported defects which were classified as 'major'. Eighty-six per cent of the Hendon families were dissatisfied with the structural condition of the dwelling as compared with 59 per cent of the general sample; 50 per cent were very dissatisfied, as compared with 34 per cent of the general sample. There follow some examples of the structural condition of dwellings in the proposed Hendon clearance area:

A single man lives here in two rooms on the ground floor. One of the rooms is unusable because of the dampness. The other room is in very poor condition; the fireplace is dropping to bits. Both the cold water tap and the w.c. are outside in the yard and are shared by two other families. The house has no electricity supply.

'Deplorable! We can't wallpaper in the bedroom because all the cement is off. The Health man says he doesn't know how the ceiling is holding up. It's like a morgue in the winter. One room can't be used at all because of beetles.'

'I would like, through the medium of your paper, to bring to the Council's notice the terrible conditions that we, the house-wives of the slum area of Hendon, have to put up with. Not only do we have to share outside toilets and have to carry in coal, then carry rubbish out of these damp hell-holes, we get our drinking water from an outside tap and have to carry it up germ-ridden yards. Hygienic? O, very! So come on, council, see when you can rehouse us.'[8]

'I'm used to this. But she is used to getting out of bed, finding hot and cold water, baths, everything. She comes from a prefab. This house is depressing her, she hates it. She is always round at her sister's or mother's—they all live in council property, the mother at Hendon Court and her sister over at Victor Court in a maisonette. She always says, "Oh! I have to come back to this dump!" We have new furniture but the dampness does it a lot of damage and when I put my shirts on they are always soaking.'

The front-room walls and the walls of the bedrooms run with moisture. The electric light in the hall has not been lit for eight years because of dampness in the ceiling.

In most respects the statistics for Hendon revealed, indeed, worse conditions than those which existed in the areas cleared in the previous programme—the 1960–5 remainder. Forty-eight per cent of the families of the 1960–5 remainder complained that the standard of maintenance provided by the landlord was low; the percentage making the same complaint in the Hendon sub-sample of the 1965–70 programme was 63 per cent. Sixty-two per cent of the families of the 1960–5 remainder said that the present structural condition of their dwelling was unsatisfactory and 31 per cent said that the structural condition was very unsatisfactory; 86 per cent of the Hendon sub-sample were dissatisfied with the structural condition of their dwelling and 50 per cent were very dissatisfied.

THE NEIGHBOURHOOD

The image of the city and the large town which probably comes most readily to mind is that of dense housing development. The 1961 Census returns show that the Dolphin ward of Westminster MB had a housing density of 224 inhabited rooms per acre. The ward of Harrow Road North in Paddington MB had a density of 151 rooms per acre. St. Domingo ward in Liverpool had a density of 139 rooms per acre. Harehills ward in Leeds had a density of 118 rooms per acre. There is nothing to match such densities in Sunderland. The Hendon area,[9] however, is developed at a density of 68 rooms per acre, which is considerably above the next most densely developed ward, Roker, with a density of 46 rooms per acre.

A second neighbourhood difficulty experienced by some of the families in the 1965–70 slum-clearance programme was the proximity of noxious industries. It is possible to belittle the importance of this. There is a feeling in some quarters that the reaction against the mixture of residences and work places has gone too far. As Nairn says, zoning–separating out areas into industrial, residential, commercial, and entertainment districts –which was intended to fight the worst excesses of the industrial revolution has degenerated into a 'bureaucratic bolt-hole' and is now the reason why the new estates don't have corner shops, or why workers in a New Town have to travel miles to a factory.[10] Rossi's influential study of American families (273) making voluntary moves for housing reasons showed that the physical features of the neighbourhood constituted the primary reason for moving in only six cases; discontent with the physical features of the neighbourhood tended to be contributory or ineffective as a reason for moving rather than primary, if present at all.[11]

There can be little doubt, however, that many families were living in thoroughly unattractive environments and that they recognised them as such. In the Ocean Road area there were complaints about the dampness even on fine days because of spray from the water tanks at the Paper Mills. 'It's always raining in Ocean Road.'

> It is serious down here. Wagons are going into the Mill at 3 o'clock in the morning. There are piggeries just down the bottom. When the chimneys start up the smell is terrible. There is a potato warehouse at the back and big lorries are always running up and down. It is awfully dirty round here, the children are never clean.

An informant in the Deptford Road area complained that he could not get to sleep during the day when he was on night shift because of the noise from the nearby engineering works. In Hendon there were frequent references to 'all the smells from the Paper Mills and the Gas Works'.

Half the informants at Hendon said that they were very dissatisfied with the physical aspect of their localities. The percentage was almost as high, however, in the Deptford Road area (48 per cent). 'Terrible! With it being an industrial area, soot and everything on the clothes.' 'Filthy, dirty from the chimneys.'

> 'Powdered glass from the Pyrex factory flies everywhere and forms a coating on everything. I am fed up with Jobling's. We want to leave the district and the only way we can do that is to have the house demolished in slum-clearance.'

> The informant claims that the dust coming from the Pyrex factory becomes embedded in the windows of the houses. If it can do that, he says, what effect does the dust have on the people in the area breathing it day and night?

> 'Until the scrap yard came about a year ago, it was perfect. All peace and quiet. It has properly upset things. How he got permission I don't know. I've been down to the Council, nothing done. You get nothing but a lot of abuse from him if you talk to him. He burns his scrap.'

There were many references to dirt in the atmosphere. 'The dirt goes to my stomach.' The most criticised district was the Wayman Street clearance area, which borders Wearmouth colliery. 'There is a lot of dirt and air pollution because it is near to the colliery.' 'It is a dirty area as it is very near to the colliery.' 'A very dirty and noisy area.' 'We get an undue share of the dirt.'

Well over half of the informants regarded the area as unsafe for pedestrians. The percentage for the general sample was 61; 44 per cent of the general sample regarded their districts as very unsafe for pedestrians. In Hendon 73 per cent thought the district was unsafe for pedestrians; 59 per cent thought the district was very unsafe. 'Oh! It's atrocious for the bairns around here–lorries to the building site.' 'I wouldn't dare let him play outside the same as I could on the estates–traffic from the docks, factories, everywhere–very busy.' 'When you have a little 'un you worry. You can't be out at them all the time. They are running straight out into the traffic.' The son of a Hendon informant was injured by a vehicle and was in hospital for eighteen weeks with a broken thigh and pelvis.

The noise, vibration and other inconveniences of traffic were also recognised as drawbacks of residence in such areas as these. 'The vibration of the traffic is beginning to bulge the wall of the house.' 'It was all right until the traffic began to get there. Lorries, vans. We couldn't get light into the house; we might as well put the shutters up! We went to the police and now it is only cars from the showroom and vans.' 'The lorries have to come onto the pavement to get round, the streets are so narrow.' 'I feel very strongly about workers from the factory parking their cars at the front and back of my house. I have been to the police and I have complained to the manager of Pyrex several times.'

Some of the dirt and dereliction of the neighbourhood was attributed by the informants to the lack of interest of the local authority in attending to the environment of an area where clearance was shortly to take place. 'Lots of houses are getting pulled down. The place is more neglected by the Corporation. Grass is just left to grow between the cobbles.' 'This is an old neighbourhood. The sewerage is bad. The air is polluted by the drainage.' One informant, a crippled old-age pensioner, had been happily living in her cottage. Now that the shop next door had been closed by the Public Health Inspectorate she was 'scared to death' when she heard the sounds of men stealing lead from the property. In the Deptford Road area the worst point was 'To have these surroundings to look at, especially the dump at the top of the street where the prefabs were demolished.'

There was very little criticism of community facilities: shops, schools, access to work places, medical services, and so forth.

Early in 1954 Michael Young addressed the Town Planning Institute on the subject of old people in central areas. There was, he argued, a fundamental problem of loneliness for old people–especially widows–who need a function and a status within a family but are deprived of these by policies which rehouse young people on housing estates and leave the old people behind in central areas. This did not appear to be a problem of great magnitude in Sunderland. There were, however, examples of it. 'I had no luck in this house. If I got to Red House with my daughter my luck would change. I am sick of living round Hendon.' An 88-year-old widow wanted to move to Hylton Castle in order to be near her daughter. An Ocean Road couple had applied 'umpteen times' to be near their son at Hillview. They were not interested in a council house anywhere else and they were 'terrified' that 'they might bang us up to Hylton Castle'.

Dissatisfaction with the behaviour of neighbours was more important in the slum-clearance areas than was either dissatisfaction with community facilities or problems of maintaining contact with relatives. Rossi found the same true of his sample of American families.[12] Twelve per cent of the sample disliked their neighbours. In Hendon this was true of 18 per cent. There were many reasons for disliking neighbours. 'Dirty people! I swill out the back with Dettol to try and kill the smell.' 'The place gets dirtied with other people's muck.' Others complained of the noise made by neighbours or their children. 'It was a nice, quiet street until we got the crowd at the bottom. They came when they heard the street was to come down.' Some objected to their neighbours because they believed they made it difficult for them to bring up their children 'decently'. They saw their neighbours' children as being less controlled than their own and having different standards of behaviour and language. 'We want to move the children to a council estate for their speech. Since we came here the daughter comes out with terrible talk.'

For some the neighbours were not friendly enough. 'They are all old people round here. There is no company.' 'I am helpful. I sat with the old woman all night. But if I was dying, no-one would come near hand! They keep to themselves. I have only lived here fifteen years! I'm not one of the old hands!' Others (especially in Hendon) disliked their neighbours because they were too friendly. 'Oh yes, they are friendly. A lot of the neighbours sit around the doorsteps from morning till night. I can't stand them. They just sit and gossip all day long.' 'Friendly—but I don't want to be friendly with them! They are the type who run into debt. I have known lots of people in trouble because they didn't keep neighbours out of their houses.' For some the neighbours were too aloof. For others again the neighbours were too interested in the family's affairs and were disliked for that reason. 'We were warned by the previous tenant that they are very nosey. They are watching behind the curtains when you go out and when you come back. Just like Coronation Street.'

OTHER BENEFITS

The majority of the families affected by the 1965–70 slum-clearance programme lacked certain internal household amenities.

Water Closets

Eighty-two per cent of the families had no indoor lavatory— 86 per cent in Hendon and 90 per cent of the tenants of private landlords. For some families an outdoor w.c. was a trial. 'The worst thing is with the children. If they get up in the middle of the night you have to take them down the yard.' 'It is a drawback because it is hard to train the kiddies.' 'Now that my husband is dead I am terrified to go to the w.c. in the yard at night in case somebody comes into the house while I am out.' One quarter of the families in the 1965–70 sample shared a w.c. with one other family and a further 4 per cent shared with two other families. In the Hendon area a young girl, her husband and three children under five were, in the period immediately preceding the interview, without a toilet in the curtilage for one whole year; they used the wife's sister's w.c. further down the street. The Health Inspector subsequently succeeded in compelling the landlord to put this family's w.c. into working order.

Baths

Two-thirds (66 per cent) of the 1965–70 families and in Hendon over three-quarters (77 per cent) were without a fixed bath in their homes.

> 'Oh! That's the main thing – especially in this area. He has to go to his family for one. I have to go to my family for one. The kids just have to get into the dish, that's all.'

> 'My husband is a coalman, so having no bath is a big drawback. He has to wash in the kitchen every night and the wallpaper gets splashed with dirty water.'

> 'Worth paying two pounds a week for a bath! I have to go to Da's at Plain's Farm. She has to go down to the Town End. Otherwise just under the tap in the yard for me or one foot in the dish for her. It is the worst thing about this house. They are talking about sending men to the moon – and we can't get a bath!'

> 'It's a big drawback. As it is I have to catch a sunny day to put the washboiler on and get a bath in the washhouse; it is too much of a mess to get bathed in the living room.'

Fewer than one in three of the families with fixed baths had those baths in a separate bathroom (31 per cent). Well over half (58 per cent) of the sample and over three-quarters (77 per cent) of the tenants of private landlords were without a supply of hot water from a tap.

Water Supply

One-third (34 per cent) did not have an internal supply of cold water. This percentage rose to 52 per cent when only the tenants of private landlords were considered and to 55 per cent at Hendon. Twenty per cent of the families shared their cold water tap with one other household and a further 4 per cent shared with two other households. At Hendon twelve of the 22 families in the sub-sample shared their cold water supply with another family and a further three families each shared with two other families.

Other Amenities

Thirty-four per cent of the general sample were dissatisfied with the utilities of the dwelling. Among the private tenants 45 per cent were dissatisfied and 21 per cent were very dissatisfied. An informant in the Hendon area reported very dilapidated wiring: 'The electricity man himself has said that he wonders how we have not all gone up in smoke.' In one dwelling there was no cupboard room at all: 'I have to have a tin box in the bedroom to keep the food in.' Thirty-five per cent of the informants regarded the heating of their dwelling as being unsatisfactory; fifteen per cent said it was very unsatisfactory. 'The fireplaces wouldn't keep a cat warm. We sit over the fire with our coats on, there is no heat from the fire because the whole house is too cold, too damp.' 'I have to paper twice a year in the living room because of the smoke from the old-fashioned range.' 'Five fireplaces, mind! But you can't keep them going—the cost—so big and old-fashioned. That is about the biggest draw-back of the lot, heating, trying to keep it warm in the winter.' Clothes washing is difficult for some families. 'I only have a washhouse so I wash at me Mam's in Moor Court.' 'I have to go to my mother at Grangetown to do my washing.'

Eighty-one per cent of the private tenants reported no modernisation whatsoever by the landlord in the previous five years or since the tenant came to the dwelling. Fifty-five per cent of private tenants said that they themselves had undertaken no modernisation. In Hendon 16 of the 21 tenants had attempted no modernisation.

Out of the 160 responses recorded in the questionnaires which related to the main advantages of a council tenure as the prospective tenants saw them, 47 mentioned a bath and a bathroom. 'Here you can't wash them every minute of the day. On a council estate if they go out and get wet they can get a hot bath when they come in.'

Overcrowding

Forty years ago Henry Mess concluded that the 'salient feature of the area' was 'not the badness of its slums but the skimping of land and houseroom endured by the vast majority of its population'.[13] Since those days there has been a transformation in the space standards of Sunderland families. Problems of space did, however, exist among the families of the 1965-70 programme and will be briefly examined here.

Thirty-four per cent of the 1965–70 families found themselves dissatisfied with the internal space of the dwelling and 14 per cent found their standards of internal space very unsatisfactory. At Hendon 57 per cent of the families were dissatisfied with their internal space and 33 per cent were very dissatisfied. Of those families whose space standards were unsatisfactory, some complained of an excess of space; the vast majority, however, felt cramped (79 per cent of the 47 families who complained of their space standards).

In certain districts and among certain groups there were families living at high occupancy rates: 17 per cent of private tenants were living at over one person per room and 4 per cent were living at more than one-and-a-half persons per room. At Hendon 19 per cent were living at over one person per room and a further 19 per cent at over one-and-a-half persons per room. A wife, her husband, two sisters-in-law and five children (another child was expected) lived in two living rooms and two bedrooms. One informant complained that the backyard was not big enough for four prams, four people's washing and four loads of coal. In a cottage in Ogden Street the cooker had to be placed in a pantry as there was no kitchen. 'If we had the money we would extend into the yard. A lovely big yard! I wish they'd do that instead of knocking it down!' Another informant said that the family needed another bedroom, an internal w.c. and a bathroom because their child had recently experienced a kidney operation and 'his penis is still painful when he passes water'. A bathroom was particularly needed because the boy suffered from eczema.

Lack of Privacy

The capacity of the family to control its relationship with other families–the problem of privacy–was also restricted in some instances. In the total 1965–70 sample 15 per cent of the families thought that their housing conditions were unsatisfactory as far as privacy was concerned and for 10 per cent of the families their conditions were very unsatisfactory. Among those families living in flats the proportion of those who were very dissatisfied was 27 per cent; among those living in rooms the proportion was 29 per cent; and in the Hendon district 7 of the 22 families (32 per cent) were very dissatisfied with the degree of privacy they enjoyed.

'They know when we go to bed, they know when we get up, they know when we go down the yard–well, they know everything we do.'

'Oh dear! There is *no* privacy. There are no locks or bolts on the doors. The front door does not even close–anybody can just walk in and walk out. There is no knocking. Even the doors to this flat don't lock. The windows drop open by themselves. There's no privacy and it's noisy. In your own house you only got yourself to blame.'

In a few other parts of the town, where the slum-clearance programme was similarly concerned with flats and rooms rather than with whole houses and cottages, there were problems of privacy similar to those found in Hendon.

High Cost

Some informants felt there was a financial advantage in moving to a council dwelling. A young family in the Deptford Road clearance area was very much in favour of their owner-occupied cottage being demolished. They were 'a bit sick of doing everything to it'. The family, because there were three young children, expected a council house rather than a flat, and expected to be financially better off 'considering what we have been paying here for repairs'. In the same slum-clearance area a couple with two young children said that they would be better off financially with a council dwelling because 'here we have a gas, coal and electricity bill; in a council house we will have to pay for electricity and gas only–here we have a fire on continuously in the bedroom from October till March because of the dampness'.

THE CONSUMER'S PREFERENCE ARRAY

Life in these dwellings and in these districts was thus a burden in one respect or another to substantial numbers of people. The families in the sample were asked to indicate in a variety of ways their overall assessment of their present housing conditions.

Twenty-eight per cent said that they were dissatisfied with them and 18 per cent were very dissatisfied; in Hendon 50 per cent were dissatisfied and 36 per cent were very dissatisfied. One-third (33 per cent) of the families interviewed had already applied for a council tenancy; 45 per cent of the tenants of private landlords in the sample had applied; nearly two-thirds (64 per cent) of the Hendon families had applied. Nearly half (46 per cent) of the informants thought they would be better off in a council district and nearly one-third (32 per cent) thought that they would be much better off; 57 per cent of the Hendon informants thought they would be better off in a council district and 43 per cent thought they would be much better off. Seventy per cent of the families thought they would be better off in a council dwelling and 58 per cent thought they would be much better off; 66 per cent of the tenants of private landlords thought they would be much better off and sixty-eight per cent of the families in Hendon thought they would be much better off in a council dwelling. Furthermore, some of the informants who were satisfied with their present conditions nevertheless stated that they would be more satisfied still with a council tenancy. The result was that over half (53 per cent) of the informants said they were in favour of demolition. The percentage was higher among the tenants of private landlords (72 per cent) and higher still among Hendon informants (83 per cent). Nearly three-quarters of the informants in Hendon were very much in favour of demolition.

Not surprisingly, the housing conditions of those favouring demolition were inferior to those who opposed it. Over two-thirds (67 per cent) of the families who were opposed to demolition lived in single-storied Sunderland cottages; this was true of under one-half (46 per cent) of the families who were in favour of demolition. Well over one-half (55 per cent) of the families who were opposed to demolition were owner-occupiers; this was true of under one-quarter (22 per cent) of those families favouring demolition. These and other comparisons are listed in Table 13.1.

The preference arrays and housing conditions of many residents in the 1965–70 slum-clearance areas, therefore, led them to reject their present neighbourhood and home in favour of a council tenancy. For the adults in the sample this was a reflection of their weakness in the housing market. For whatever reason—the level of their skill, education or personal competence in managing their everyday affairs—they had been unable to obtain housing conditions for themselves which (in their opinion) equalled those provided by the local authority.

Differences in housing conditions were associated to some extent with income differences. Owner-occupiers, for example, tended to be somewhat better off than tenants of private landlords. Among private tenants 30 per cent of the household heads had an income of between £5 and £10 a week; only 18 per cent of the heads of households in the sample of owner-occupier families had a weekly income in this range. By contrast, only one of the heads of households in the sample of tenants had a weekly income of £20 or more; this was the income of 12 per cent of heads of households among owner-occupiers. Among the private tenants nearly one-third (32 per cent) had no member 'economically active' (that is, available for work even if temporarily unemployed); this was true of only 21 per cent of the owner-occupiers. One-third of the owner-occupiers, furthermore, had two or more members of the family economically active; this was true of only 25 per cent of the private tenants.

Among the owner-occupiers fifty per cent of the heads of households were in skilled occupations; among the private tenants this was the case with only 33 per cent of the heads of households. Among owner-occupiers, only three (7 per cent) of the 42 heads of households were in unskilled occupations; fourteen (19 per cent) of the 73 heads of households in the families of tenants were in unskilled occupations.

While these differences existed, it must also be pointed out that they were not as large as is perhaps generally supposed. For example, among both owner-occupiers and tenants, one in five (21 per cent in both cases) of the heads of households received under £5 a week income—in the form of old-age or other types of pension. In Hendon, the area of worst housing conditions, the proportion of heads of households receiving a weekly income of under £5 was considerably less than this, 10 per cent. With regard to occupational grade, too, differences must not be exaggerated. They existed only between various grades of manual workers. No heads of households were in the

Registrar General's socio-economic grades 1, 2, 3, 4, or 13 (professional workers, employers and managers). Only three (4 per cent) of the 126 heads of households in the sample were in socio-economic grades 5 and 6 (skilled non-manual workers– clerks etc.). When those families favouring demolition were compared with those opposing it, the largest percentage-point difference was found in those families where the head of the household had retired. (Table 13.2.)

The statistics show that the children, whose preference arrays must in any case be met by their parents, tended to belong to families which were discontented with their housing conditions. Among the families in favour of demolition 44 per cent contained four persons or more, as compared with 28 per cent among the families opposed to demolition. Forty per cent of the families in favour of demolition had at least one child under the age of five as compared with 14 per cent of the families who were opposed to demolition and eighteen per cent had two children under the age of 5 as compared with 2 per cent among the families opposed to demolition.

NOTES TO CHAPTER 13

1 Paul F. Wendt, *Housing Policy: The Search for Solutions*, University of California Press 1962.
2 J. B. Cullingworth, *Housing in Transition*, London 1963.
3 David V. Donnison, *Housing Policy since the War*, Codicote, July 1960, p. 20.
4 *Ibid.*, p. 20.
5 *Sunderland Echo*, 5 October 1965.
6 *Ibid.*, 8 October 1965.
7 One-third of the general sample of dwellings in the 1965–70 programme were owner-occupied and in the sub-sample relating to the Deptford Road area the proportion was nearly one-half (22 out of 48 dwellings). In Hendon, by contrast, only one of the 22 dwellings of the sub-sample was owner-occupied. Well over half of the dwellings (56 per cent) in the general sample were single-storied cottages. (Cottages with attic rooms and dormer windows were counted as 'single-storied'.) In the Deptford area nearly three-quarters were cottages (73 per cent). In the Hendon sub-sample, by contrast, only 2 of the 22 dwellings were cottages. There was only one informant not in single-family occupation in the sub-sample for the Booth Street area and only 10 per cent of the informants in the Deptford Road area were not in single-family occupation; by contrast

10. 'Hendon has presented problems of sub-divided houses as compared with single-family cottages for many years.' (p. 195)

11. A typical street in the area of Hendon covered by the slum-clearance proposals 1965–70. (pp. 195–7)

12. 'With it being an industrial area.' River Wear at Sunderland—Wearmouth Colliery left, Laing's Shipyard right. (p. 198)

over one-quarter (27 per cent) of the informants in the Hendon sub-sample were in rooms, and a further 64 per cent were in self-contained flats.

8 *Sunderland Echo*, 21 October 1965.

9 Park ward.

10 Ian Nairn, 'Stop the Architects Now', *Observer*, 13 February 1966.

11 Peter H. Rossi, *Why Families Move*, Free Press 1955.

12 Thirty-seven of his 273 families complained about the social composition of their former neighbourhood and in 60 per cent of these cases this was a primary complaint—that is, it was sufficient to motivate the family to move from their former home. 'Complaints about the neighbourhood's social composition were much more effective in bringing about residential shifts than all other types of complaints about the neighbourhood.' Peter H. Rossi, *op. cit.*, p. 146.

13 Henry A. Mess, *Industrial Tyneside*, London 1928, p. 93. The reasons for large differences in average size of dwellings between towns is not clear. Bowley and Burnett-Hurst for example, were struck by the difference in the size of the predominant house in the towns they studied; it contained six rooms in Northampton, five at Reading, four at Warrington, and only three at Stanley. They insist that the causes are not only economic but the possible other causes are grouped under 'custom and habit of mind'. (A. L. Bowley and A. R. Burnett-Hurst, *Livelihood and Poverty*, 1915.) Mess in his study of Tyneside in 1928 noted that 'the small and congested house is accepted as a matter of course in this corner of England to a degree greater than elsewhere. Standards of house accommodation in different parts of the country are to a considerable extent conventional'. Henry A. Mess, *op. cit.*, p. 88. Mess himself offers an explanation in terms of historical circumstances.

Table 13.1

Housing Conditions of Families For and Against Demolition: Slum-clearance Programme 1965–70: Sunderland CB

Housing Condition	Families For Demolition per cent (n=65)	Families Against Demolition per cent (n=42)
Single-storied cottage	46	67
Owner-occupation	22	55
Access to work 'very satisfactory'	45	81
Access to shops 'very satisfactory'	78	88
Access to medical services 'very satisfactory'	54	69
Access to town centre 'very satisfactory'	77	88
Neighbours 'very sociable'	40	57
Neighbours 'very helpful'	40	52
Neighbours liked 'very much'	31	50
Neighbourhood amenity 'very satisfactory'	9	26
Privacy 'very satisfactory'	66	81
Internal space 'very satisfactory'	36	64
Occupancy rate 0–$\frac{1}{2}$ persons per room	35	50
Internal cold water tap	58	76
Exclusive use of cold water tap	68	83
Indoor w.c.	14	31
Exclusive use of w.c.	62	83
Fixed bath	26	55
Structural condition 'very satisfactory'	6	33

Source: Interview material

Table 13.2

Socio-economic Grade of Household Heads: For and Against Demolition: Slum Clearance Programme 1965–70: Sunderland CB

Socio-economic Grade	Families For Demolition per cent (n=65)	Families Against Demolition per cent (n=42)
Skilled manual and non-manual	45	38
Semi-skilled	14	10
Unskilled	15	12
Retired	11	21
Housewives etc.	15	19

Source: Interview material

CHAPTER 14

OPPOSITION TO THE SLUM CLEARANCE PROPOSALS 1965–70

I. Structural Condition, Structural Form and Internal Facilities

---

The deficiencies of the dwellings and districts included in the 1965–70 proposals were, therefore, clear and considerable. The interview material shows that they were recognised and disliked as deficiencies by the people who suffered from them.

It is necessary now to examine the other side of the picture, namely, the experience and attitudes of informants who were favourably disposed to one or more elements in their housing situation. As might be expected, some families were reluctant to lose certain advantages of residence in their present home and location; and for some the deficiencies were so slight or the prospective losses were so large that they were more or less seriously opposed to being rehoused at all.

The first aspect to be considered is the structural condition of the dwelling. Sixty-four per cent of the owner-occupiers and half of all the informants in the Millfield clearance area, in small slum-clearance areas elsewhere and in the sub-sample of Sunderland cottages were satisfied with the structural condition of their dwelling. (Table 14.1.)

All the cribbing in the world won't stop them coming down if they are scheduled. That's logical. No good shedding tears! 'The

13. 'The exclusive use of a water closet in a private, walled backyard.' (p. 221)

14. 'You can see that we've cemented the front and put in modern windows. We have practically rebuilt the house.' (p. 213)

15. 'Flats . . .' (p. 215)

16. '. . . We'll stop in our old houses!' (p. 215)

old homestead's going . . .' Thirty-five years . . .! But they are jolly good cottages here.

Ever since 1957 Sunderland's development plan had shown these areas as being 'programmed for redevelopment by the end of 1971'. In spite of the discouragement that could be expected in the face of the long-standing prospect of demolition, most of the families who were satisfied with its condition had maintained and improved their dwelling.

> I do not expect the house to be demolished. I expected it to go to my son. I don't see how they can, they're all good houses, all owner-occupied houses.

> You can see that we've cement-faced the front and put in modern windows. We have practically rebuilt the house.

In November 1965 the Prime Minister was reported as saying that housing was the great social evil of the nineteen-sixties, as unemployment had been the great social evil of the nineteen-thirties. This brought a response in the local newspaper which seemed to summarise very well the attitude of many of the families in well-maintained cottages and other dwellings in slum-clearance areas:

> How right he is! Unfortunately he has got hold of the wrong end of the stick. Unemployment was a social evil because men were ruthlessly thrown out of work by employers in so-called 'rationalisation' schemes. Housing today is a social evil because families are turned out of their cherished cottages in mis-named 'slum-clearance' schemes. Why is it that having been brought from under the shadow of the dole, we now have to live under the shadow of the bulldozer?[1]

The press, too, tended to report at length on the structural defects of council dwellings.[2] The slum-cleared owner-occupier or tenant did not know where he would be rehoused, and had in fact minimal choice. Unfavourable newspaper reports about council accommodation, however unrepresentative, were likely, therefore, to reinforce attachment to their existing accommodation.

To reservations about the degree to which rehousing would mean an improvement in freedom from damp, sunlighting, ventilation, and other structural features were added doubts about the basic structural form of the dwelling they might be allocated. A high proportion of the dwellings in the 1965–70 areas were Sunderland cottages.[3] Informants were asked which type of council dwelling they thought would be best for themselves. In the Wayman Street area 70 per cent said that the bungalow—i.e. the single-storied cottage—was the best type of council dwelling. In the Deptford Road area the proportion was 49 per cent and in the Booth Street area the proportion was 38 per cent. (Table 14.2.) Ninety-three per cent of the informants in the Booth Street area, 91 per cent in the Wayman Street area, 87 per cent in the Hendon area and 81 per cent in the Deptford Road area said the flat or maisonette was the worst type of council dwelling.[4]

Publicity about 'flats' tends to refer to the conspicuous 'multi-storied' type, those of perhaps twelve, fifteen or twenty storeys. In discussing with the relevant officers of the local authority the reasons for choosing flats as a form of development in Sunderland the interviewer was told that 'high-rise blocks are essential to the skyline of the town'. Seven blocks of 16-storied flats were built at Gilley Law, on the outskirts of the town, as a result of 'an aesthetic choice'.[5] Attacks also tend to concentrate on high-rise developments.[6]

In Sunderland the centrally located high-rise flats,[7] however, had lifts and resident caretakers, and tenancies were allocated only to families without children. There was also what might be termed 'the Dagenham effect'.[8] Multi-storied flats formed such a small proportion of its stock that the council could afford to go far down the housing list in order to find tenants. There had been somewhat freer consumer choice, and the inhabitants, therefore, were by and large families which desired dwellings of this type, cost and location.

Problems arose in, and slum-clearance families were more fearful of flats of two, three or four stories (i.e. tenements) with their problems of noise, staircases, shared courtyards and unsupervised internal spaces. Multi-storied flats formed a small though growing fraction of the council's stock while tenements had in recent years become a very important part of the council provision in Sunderland.

The 1921 census records two per cent of the town's housing stock as 'maisonettes, flats and tenements'. Between 1919 and

1945 the council built 4,800 dwellings, 5 per cent of which were tenements.[9] Between March 1945 and March 1955 the council built 9,400 dwellings, 9 per cent of which were tenements. By March 1966, of 20,800 post-war dwellings which had been built, no less than 21 per cent were tenements (4,400).[10]

I don't like the idea of being up aloft at all. I have bad legs. I'm under the doctor for my chest and heart.

Flats! They say it's just like going into hospital when you go. We know two or three who want to be out. You've only got to set fire to one of them and they're all gone. We'll stop in our old houses!

We've been offered three or four and we wouldn't take them. We were offered a place in Leechmere Road. He has angina heart, chronic bronchitis and bloodpressure. He *couldn't* trail upstairs.

I would die if I had to go into a flat.

I am against flats. Once you're locked in, you're locked in. Here you can walk out of the front or into your own backyard.

I don't believe in flats or maisonettes. My mother moved to a flat. It didn't work, having to climb stairs. There was somebody above her with kiddies. There was always rows over not taking turns cleaning the stairs.

If you have an argument or a fight with your wife it ought to be private. In a flat everybody in the building hears—it becomes everybody's fight.

Another possible source of loss for the 1965–70 families was in size and number of rooms. Some housewives, referring to the experience of friends, would regret having to dispose of items of furniture to which they had for one irrational reason or another become attached, but which might be too large to be accommodated in their new dwelling. Sunderland council, too, at the time of the SHN study was operating its 'tailor made' policy of house-size allocation. Under this system a man and wife with, say, two bedrooms, one of which they used for occasional visits from sons or daughters and their families, would be allocated a dwelling with only one bedroom. They would be entitled, that is, to a 'two-person' dwelling and they would not be allowed

215

anything larger even if they were prepared to pay for it and no matter what the size of the dwelling they had given up.

In principle this is, of course, simply a matter of housing management, and the policy could be changed. As a result of the policy, however, certain constraints would continue to operate. Sunderland's dwellings are in general the smallest in average size among the twenty-nine largest towns of England and Wales, 4·07 rooms per dwelling as compared with the median town Wolverhampton (4·72) and the towns with the largest dwellings Birkenhead (5·01) and Cardiff (5·25).[11] (Diagram 14.A.) Yet Sunderland, with the *highest* proportion in 1966 of post-war council dwellings among these towns (113 per thousand population), as compared with the median town Manchester (with 62) and Blackpool, the lowest (with 27), (Diagram 14.B) was also second from the bottom in size of council dwellings (59 per cent one- and two-bedrooms) as compared with the bottom town Brighton (60 per cent), the median town Blackpool (42 per cent) and the town with the smallest proportion of small council dwellings, Nottingham (15 per cent).[12] (Diagram 14.C.) In Sunderland's newest council housing development at Mill Hill, Silksworth New Township (Doxford Park), no less than 30 per cent of the 670 dwellings will have only one bedroom.

The degree to which the 1965–70 dwellings lacked certain internal fixtures was demonstrated in Chapter Thirteen. There were complaints about, for example, defective wiring and about unsatisfactory arrangements for clothes-washing; only one-fifth had an indoor water closet; there was a fixed bath in only one-third of the dwellings.[13] Because of the inadequacies of their household amenities many families wished to be rehoused.

It could be expected, on the other hand, that the families already possessing these amenities would be so much the less inclined to move into council accommodation. Fifty-four per cent of the sample and 74 per cent of the owner-occupiers had modernised their dwellings.[14] They had 'brought the water in' (i.e. laid on an internal supply of cold water to replace the tap in the backyard); former wash houses (small outhouses with coal heated boilers, attached to the main cottage but with access only through a door in the backyard) had been converted into bathrooms; gas geysers or other sources of hot water had

Diagram 14.A

SIZE OF DWELLINGS : SUNDERLAND AND COMPARABLE* TOWNS CENSUS 1961

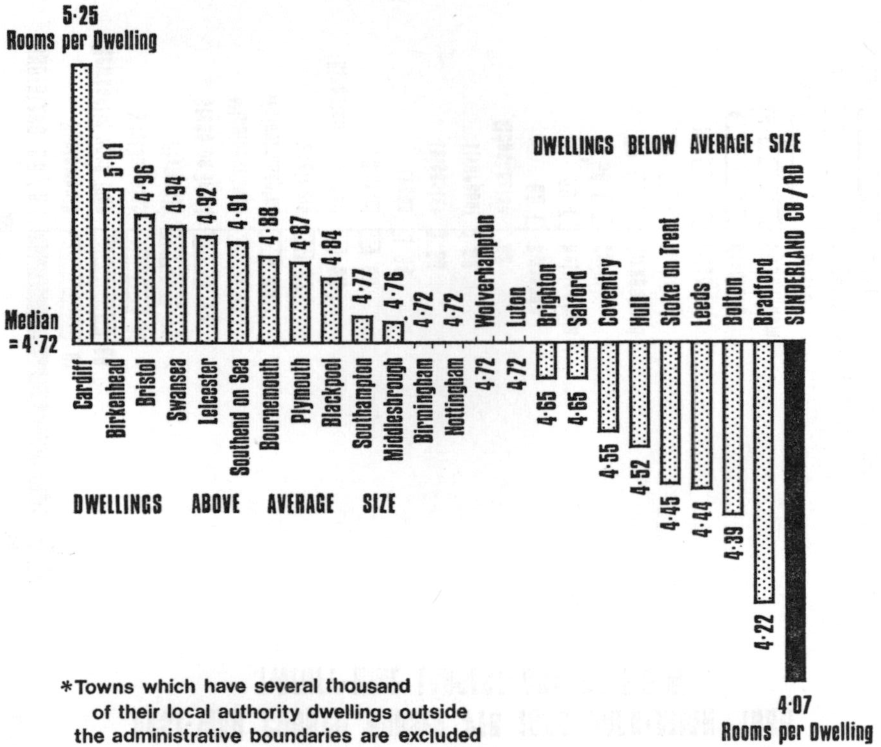

5·25 Rooms per Dwelling

Median = 4·72

Town	Rooms per Dwelling
Cardiff	
Birkenhead	5·01
Bristol	4·96
Swansea	4·94
Leicester	4·92
Southend on Sea	4·91
Bournemouth	4·88
Plymouth	4·87
Blackpool	4·84
Southampton	4·77
Middlesbrough	4·76
Birmingham	4·72
Nottingham	4·72

DWELLINGS ABOVE AVERAGE SIZE

Rooms per Dwelling	Town
4·72	Wolverhampton
4·72	Luton
4·65	Brighton
4·65	Salford
4·55	Coventry
4·52	Hull
4·45	Stoke on Trent
4·44	Leeds
4·39	Bolton
4·22	Bradford
4·07	SUNDERLAND CB / RD

DWELLINGS BELOW AVERAGE SIZE

4·07 Rooms per Dwelling

*Towns which have several thousand of their local authority dwellings outside the administrative boundaries are excluded

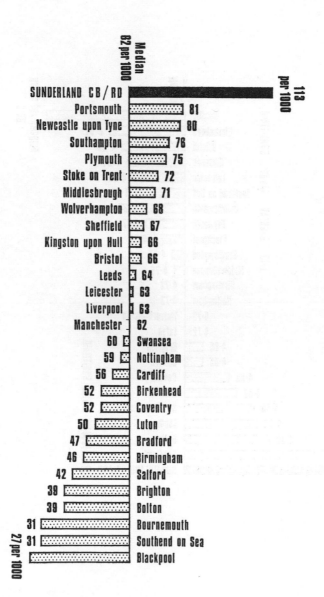

Diagram 14.B

POST-WAR COUNCIL HOUSES PER 1000 POPULATION 1966
TWENTY-NINE LARGEST CBs OF E & W

Median
62 per 1000

113
per 1000

SUNDERLAND CB / RD	
Portsmouth	81
Newcastle upon Tyne	80
Southampton	76
Plymouth	75
Stoke on Trent	72
Middlesbrough	71
Wolverhampton	68
Sheffield	67
Kingston upon Hull	66
Bristol	66
Leeds	64
Leicester	63
Liverpool	63
Manchester	62
60	Swansea
59	Nottingham
56	Cardiff
52	Birkenhead
52	Coventry
50	Luton
47	Bradford
46	Birmingham
42	Salford
39	Brighton
39	Bolton
31	Bournemouth
31	Southend on Sea
27 per 1000	Blackpool

Source : Institute of Municipal Treasurers and Accountants

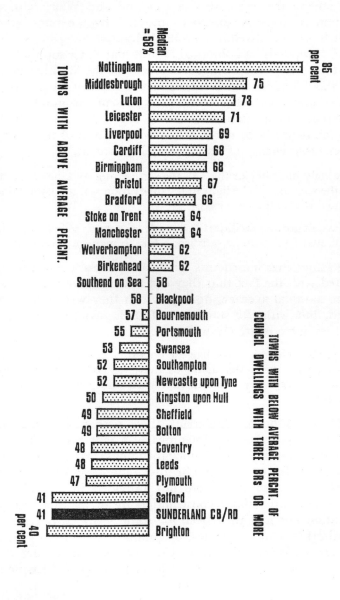

Diagram 14.C

PERCENTAGE OF COUNCIL DWELLINGS HAVING 3 BRs OR MORE: 29 LARGEST CBS OF E & W

SIZE OF COUNCIL HOUSES IN 1966

85 per cent

Median = 58%

TOWNS WITH ABOVE AVERAGE PERCNT.

Nottingham	85
Middlesbrough	75
Luton	73
Leicester	71
Liverpool	69
Cardiff	68
Birmingham	68
Bristol	67
Bradford	66
Stoke on Trent	64
Manchester	64
Wolverhampton	62
Birkenhead	62
Southend on Sea	58

TOWNS WITH BELOW AVERAGE PERCNT. OF COUNCIL DWELLINGS WITH THREE BRs OR MORE

58	Blackpool
57	Bournemouth
55	Portsmouth
53	Swansea
52	Southampton
52	Newcastle upon Tyne
50	Kingston upon Hull
49	Sheffield
49	Bolton
48	Coventry
48	Leeds
47	Plymouth
41	Salford
41	SUNDERLAND CB/RD
40	Brighton

per cent

Source : Institute of Municipal Treasurers and Accountants

been installed. 'There are no advantages in a move to a council house. We have everything here.' In 1951 one-quarter of all Sunderland's dwellings were without an internal water supply. This was the highest proportion of dwellings lacking such a facility among the 157 towns of England and Wales with a population in 1951 of 50,000 or more.[15] By the mid-sixties two-thirds of the dwellings covered by the 1965–70 slum-clearance proposals had obtained an internal water supply.[16]

What is perhaps surprising, however, was the fact that even among those families which lacked one or more of these 'basic' amenities, many wished to retain their present accommodation in preference to a council dwelling. An explanation which springs immediately to mind is 'the wantlessness of the poor', that venerable enemy of reform and betterment.

> I've only one plug for the TV, the refrigerator and the vacuum. I use the vacuum off the light in the other rooms. Can't complain! I've used them all these years.

> I haven't got any facilities! It doesn't take much to heat a kettle or pan, man! I *have* to be satisfied. I *have* to manage without it.

Among some older informants this 'wantlessness' seemed to be connected with the fact that they did not compare themselves with the national average, against which they were relatively deprived, but with the standards of their own past, against which they were relatively well-off.

> Days have changed. Not like the poss-stick and the poss-tub. It is changed for the better as far as that was concerned, because that was slavery. I've stood in that yard and scrubbed claes in the snaa!

A second reason for preferring their present dwellings in spite of their poor 'basic' amenities was that they possessed other amenities which some council dwellings lacked, and which they therefore feared they might lose. One example of this is the coal fire. Open fires were not provided in any of the dwellings currently under construction by or for Sunderland Corporation nor had they been for some years past. Certain large suburban council estates, originally designed with open fires, were governed by Smoke Control Orders. During the winters of 1966–7 and 1967–8 the local press carried frequent

17. 'Some housewives would regret having to dispose of items of furniture to which for one irrational reason or another they have become attached.' (p. 215)

18. 'Complaints about physical amenity of Council areas.' (p. 260)

19.
'Living next to
Corporation
slums.' (p. 260)

20.
'Satisfaction with
access to places
of entertainment.'
(p. 271)

complaints from tenants about the cost and scarcity of smokeless fuel and the inefficiency of their grates. Publicity, agitation and the plausibility of the complainants' case resulted in the Orders being suspended for several months. On their reimposition the local newspaper again carried bitter complaints of the failure of supplies, of penury and of cheerlessness.

> What's a house without a bit of fire? An electric fire or under-heating is all right in the summer but not in the winter.

> A lot of people down in Dame Dorothy Street are putting up mock fireplaces with hardboard—the mantelpiece, the lot—just to pretend there is a fire. That's what my nephew has done, so they have a place to put their furniture around.

In this matter it is possible to argue strongly that families who felt worse off with the room-heating facilities of the new council developments, or the Smoke Control Orders of older council estates 'suffered for the public good'. It is nevertheless understandable that families which were not so suffering should be reluctant to give up what they saw as the homeliness they for the moment enjoyed.[17]

No informant preferred to be without a bath or without a bathroom. Only one informant, a young man, preferred his water tap to be in the backyard—he enjoyed the daily in-vigoration of a 'swill' in the open air. Among those without an indoor toilet (n = 66), however, the majority (65 per cent) did not feel this to be a drawback. 'It's not hygienic. It's not *polite*! A toilet *inside* the home? O, no, thank you!' It was felt 'not nice' to bring the sound of, for example, the emptying cistern into the home, and desirable that the use of the lavatory should be more strictly a private matter than is now usual, perhaps, in general society. The exclusive use of a water closet located a few feet from the main rooms of the house in a private, walled backyard achieved this for the families holding this view.

NOTES TO CHAPTER 14

1 *Sunderland Echo*, 11 November 1965.
2 'Couple Driven From Flat By Water', *Sunderland Echo*, 23 October 1967. '"Bedrooms Too Damp To Sleep In", Say Tenants', *Sunderland Echo*,

21 January 1966. To take some examples almost at random, the *Sunderland Echo* of 10 February 1966 contains an item on leaking flats at Monkwearmouth and a letter from Red House estate complaining of 'dampness which turns wallpaper black, pantries so wet and damp they are just a waste of space'. A letter from Town End Farm in the issue of 4 April 1967 complains: 'My bedroom is damp, my boxroom has a fusty smell'. An item in *The Journal* (Newcastle) 18 April 1967, as well as at the same time in the *Echo*, reports complaints about the draughts and noisiness of Lambton Tower, High Street East. A writer from Millfield, referring to the well-known local legend of John Lambton and the Lambton Worm, wrote in a letter to the *Echo*:

> Who hasn't heard in his home town
> Of the famous Lambton beast?
> Young Johnny Lambton cut it down—
> But it's back in High Street East!

Another verse reads, again referring to the legend,

> If they think we are sheep they're mistaken,
> We're all Millfield men of proud breed!
> We won't have our tenancies taken—
> And the Town Hall had better take heed!

Sunderland's 642 flats at Gilley Law are of similar design and construction to the flats which collapsed in the Ronan Point disaster, 16 May 1968, as are the 216 in the Lambton Tower group.

3 Seventy-three per cent in the Millfield (Deptford Road) area, 70 per cent in the Southwick (Wayman Street) area and 69 per cent in the Millfield (Booth Street) area.

4 The Ministry of Housing researchers made the same finding in Rochdale. 'Hardly anyone trying to move wanted a flat rather than a house or a bungalow.' MHLG, *The Deeplish Study*, HMSO 1966, p. 24.

5 Only one other reason was given for the provision of flats rather than houses, namely, the need for high density in central redevelopment.

6 See, for example, W. H. Whyte Jnr., 'Are Cities Un-American?', *The Exploding Metropolis*, Ed. the Editors of *Fortune*, N.Y. 1957; Terence Bendixson, 'Cosier than Corbusier', *The Spectator*, 25 March 1966; R. E. Nichol, Chief Planning Officer, Scottish Development Department (quoted in *The Journal* (Newcastle), 16 September 1965).

7 The peripheral multi-storied flats at Gilley Law were not investigated in the SHN surveys. At the time of the SHN fieldwork they were under construction.

8 Because the vast inter-war LCC estate at Dagenham was so defective in many respects (see Terence Young, *Becontree and Dagenham*, London 1934, and Robert Sinclair, *Metropolitan Man: The Future of the English*, London 1937), there were usually, before 1945 'more empty houses than prospective tenants. Those, therefore, who did want to live there were free to do so. Sons and daughters of residents, for example, could

reside on the estate near their own parents. The result is that matri-locality is almost as marked in Dagenham as in the East End.'

Peter Willmott, *The Evolution of a Community: Dagenham after 40 years*, London 1963, p. 31.

9 A further 2,100 dwellings were built by the North Eastern Housing Association one-quarter (524) of which were tenements. The tenancies of the NEHA dwellings are allocated by the local authority's Housing Department on the same basis as allocation to the local authority's own dwellings.

10 A further three per cent were multi-storied flats (700), mainly 13 to 20 stories high, and 5 per cent were maisonettes (1,100). In the post-war stock there were, on the other hand, only 370 bungalows; the majority of these (306) had one bedroom, i.e. they were smaller than the normal Sunderland cottage.

11 *Census*, 1961.

12 Institute of Municipal Treasurers and Accountants, *Housing Statistics 1965–66.*

13 GRO, *Sample Census 1966: County Report; Durham*, HMSO 1967.

14 These figures refer to families which had undertaken one or more of the following improvements or improvements of approximately the same magnitude: provision of a fixed bath, provision of a bathroom, provision or renewal of the electricity circuit, provision of an internal water supply, provision of a hot water supply other than a simple hot-water geyser, etc. Structural repairs and improvements and minor 'modernisation' such as the replacement of a high-level by a low-level cistern do not appear in the above figures.

15 Claus A. Moser and Wolf Scott, *British Towns*, London 1961, p. 29.

16 In the county borough as a whole 22 per cent (12,000) of the house-holds had been without a fixed bath and 21 per cent (11,700) had been without a hot water supply in 1961. Due partly to demolition and replacement, but partly due also to modernisation, these figures had been reduced to 15 per cent (8,800 households) and 13 per cent (7,700 households) by 1966. GRO, *Census 1961: County Report; Durham*, 1963; and GRO, *Sample Census* 1966, HMSO 1967. The readiness to modernise were it not for the expressed intention of the local authority to clear these dwellings, was not systematically investigated. It did emerge in the course of the interviews, however, that it was only the prospect of demolition that prevented some families from providing these amenities for themselves. 'Before we heard it was coming down we were ready to . . .' provide a bath, or install a hot water system, etc., was a 'frequent' response not, however, quantified.

17 A second example of a feature of the home defined as an amenity by some families in slum-clearance areas, which they might lose were they to be allocated a council dwelling, is the television aerial. Such families regard the communal aerials and wired television now required in some areas by the local council as less efficient and less reliable than the individual aerials they already possess.

Table 14.1

Families Satisfied with the Structural Condition of their Dwelling: Sunderland CB Slum-clearance Proposals 1965–70

Sub-sample	Families satisfied with structural condition	Number of families in the sub-sample (=100 per cent)
Owner-occupiers	64	42
Tenants of private landlords	32	73
Millfield (Booth St.) area	53	13
Elsewhere	50	20
Millfield (Deptford Rd.) area	48	48
Southwick (Wayman St.) area	39	23
Hendon	14	22
Old single-person or two-person families	47	34
Adult large families	42	24
Mature single-person or two-person families	40	20
Young small families	35	31
Young large families[1]	35	14
Single-family cottages	50	71
Single-family houses	42	19
Flats	23	22

Source: Interview Analysis

[1] Families were classified according to the schema—(after Cullingworth) on page 225.

Stage of Family Development		Persons aged 0–15		Persons aged 16 and over
Young single-person or two-person family		Nil		One or two 0–44
Young small family		One or two	AND	One or two
Young large family	EITHER	Three or more	AND	Any number
	OR	Two	AND	Three or more
Adult large family		Nil or one	AND	Three or more
Mature single-person or two-person family		Nil		One 45–64 OR Two (i) both of whom are 45–64; (ii) one under 45, other 45–64
Old single-person or two-person family		Nil		One or two, at least one of whom is 65 or older

Table 14.2

'Best Type of Council Dwelling'

'Best Dwelling Type'	Hendon per cent	Millfield (Booth St.) area per cent	Millfield (Deptford Rd.) area per cent	Southwick (Wayman St.) area per cent
Semidetached house	50	38	30	26
Terraced house	14	0	6	0
Bungalow	23	38	49	70
Other	13	24	15	4
	n=22	n=13	n=47	n=23

Source: Interview Analysis

OPPOSITION TO THE SLUM CLEARANCE PROPOSALS 1965–70

II. Cost and Tenure

Cost

One reason for living in an old dwelling is that the family cannot or does not want to bear the cost of a more modern one. On certain assumptions of what a family can afford only 25 per cent of households in this country could rent a new three-bedroom dwelling, only 10 per cent could purchase such a dwelling out of income and most people now living in houses built before 1880 could neither rent nor buy such a new house.[1] There is a tendency for housing costs to rise faster than incomes in most countries of Europe. A working-class dwelling costs more in terms of average wages than it did in 1900[2] and these families have not the income to purchase decent housing without state assistance.[3] Other writers point rather to the failure even of people who could afford decent accommodation to seek it. 'Large sections of the population aspire to live and feel entitled to live in accommodation much superior to that for which they are willing to pay.'[4] The proportion of total national investment which goes into housing is 'by no means excessive in comparison with other European countries', and slums and areas of very old and decaying houses are 'a disgrace' in a wealthy country such as Britain.[5] The purpose of subsidy is to bridge the gap between the cost of the better dwelling and the amount 'poorer people' might 'reasonably be expected to pay'.[6]

Housing subsidies make up the difference between the rent actually charged and the economic rent, i.e. the amount which would have had to be charged to meet the full cost of interest, amortisation, maintenance and management. When an equivalent dwelling would bring more on the open market than the economic rent, then the council tenant, as Kaim-Caudle points out,[7] is in fact subsidised further by an amount equal to the difference between what he pays and his notional 'market rent'. These subsidies have allowed council dwellings to be provided (with certain interruptions) at an ever higher standard of construction and amenity.[8]

Table 15.1 shows the number of houses built under different conditions of subsidy in Sunderland from the early years of the twentieth century to 1965. As compared with the other large towns and cities of England and Wales council tenants in Sunderland were very well off. Sunderland in the first place received more government grants per head of the population for housing than any other of these towns except Newcastle upon Tyne and Salford. (Table 15.2.) Exchequer subsidies constituted twenty-one per cent of the total income of Sunderland's housing revenue account in the financial year 1965–6—a higher proportion than for any other town except Salford, Newcastle and Sheffield.[9] The exchequer subsidy per head of the population was higher for Sunderland CB/RD than for any other town.[10] During the year 1965–6 rates levied per head of the population for housing purposes were higher only in Salford, Hull, Leeds and Sheffield.[11] Rates levied per £ for housing purposes were higher only in Salford and Hull.[12] As a result of exchequer and rate subsidies, rent paid by tenants formed a less than average proportion of housing revenue account income in Sunderland: in only seven of the 29 largest towns of England and Wales did rent constitute a smaller proportion of the housing revenue account.[13]

The extent to which his dwelling is a bargain for the Sunderland council tenant is demonstrated also by the fact that a very low proportion of the council's stock is composed of old property formerly owned by private landlords. In 1965–6 under two per cent of Sunderland's 26,000 council dwellings were not built by or for the Corporation. Birmingham, by contrast, owned 35,000 old dwellings which had been acquired or purchased from private owners (26 per cent of the council's housing stock).[14]

Sunderland's council houses are, furthermore, predominantly of post-war rather than inter-war construction. Only in Bournemouth, Luton, Portsmouth and Southend do post-war council houses form a higher proportion of all houses built by or for the council (Table 15.3) and whereas three of these towns are among the bottom four with regard to the number of council dwellings built per thousand population, Sunderland has built more council houses in total and more post-war council houses than any of the 29 towns with which it is being compared. (Table 15.4 and Table 15.5.)

The cost of construction of a typical traditional three-bedroom house built by Sunderland Corporation during the year 1965–6 was £2,070. Square foot for square foot this was below the average for the large towns of England and Wales indicating, again, a bargain for Sunderland council tenants. (Table 15.6.)[15] Notwithstanding this fact, some developments in the 1960s were designed to reach high standards, and were correspondingly expensive. The Dame Dorothy Street area can be taken as an example.[16] Gas appliances provide ducted warm-air central heating, water heating, clothes drying facilities and convector gas fires, and the dwellings are insulated to Scandinavian standards with floors of polystyrene foam under plaster, glass fibre and wood-on-concrete, and double-glazed windows.[17] Another example is provided by three 21-storied blocks in Sunderland's central redevelopment area. The average cost of each of the 270 flats was £3,977.[18] At Downhill (68 dwellings) the estimated cost of three-bedroomed houses, exclusive of land, was £2,918,[19] and at the estate at Witherwack (601 dwellings, 2,150 persons) the standard of dwellings was superior to those laid down in the Parker Morris Report.[20]

For the family, therefore, which wishes to move from its present dwelling (characteristically the family on the council's housing list) there is hope of becoming the tenant of an expensive house or flat at very reasonable cost to itself in terms of weekly rent. Only Bradford and Hull have lower average weekly net rents for post-war dwellings. (Table 15.7.) Is it nevertheless possible that financial considerations enter into the decision of some householders in the 1965–70 areas to cling to their old dwellings? There are several reasons why they should.

Sunderland, in the first place, has been a local authority in the forefront, not only of council house construction, but also the demolition of old property. Among the 29 largest towns of England and Wales it has the ninth highest proportion of houses demolished or closed since 1955. (Table 15.8.) The old dwellings which remain compare more favourably with new dwellings, therefore, than is the case in towns where slum-clearance programmes have been less progressive.

The second thing to notice is that not all families housed by the corporation in a particular year go into the newest dwellings. Of the 1,359 new houses let by the Corporation Housing Department in the year 1 April 1965–31 March 1966, 20 per cent were allocated to existing council tenants. (Table 15.9.) Among those rehoused from slum-clearance areas, on the other hand, nearly one-half (47 per cent) were allocated relet dwellings. (Table 15.10.)

Thirdly, although the long waiting lists for council houses are frequently regarded as evidence for an intense unsatisfied demand for *anything* the council can offer,[21] the housing stock (old or new) is not regarded as homogeneous by either housing-list or slum-clearance families. A dwelling may have been expensive to build, but that is no guarantee that it will be acceptable to the families to which it is offered. This can be shown from an analysis of Sunderland's experience in the allocation of council houses to waiting-list families–i.e. to families actively seeking a council tenancy. In January 1965, there were 5,335 families on Sunderland's housing list. Of these just one-third (1,741) had been registered in the previous twelve months. This is the normal rate of applications received.[22] Applications come mainly from newly-married couples. They are not saying 'we want anything the council will offer us'; they are simply opening one housing option among others, an option which requires very little effort on their part. Their names remain on the housing list, but many hundreds in fact take up other options and 'leak away' into non-council accommodation before the time comes for them to be offered a council tenancy. Thus, in the year 1 January 1965–31 December 1965, of the waiting-list cases visited 642 had decided to cancel their applications: 155 of the applicants had withdrawn their forms; 254 had moved house and their address was unknown; the remainder (233) refused the particular house offered in terms which showed a desire not to move at all.

The fact that slum-clearance and waiting-list applicants are offered dwellings, including expensive dwellings, which are not acceptable to them is further illustrated by the fact that 132 old age pensioners refused what was offered to them for every 100 OAP dwellings which were allocated. There were 81 refusals per 100 lettings among one- and two-person families, 77 refusals per 100 lettings among three-person families and 61 refusals per 100 lettings among four-person families. At the other extreme, there were only 33 refusals per 100 lettings among eight-person families. (Table 15.11.)

Among waiting-list applicants the average number of points on allocation of a tenancy in the year 1 April 1965–31 March 1966 was 55; for three-person dwellings the average was 57 points; for four-person dwellings the average was 72 points; and for seven-person dwellings the average was 77 points. Smaller families, that is, were less willing than large families to accept what the council had to offer, and it was therefore easier for those among the small families who did want a council tenancy to obtain one. This can be further demonstrated by contrasting different family sizes on the waiting-list with regard to the ratio between the number of points at which applicants were visited as potential tenants and the points of the families of the same size at the top of the waiting-list. Among old age pensioners there were families with 82 points at the top of the list who were unwilling to accept anything the council had to offer; OAP families with only 35 points were therefore being visited with a view to offering them a tenancy.[23] (Table 15.12.)

While the housing-list applicant can afford to express his preferences by waiting indefinitely, or even by choosing to forgo his application altogether (see below, p. 303), the slum-clearance family is deprived of its existing dwelling and is offered over a short period of time a limited number of alternatives. The fact that the Corporation has a proportion of expensive and well-equipped dwellings at its disposal does not, therefore, mean that either waiting-list applicants or dwellers in slum-clearance areas can reasonably be attracted to a council tenancy on those grounds. They may not be offered a new dwelling; if a new, expensive dwelling is offered, it may be unsuitable for other reasons; they have no way of knowing at all, indeed, that they will be fortunate enough to secure the tenancy of a dwelling which they would voluntarily choose as being 'worth the money':

It appears to me that Sunderland Corporation Housing Department is applying, or is trying to apply, some sort of class distinction in its allocation of new homes. I have had the department's visitor and have questioned several others who have been visited and one common factor emerges, all have been asked if they will take a 'relet'. The question naturally arises, where are the tenants going to out of all these relets? The answer can only be—into new houses. We are asked to graciously take over their 'cast-offs' so that they can move into brand-new homes! What effrontery![24]

Police were last night called to Sunderland Town Hall to remove about twenty people, mostly housewives, seeking new homes. Some of the women said they had been offered relets. 'But why should we have to take second best when people in other areas are being given new houses?' said 26-year-old Mrs. Winifred Dale. 'I was offered a house at Pennywell but the front room was so small it would only take a table and chair. It would have meant selling most of our furniture.' Said Mrs. Gertrude Bennet, 'I was offered a council house at Farringdon, but the sink was broken and the doors were off the hinges.'[25]

Not only are the residents of the areas covered by the 1965–70 slum-clearance proposals uncertain that they will be allocated one of the higher standard dwellings: were they to be allocated one of the poorer dwellings, they would find that they would have to pay almost as much in rent as if they had. The statutory basis for rent determination is worded in deceptively simple terms. Local authorities are simply required to fix 'reasonable' charges and are permitted to grant rent rebates. Since 1936 local authorities have been permitted to pool all subsidies and treat their housing stock as a whole, instead of relating the rent of different groups of dwellings to the subsidy provisions under which they were built. Since 1949 (when the term 'working-classes' was dropped from housing legislation) it has been unnecessary for local authorities to take account of working-class rents in the locality. Sunderland's policy has been to equalise the rents of the old, more poorly equipped dwellings with the rents of its newer, more expensive dwellings. The difference between the highest and lowest rents is smaller in Sunderland than in any comparable town except Blackpool (which has very few council houses) and Newcastle. (Table 15.13.)[26]

Whether or not any or all council dwellings are a 'bargain' in the sense that they are rented at below economic, replacement or market levels, and whether or not state housing subsidies are fair or efficacious are not at issue. Contributors to that discussion come from all bands of the political spectrum, from those who still argue in favour of the free market[27] to those with extreme collectivist views. Nor is the equity of any particular structure of contributions and subsidies under scrutiny. In this chapter the problem is being approached from a different viewpoint, the viewpoint of the family which, however generous the subsidies, prefers the cost-benefit of their present dwelling to the cost-benefit of its likely replacement in the council stock.

The gross rents of Sunderland's council dwellings range from 9s. 8d. to £3 7s. od. a week. (Table 15.14.) Among the tenants in the 1965–70 sample (n = 71) 76 per cent paid less than 25s. od. a week in rent and rates. Among owner-occupiers (n = 39) no less than 82 per cent were in unmortgaged property.[28] (Table 15.15 and Table 15.16.) Although the cells are extremely small, it may be of some interest to record the distribution among certain social categories of families living in low-cost accommodation. (Table 15.17 and Table 15.18.)

The main disadvantage of a council tenancy was, for sixteen families, the high rent. 'I wouldn't like to have to pay the big rent.' 'I would have rent to pay.' 'I couldn't afford the rent.' 'Bigger rent.' 'We won't shift now unless it's pulled down. The rent suits us too well. What's the use of big rents when you can't feed y'sell?' 'Very high rent as compared with only rates here.' Some families looked upon a present low-cost dwelling as only a temporary expedient. 'I want to stay here for the present until we get the furniture paid for and gone in for a bedroom suite.' 'I don't feel ready for an estate yet, I would rather get this furniture paid for, then get a bedroom suite.' Other families, while they disliked their present accommodation, felt they would always be too poor to afford a council dwelling. 'We were in Norman Street. The council asked us if we would take this flat in Rosalie Terrace so that the family there could take the Norman Street slum-clearance council house. I was willing as we only had a little bit of furniture, and we were frightened of the big rents.' In one case the informant and her husband had left a three-bedroom council house at Thorney Close three years previously. Three of their children who had been contributing to the household expenses married and left home in the space of a single year. The informant and her husband could no longer afford the rent. They therefore gave up their tenancy and moved to share their present cottage with their daughter (who is separated from her husband) and their two grandchildren.

An additional cause for hesitation on the part of those families who regard the low cost of their present accommodation as important is the fact that householders in the proposed slum-clearance areas are periodically presented with the spectacle of council-house rents being *raised* by more than their own *total* weekly outlay.[29] The same problem arises when other costs are publicised. The Gilley Law flats, for example, were initially advertised as having one of the cheapest forms of central heating in the country.[30] A standard weekly charge of 17s. od. to £1 5s. od. was levied in the first year of operation. The amount of heat actually used by each household was metered and the annual cost balanced by means of a rebate or an excess cost charge. At the end of the first year surcharges were levied on one-third of the households, the highest being £92 os. od.[31]

There may be, of course, a case in terms of public well-being in the here-and-now or in terms of the long-run interests of the families themselves for preferring a high to a low level of personal expenditure on housing. If the situation is seen from the point of view of the 1965–70 families, however, the reluctance of some of them to take on higher and unpredictably rising housing costs is at least understandable.

Tenure

Modern notions of 'private property' are associated with the work of John Locke. The heavens are the Lord's, as King David says (Psalm 125), 'but the earth he has given to the sons of men', to mankind in common. God has also given men reason to make use of this common property to the best advantage of life and convenience. 'The earth and all that is therein is given to men for the support and comfort of their being.'[32] In order to attend to his own support and comfort anyone can annex to himself by his own labour, by the work of his own hands, as much of the common property as he can make use of before it spoils. 'Whatever is beyond this is more than his share, and belongs to others.'[33] This philosophical position was not substantially different from that of the mediaeval church nor from the labour theory of value.[34]

Certain types of private ownership, however, especially the private ownership of the means of production, led to 'the free exploitation of men by men'[35] and to on the one hand, the poverty of the great majority in spite of their labour and, on the other, to 'the wealth of the few although they have long since ceased to work'.[36] Various techniques of control have therefore been developed in all advanced industrial societies to modify in some degree, or lodge with an agency of the state, certain of the rights attached to private ownership. The same argument applied to all property 'usable for returns', including the ownership of domestic buildings[37] i.e. private landlordism, which so often seemed to lead to that 'most foule offence, which the Prophet has called in a very energeticall phrase "grynding the faces of the poore" '.[38]

Before the first world war virtually all wage-earners lived in rented property[39] and it seemed that the only solution to the problems both of housing shortage and of housing quality would be to put a public body in the place of the private landlord.[40] Since the second world war, however (partly as the result of a higher standard of living, partly because legislation has rendered private landlordism unattractive), wage-earners in increasingly large numbers have been able to become the owners of their homes 'for the support and comfort of their being' and free from exploitation.[41]

Sunderland cottages, in particular, have been sold by defeated landlords at modest prices. They have typically been bought by sitting tenants for £120–£150 each, involving the family in interest payments and capital redemption of under

10s. od. a week.[42] In the areas covered by the 1965–70 proposals there is almost the same proportion of owner-occupiers
as in the town as a whole.[43] The 1966 sample census shows that
twenty thousand of the household spaces in Sunderland CB
were owner-occupied (35 per cent), 27,000 were rented from
the local authority (45 per cent) and 9,000 were rented unfurnished from private landlords (16 per cent). As compared
with 1961 owner-occupation had increased by 5 per cent,
council tenures had increased by 24 per cent and tenures of
privately rented unfurnished accommodation had declined by
36 per cent. At the time of the SHN survey 46 per cent of the
households in the largest of the proposed slum-clearance areas,
Millfield (Deptford Road), were owners of their accommodation. Forty-seven per cent of households in single-family houses
and 45 per cent of households in single-family cottages were
owner-occupiers. Fifty per cent of the young large families
were owner-occupiers. (Table 15.19.)

What are the reasons for becoming or remaining an owner
of one of the dwellings in the 1965–70 areas? Certainly, some
of the normal advantages are inoperative. Few, for example,
profit from tax rebates on interest repayments, the home-
owner's usual 'subsidy'. The same applies to ownership,
especially on borrowed money, as a hedge against inflation.
The home cannot be valued as a tangible object to be handed
down in the family, nor can owner-occupation be regarded
as a means of obtaining security of tenure.

Obviously this is the case in the 1965–70 areas. Nor can it be
valued for these purposes, indeed, in any of the areas developed
before 1914. At the time of the SHN study a planning exercise
was completed designed to estimate the number of houses that
would be 'unfit by 1981'. The result of the exercise was an
assumption that, with certain exceptions, all dwellings built
before 1890 would be unfit by 1981. Those built between 1895
and 1914 at more than 90 rooms an acre, or not in possession of a
bath, an internal toilet and a hot water supply were included
in the 'unfit by 1981' category. Houses built between 1895 and
1914 were also judged 'unfit by 1981' if they fell below a certain
level on an 'environmental deficit score'. This score was based
on entirely *ad hoc* items and weights such as 'detrimental uses
in the neighbourhood–minus 22; lack of garden space–minus

18; lack of playing space—minus 15; unattractive outlook—minus 2; more than 15 minutes on foot to shops—minus 2'. On these calculations, out of the 21,610 pre-1914 houses in Sunderland CB 15,250 were expected to be unfit by 1981 and anxiety was expressed that the less satisfactory solution of revitalisation might be unwisely adopted and hinder the wholesale demolition of these properties.[44]

The main advantage is that, *given* its circumstances of income and job security (neither of which would be improved on transfer to a council house) the family is in control of more aspects of its domestic life. In the light of the age of its members, their wages, their employment prospects and the pattern of other claims on their expenditure, they can decide to improve and maintain the property at a rate and to a standard they themselves deem desirable and expedient. Another aspect of independence valued by owners (and by tenants of private landlords to a lesser degree) is the right to behave inside their own homes with greater freedom than in a council dwelling. Though very far from the state of affairs described by the elder Pitt in which 'the poorest man in his cottage may bid defiance to all the forces of the Crown', they are at least able to keep cats, dogs and other household pets without permission.[45]

> Why should a middle-aged couple, whose home has been demolished under a slum-clearance order, be forced against their will to live in a council flat? Their only 'crime' is that they have no children, but they do own dogs. I have known the lady concerned for many years. She attends three dog-training classes a week to ensure that her dogs are well-behaved. Now after six miserable months of living in her 'unwanted prison' this couple have been ordered to dispose of their beloved pets because some interfering person has reported them to the housing authority. What is there for them now? Who are the heartless dictators on the Housing Committee, who allow decent, hard-working, law-abiding people to suffer such heartbreak?[46]

Pride of ownership in these small cottages and old houses looks petty, droll and even ridiculous, no doubt, to men of professional status.

> We are proud of our trim little palace,
> We've worked hard to make it just that.
> Can the council be cruel and callous
> And force us to fret in a flat?[47]

But such pride does exist, based largely on the feeling that it is better not to rely on such benefits as officials may happen to make available at a particular time. Such a view may be anti-social or merely ill-judged, but it is perhaps helpful to understand that it forms part of the total situation which has to be altered in the processes of slum clearance.

NOTES TO CHAPTER 15

1 Lionel Needleman, 'A Long Term View of Housing', *National Institute Economic Review*, November 1961.
2 United Nations, *Government Policies and the Cost of Building*, Part I, Geneva 1959, p. 3.
3 J. B. Cullingworth, 'Some Aspects of the Housing Problem', *Housing*, 1, 2, July 1965, p. 64.
4 P. R. Kaim-Caudle, 'A New Look at Housing Subsidies', *Local Government Finance*, 68, 3, March 1964, p. 91; see also Peter C. Collison, 'Occupation, Education and Housing in an English City [Oxford]', *American Journal of Sociology*, 65, 6, May 1960.
5 Political and Economic Planning, *Growth in the British Economy*, London 1960.
6 Working Party on Local Authority Housing Finance, *Report*, September 1964.
7 P. R. Kaim-Caudle, *op. cit.*, p. 88.
8 At the time of writing the standards are those based upon the recommendations of the Parker Morris Committee (1961) and are the highest ever required. After the end of 1968 schemes not meeting the standards indicated in the MHLG circular of April 1967 receive neither loan sanction nor subsidy.
9 The highest proportion was in Salford (25 per cent). The median town was Coventry (18 per cent). The town with the lowest proportion was Brighton (13 per cent).
10 Institute of Municipal Treasurers and Accountants, *Housing Statistics 1965–66*, 1967. This refers to the exchequer subsidy 1965–66 per head of the estimated mid-year population 1965. The figure for Sunderland was £2·86. The median town was Middlesbrough (£1·93). The town with the lowest exchequer subsidy per head was Bournemouth (£0·57).
11 Under section 8 of the Housing Subsidies Act 1956 rate subsidies became optional. Sunderland Corporation chose to subsidise every house completed after 31 March 1956 to the extent of £7 7s. od. per annum and to continue the various rate contributions in existence before March 1956. Sunderland Town Council decision, 10 October 1956. By 1965–66 the rates levied per head of population for housing amounted to 76s. 9d. The figure for the top town, Salford, was 119s. od. The median

town was Swansea (51s. od.). The town with the lowest housing rate per head was Southend on Sea (2s. 3d.). Institute of Municipal Treasurers and Accountants, *Return of Rates 1965–66*, 1967. The figure for Sunderland RD was 87s. 8d.

12 *Ibid.*

13 *Ibid.* Rent constitutes 72 per cent of the total housing revenue account income in Sunderland. The lowest proportion is in Salford (43 per cent). The highest proportion is in Bournemouth (86 per cent). The median town is Coventry (76 per cent).

14 The council houses of other large cities included a substantial proportion of old property formerly privately owned. Out of Bristol's stock of 44,500 council houses 4,800 (11 per cent) were of this kind. In Leeds the number was 5,452 (9 per cent). In Newcastle upon Tyne the number was 3,410 (10 per cent). In Salford the number was 2,079 (19 per cent).

15 The Institute of Municipal Treasurers and Accountants, *Housing Statistics 1965–66*, 1967.

16 This development is composed of five 14-storied blocks (260 dwellings). Half are one-bedroom and half are two-bedroom flats. There are also 173 four-storied maisonettes of which 42 have two bedrooms and nearly all the remainder three bedrooms.

17 The MHLG approved the costs of these dwellings in 1961. They were, however, 25 per cent higher than the 'housing costs yardstick' which was issued shortly afterwards and the MHLG intimated that no more blocks of this design should be planned.

18 Information supplied by the Borough Architect to Sunderland Corporation's Housing Committee, 20 February 1967.

19 This information was supplied by the MHLG in a letter to Coun. John Quayle, 3 February 1967.

20 It must be borne in mind, of course, that the high price of flats is partly due to the fact that, other things being equal, they are more expensive to construct than are two-storied dwellings. To the basic £24 a year exchequer subsidy, however, is added £8 a year for four-storied development, £14 for five-storied development, £26 for six-storied development and £1 15s. a year for each storey over six (Housing Act 1961).

21 'These long waiting lists should be considered as *prima facie* evidence that the rents are well below open market rents—not a mere 20 per cent or so.' Kaim-Caudle, *op. cit.*, p. 88.

22 Cf. Applications received 1 April 1964 to 31 March 1965 = 1,882. Applications received 1 April 1965 to 31 March 1966 = 1,999.

23 The ratio was highest among four-person families, 65 per cent. Formally the system would require that allocations be made always to families with the same number of points.

24 *Sunderland Echo*, 6 October 1966.

25 *Sunderland Echo*, 25 August 1967.

26 The effect of Sunderland's pooling its subsidies can be clearly seen by comparing the rents of its pre-war dwellings with those of very similar dwellings built by the North-Eastern Housing Association at the same time. NEHA rents are related to the financial conditions at the time at

which they were built. The 531 NEHA houses on the Hylton Lane Estate rent at between £1 2s. 0d. and £1 3s. 0d. a week (net rent 9s. 8d. to 9s. 11d. a week). The rent and rates of the 1,062 NEHA houses at Plains Farm range from £1 2s. 2d. to £1. 5s. 10d. (net rent 9s. 8d. to 10s. 1d.). The equivalent house in the council's stock would be rented for approximately £2 10s. 0d. gross.

27 Milton Friedman and George Stigler, *Roof or Ceilings?*, New York 1946.

28 Only one of the owner-occupiers paid as much as 25s. 0d. a week in interest repayments and amortisation.

29 At the meeting of Sunderland's Housing Committee of 23 October 1967, for example, the Borough Treasurer showed that if council rents were unchanged there would be a deficit of £526,000 in the financial year 1967–68 and of £844,000 in the year 1968–69. The Committee agreed, therefore, to raise rents by amounts ranging from 1s. 9d. to 17s. 7d. a week.

30 When he opened the N.C.B. installation Lord Robens, the Chairman of the National Coal Board, forecast that the cost of hot water and heating for a four-bedroom flat would be £1 0s. 0d., as compared with a 'normal' coal bill of £1 6s. 0d. See also 'Gilley Law Pioneers District Heating Scheme', *Sunderland Echo*, 9 September 1966.

31 'Women Threaten Rent Strike Over Central Heating Bills', *Sunderland Echo*, 20 March 1968. 'M.P. Seeks Inquiry On Heating Bills', *Sunderland Echo*, 6 April 1968.

32 John Locke, *Two Treatises of Civil Government* (1691), Everyman Library 1924, p. 129.

33 *Ibid.*, p. 131.

34 'The last of the Schoolmen was Karl Marx.' R. H. Tawney, *Religion and the Rise of Capitalism* (Holland Memorial Lectures 1922), Penguin Books 1938, p. 48.

35 Karl Marx, *Capital* (1863), Volume I, Moscow 1958, p. 715.

36 *Ibid.*, p. 713.

37 Max Weber, *Wirtschaft und Gesellschaft*, quoted in *From Max Weber*, Hans H. Gerth and C. Wright Mills (Eds.), London 1948, p. 182.

38 Quoted in Tawney, *op. cit.*, p. 178.

39 At the time of the first rent-control legislation (1915) 90 per cent of *all* houses in Britain were let to private tenants.

40 Not only did owner-occupation for working people seem an unrealistic policy, some socialist thinkers poured scorn on the notion. They preferred the wage-earner, now 'driven from his hearth and home', to remain a completely propertyless 'free outlaw' rather than once again resemble the quiet and contented owner-occupier, 'godly and honourable'. Frederick Engels, 'The Housing Question' (1874), in Marx and Engels, *Selected Works*, Volume I, Moscow 1958, p. 563.

41 The MHLG's Deeplish study emphasises 'the effect of the post-war domestic revolution of which so little notice has been taken – the shift from tenancy to home-ownership in hundreds of thousands of these older homes up and down the country. Not so long ago the normal house in Deeplish was landlord owned. Now over 60 per cent of the residents

own their own homes and many of them have carried out big improvements.' *Op. cit.* Preface.

42 A glass-works labourer, for example, bought his cottage in 1954 for £150. It had been rented since 1904 first by his father and then by himself and his sister. The property was mortgaged to the Sunderland Workingmen's Building Society. Repayments were 12s. od. each half-month for 14 years 6 months, plus 11s. od. a year premiums for a £500 fire insurance policy. By paying 7s. 6d. a week for a time, instead of 6s. od. he was able to pay off the mortgage by Christmas Day 1966.

43 The distribution of types of tenure varies greatly even in the same region. Among the county boroughs of Durham, for example, the proportion of owner-occupiers at the time of the 1961 census was 55 per cent in Darlington, 47 per cent in West Hartlepool, 32 per cent in Sunderland, 25 per cent in Gateshead and only 22 per cent in South Shields.

44 Joint Consultative Committee as to Regional Planning: Technical Subcommittee of Planning Officers, *Final Report of Working Party on Method of Assessment of North East Housing Need*, February 1965. See also the account of the meeting of Planning Officers, a year or so later, at which this document was discussed: the Planning Officer of Northumberland County Council is reported as saying that 'Renewal of some of the old houses would have to be very seriously considered'. The report continues, '*In this respect the Committee was concerned lest renewal be substituted as a policy for the redevelopment of this area*'. (Emphasis added.) *Sunderland Echo*, 29 July 1966. The environmental deficit score was revised in April 1965.

45 See Brian Abel-Smith, *Freedom in the Welfare State*, Fabian Society Tract, March 1964 for a criticism of such restrictions.

46 *Sunderland Echo*, 8 July 1967.

47 *Sunderland Echo* 20 June 1966.

Table 15.1

**Dwellings Built under Various Subsidy Provisions:
Sunderland CB 1903-65**

Housing Act	Dwellings built in Sunderland under each Act Per Cent (n=23,750)	Housing Act	Dwellings built in Sunderland under each Act Per Cent (n=23,750)
1891	0·4	1946	47·8
1919	1·5	1951	
1923	0·8	1956	22·9
1924	9·4	1961	9·4
1925	1·0		
1927	0·6		
1930			
1935	6·8		
1936			
1938			

Source: Sunderland CB Treasurer's Department

242

Table 15.2

Government Housing Grants per Head of Population: 1965–66, Sunderland and Comparable Towns

	s.	d.		s.	d.
Newcastle upon Tyne	57	8	Middlesbrough	40	1
Salford	57	0	Birkenhead	37	6
SUNDERLAND CB	55	2	Leicester	37	5
(SUNDERLAND RD	71	9)	Kingston upon Hull	37	4
Sheffield	54	8	Bradford	33	8
Leeds	50	3	Coventry	33	5
Southampton	48	4	Swansea	33	5
Liverpool	45	10	Nottingham	31	5
Manchester	45	8	Cardiff	28	1
Portsmouth	45	0	Bolton	27	4
Stoke	44	1	Brighton	26	1
Wolverhampton	42	11	Southend on Sea	15	10
Plymouth	41	11	Blackpool	13	10
Birmingham	41	4	Bournemouth	12	0
Bristol	41	1			

Source: Institute of Municipal Treasurers and Accountants, *Return of Rates 1965–66,* 1967

Table 15.3

Post-war Council Dwellings as a Percentage of all Dwellings Built By or For the Council
Sunderland and Comparable Towns

	per cent		per cent
Bournemouth	91	Swansea	68
Luton	88	Birkenhead	66
Portsmouth	87	Leicester	66
Southend	86	Kingston upon Hull	65
SUNDERLAND CB/RD	80	Newcastle upon Tyne	64
Plymouth	77	Brighton	62
Southampton	77	Leeds	62
Blackpool	76	Bradford	59
Coventry	74	Manchester	57
Middlesbrough	73	Wolverhampton	56
Bristol	72	Liverpool	55
Salford	71	Sheffield	54
Stoke on Trent	71	Bolton	53
Cardiff	70	Nottingham	52
		Birmingham	51

Source: Institute of Municipal Treasurers and Accountants, *Housing Statistics 1965–66*, February 1967

Table 15.4

**Dwellings Built by or for the Corporation to 31 March 1966
per Thousand Population (mid-1965)
Sunderland and Comparable Towns**

	Council dwellings per thousand population		Council dwellings per thousand population
SUNDERLAND CB/RD	141	Portsmouth	92
Sheffield	126	Birmingham	90
Newcastle upon Tyne	125	Swansea	88
Wolverhampton	121	Cardiff	79
Liverpool	114	Birkenhead	78
Nottingham	113	Bradford	78
Manchester	110	Bolton	74
Leeds	103	Coventry	71
Kingston upon Hull	102	Brighton	64
Stoke on Trent	102	Salford	59
Middlesbrough	98	Luton	57
Southampton	98	Blackpool	36
Plymouth	97	Southend on Sea	36
Leicester	96	Bournemouth	34
Bristol	92		

Source: Institute of Municipal Treasurers and
Accountants, *Housing Statistics 1965–66*, February 1967

Table 15.5

Post-war Council Dwellings per Thousand Population: Sunderland and Comparable Towns

	Post-war dwellings per thousand population		Post-war dwellings per thousand population
SUNDERLAND CB/RD	113	Swansea	60
Portsmouth	81	Nottingham	59
Newcastle upon Tyne	80	Cardiff	56
Southampton	76	Birkenhead	52
Plymouth	75	Coventry	52
Stoke on Trent	72	Luton	50
Middlesbrough	71	Bradford	47
Wolverhampton	68	Birmingham	46
Sheffield	67	Salford	42
Kingston upon Hull	66	Brighton	39
Bristol	66	Bolton	39
Leeds	64	Bournemouth	31
Leicester	63	Southend on Sea	31
Liverpool	63	Blackpool	27
Manchester	62		

Source: Institute of Municipal Treasurers and Accountants, *Housing Statistics 1965–66*, February 1967

Table 15.6

Cost of Construction[1] of Three BR Council Houses Completed during 1965–66 per Square Foot Super Sunderland and Comparable Towns

	Shillings		Shillings
Newcastle upon Tyne	69	Southampton	53
Plymouth	62	Sheffield	52
Bristol	60	Cardiff	51
Leeds	58	Leicester	51
Birmingham	57	Portsmouth	50
Bradford	57	SUNDERLAND CB	50
Birkenhead	56	Middlesbrough	49
Manchester	56	Stoke on Trent	49
Bolton	55	Liverpool	46
Coventry	55	Luton	44
Blackpool	54	Nottingham	42
Swansea	54	Salford	35
Kingston upon Hull	53		

Source: Institute of Municipal Treasurers and Accountants, *Housing Statistics 1965–66*, 1967

1 The cost of construction is defined as the cost of erecting and equipping a typical traditional house ready for occupation according to the practice of the authority. Architects and quantity surveyors fees, the cost of land and the cost of providing roads, sewers, water, gas and electricity services are excluded. The figures quoted for houses completed during 1965–66 are the best available estimates and they are not necessarily final.

Table 15.7

Average Weekly Net Rents Charged at 31 March 1966: Two BR Houses Completed 1 April 1945–31 March 1964 Sunderland and Comparable Towns

	s.	d.		s.	d.
Southend on Sea	63	3	Sheffield	32	5
Portsmouth	49	4	Blackpool	31	11
Southampton	45	5	Leicester	31	11
Bournemouth	43	9	Salford	30	10
Luton	41	1	Stoke on Trent	30	9
Bristol	40	9	Liverpool	29	9
Brighton	40	8[1]	Middlesbrough	29	1
Cardiff	37	6	Birkenhead	28	11
Swansea	37	0	Newcastle	27	11
Manchester	36	9	Bolton	27	10
Coventry	35	8	Wolverhampton	26	6
Leeds	35	0	SUNDERLAND CB	27	5
Plymouth	34	4	Bradford	26	6
Birmingham	34	0	Kingston upon Hull	22	6

Source: Institute of Municipal Treasurers and Accountants, *Housing Statistics 1965–66*, 1967

1 All dwellings, pre-war as well as post-war.

Table 15.8

Dwellings Slum-cleared 1 January 1955–30 June 1965, per Thousand Population (mid-1965) Sunderland and Comparable Towns

	Population mid-1965	Dwellings demolished or closed	Dwellings demolished or closed per thousand population
Salford	148,260	6,490	44
Leeds	509,290	17,820	35
Manchester	638,360	20,180	32
Bradford	298,090	8,920	30
Wolverhampton	150,210	4,530	30
Leicester	267,030	6,960	26
Bolton	157,990	3,740	24
Stoke on Trent	276,630	6,000	22
SUNDERLAND CB	188,340	3,980	21
Sheffield	488,950	10,194	21
Liverpool	722,010	13,350	19
Kingston upon Hull	299,570	4,975	17
Newcastle upon Tyne	257,460	4,330	17
Birmingham	1,102,700	17,200	16
Middlesbrough	157,180	2,390	15
Portsmouth	216,280	3,090	14
Birkenhead	143,660	1,830	13
Bristol	430,900	5,180	12
Nottingham	310,990	3,360	11
Southampton	209,020	2,390	11
Swansea	170,990	1,620	9
Brighton	162,520	1,450	9
Plymouth	212,550	1,400	7
Coventry	330,270	1,560	5
Cardiff	260,170	1,020	4
Southend on Sea	166,390	440	3
Blackpool	150,440	280	2
Bournemouth	151,050	190	1

Source: Institute of Municipal Treasurers and Accountants, *Housing Statistics 1965–66*, 1967; and MHLG, *Housing Return*, Appendix, 30 September 1965

Table 15.9

Allocations to New Dwellings and to Relet Dwellings: Sunderland CB 1 April 1965–31 March 1966

Type of Tenant	To New Dwelling per cent (n=1,359)	To Relets per cent (n=940)	Total per cent (n=2,299)
Waiting-list and slum-clearance	80	76	78
Transferees from council dwellings	20	24	22

Source: Sunderland CB Housing Department

Table 15.10

Allocations to New Dwellings and to Relet Dwellings: Sunderland CB 1 April 1965–31 March 1966

Type of Dwelling	From Waiting-list per cent (n=1,225)	From Slum-clearance Areas per cent (n=579)	From Existing Council Dwellings per cent (n=495)	Total per cent (n=2,299)
To new houses	64	53	54	59
To relets	36	47	46	40

Source: Sunderland CB Housing Department

Table 15.11

Refusals per 100 Lettings: Sunderland CB 1965
(Waiting-list and Slum-clearance cases)

Family Size	Refusals	Lettings	Refusals per 100 lettings
OAP	210	159	132
Other one and two persons	350	434	81
Three persons	445	576	77
Four persons	220	359	61
Five persons	45	156	29
Six and seven persons	42	92	46
Eight persons and more	12	36	33

Source: Sunderland CB Housing Department

Table 15.12

Housing Points of Families at Top of Waiting-list and Housing Points of Families Regarded as Potential Tenants: Sunderland CB 15 March 1966

Family Type	Points at which Families visited as Potential Tenants (a)	Points of Family at Top of Waiting-list (b)	Column (a) as Percentage of Column (b)
OAP	35	82	43
Other one- and two-person	35	79	44
Three-person multi-storey	39	75	52
Four-person	51	79	65
Five-person	54	87	62
Six- and seven-person	54	88	61
Eight persons and more	59	119	50[1]

Source: Sunderland CB Housing Department

1 In this case the discrepancy between the number of points at which applications come under active consideration and the number of points of families at the top of the waiting-list is due rather to the reluctance of the Corporation to house 'undesirable' tenants than the reluctance of tenants to accept what the Corporation has to offer.

Table 15.13

Difference in Average Net Rent charged for Two-bedroom Dwellings Completed 31 March 1945 or before and Completed 31 March 1945–31 March 1965. (Net Rents Charged 31 March 1966): Sunderland and Comparable Towns[1]

	Difference in Average Net Rent			Difference in Average Net Rent	
	s.	d.		s.	d.
Southend on Sea	16	9	Plymouth	5	8
Swansea	12	2	Middlesbrough	5	8
Southampton	11	10	Leicester	5	5
Salford	11	10	Bradford	4	9
Leeds	10	9	Bristol	3	10
Sheffield	9	7	Liverpool	3	10
Wolverhampton	9	4	Portsmouth	3	8
Birmingham	8	3	Cardiff	3	7
Birkenhead	7	7	Bolton	3	7
Kingston upon Hull	6	9	Brighton	3	6
Luton	6	9	SUNDERLAND CB/RD	3	6
Coventry	6	4	Newcastle upon Tyne	2	7
Manchester	6	3	Blackpool		2
Stoke on Trent	6	0			

Source: Institute of Municipal Treasurers and Accountants, *Housing Statistics 1965–66,* 1967

1 The figures for Bournemouth and Nottingham are not given in the relevant Table of *Housing Statistics.*

Table 15.14

Weekly Gross Rent of Council Dwellings: Sunderland CB: From 5 April 1966

Pre-war Dwellings		
Number of Rooms	Lowest Rent/Rates	Highest Rent/Rates
One room	9s. 8d.	
Two rooms	17s. 8d.	£1 7s. 8d.
Three rooms	£1 2s. 1d.	£1 19s. 9d.
Four rooms	£1 16s. 9d.	£2 10s. 7d.
Five rooms	£1 19s. 11d.	£2 17s. 7d.

Post-war Dwellings		
Size of Dwelling	Lowest Rent/Rates	Highest Rent/Rates
One person	£1 4s. 9d.	£1 16s. 0d.
Two persons	£1 7s. 5d.	£2 4s. 3d.
Three persons	£1 13s. 7d.	£2 6s. 11d.
Four persons	£1 11s. 5d.	£2 11s. 8d.
Five persons	£2 6s. 1d.	£2 10s. 7d.
Six persons	£2 8s. 5d.	£3 7s. 0d.
Eight persons	£2 18s. 8d.	

Source: Sunderland CB Housing Department

Table 15.15

Mortgage Repayments by Owner-occupiers and Rent and Rates of Tenants: SHN 1965–70 Sample

	Mortgage Repayment by Owner-occupiers (n=39) per cent	Rent and Rates of Tenants (n=71) per cent
Nil	82	0
Up to 14s. 11d.	8	14
15s. 0d. to 24s. 11d.	8	62
25s. 0d. to 34s. 11d.	3	11
35s. 0d. to 44s. 11d.	0	8
45s. 0d. to 54s. 11d.	0	1
55s. 0d. or more	0	3

Source: Interview Analysis

Table 15.16

Annual Rate Payment by Owner-occupiers: SHN 1965–70 Sample

	per cent (n=35)
Under £10	0
£10 under £25	69
£25 under £50	26
£50 and more	6

Source: Interview Analysis

Table 15.17

Tenants with Rent/Rates under 25s. od. a week: Sunderland CB Slum-clearance Programme 1965–70

Sub-sample	Tenants with Rent/Rates under 25s. od. a week per cent	Number of Families in the sub-sample (=100 per cent)
1965–70 Programme	77	83
Southwick (Wayman Street) area	100[1]	60
Slum-clearance areas elsewhere	84	12
Hendon	72	21
Millfield (Deptford Road) area	68	25
Millfield (Booth Street) area	67	9
Flats	81	
Single-family cottages	74	
Single-family houses	60	
Old single-person or two-person families	95	20
Mature single-person or two-person families	87[2]	15
Young small families	80	25
Adult large families	63[3]	16
Young large families	34	6
15–20 years in present dwelling	100	3
20 years plus in present dwelling	92	37
5–10 years in present dwelling	67	6
1–5 years in present dwelling	65	17
10–15 years in present dwelling	60	10
Under 1 year in present dwelling	60	10

Source: Interview Analysis

1 Thirty-eight per cent are National Coal Board tenants and pay either nothing or a very low rent.
2 Thirteen per cent are NCB tenants.
3 Nineteen per cent are NCB tenants.

Table 15.18

Owner-occupiers whose Dwellings are not Mortgaged: Sunderland CB: Slum-clearance Programme 1965–70

Sub-sample	Owner-occupiers whose dwellings are not mortgaged (per cent)	Number of Families in the sub-sample (=100 per cent)
1965–70	82	39
Millfield (Booth Street) area	100	3
Slum-clearance elsewhere	88	8
Southwick (Wayman Street) area	86	7
Millfield (Deptford Road) area	76	21
Hendon	No owner-occupier	
Single-family houses	88	8
Single-family cottages	81	31
Flats	No owner-occupier	
Mature single-person and two-person families	100	5
Old single-person and two-person families	92	13
Young large families	86	7
Young small families	80	5
Adult large families	57	7

Source: Interview Analysis

Table 15.19

Owner-occupiers: Sunderland CB Slum-clearance Proposals 1965-70

Sub-sample	Owner-occupiers per cent	Number of Families in the sub-sample = 100 per cent
1965-70 Programme	33	126
Millfield (Deptford Road) area	46	48
Elsewhere	40	20
Millfield (Booth Street) area	31	13
Southwick (Wayman Street) area	30	23
Hendon	5	22
Single-family houses	47	19
Single-family cottages	45	71
Young large families	50	14
Old single-person and two-person families	38	34
Adult large families	33	24
Mature single-person and two-person families	25	20
Young small families	23	31

Source: Interview Analysis

OPPOSITION TO THE SLUM CLEARANCE PROPOSALS 1965-70

III. Neighbourhood Amenity, Neighbours and Relatives, Privacy and Accessibility

---

Few people regarded the 1965–70 areas as physically salubrious. Even here, however, it is necessary to recognise variations in personal taste. 'I went to Peterlee. It was a load, terrible! It was quiet and . . . oo!' 'Town End Farm? Just all green and that—we just don't like it.' 'I like it here, me! I like a noisy place, me!' To some informants the much canvassed advantages of a modern housing layout seem quite irrelevant. A 63-year-old man in the Deptford Road area ('I sleep in the bed I was born in') said that he had never known a road accident during his lifetime in the street. Understandably, he regarded increased pedestrian safety as an advantage of no importance whatsoever to him, and he felt, therefore, that he was being compelled to give up a multitude of real for a handful of uncertain advantages.

Unfortunate and unforeseen side-effects of housing innovations are publicised and they influence the attitude of some families to the prospect of rehousing out of all proportion to their actual frequency and importance. The layout of all the 1965–70 areas is that of front streets, a house with a curtilage which includes a backyard, and a back lane. Motor cars can therefore be garaged in the backyard or temporarily in the front or back street. In either case there is supervision by the

259

owner or neighbours. At Hahnemann Court, a block of council flats,[1] cars are parked at ground level underneath the building. The following report describes the unexpected consequences of the arrangement:

> Thugs pillaging a car park at Hahnemann Court turned on a caretaker who tried to stop them, butted him in the face, threw him on the ground and ran away. Since the flats were completed two years ago tenants have suffered the depredation of vandals who have broken into cars, removed batteries, wheels and tyres and anything else they could lay their hands on. 'It is so bad around here that we do not know what to expect when we get up in the morning.'[2]

Such reports, like the reports on defective structural condition, damage what is equivalent to commercial goodwill. Families are discouraged from 'patronising' such a 'firm'. The same point applies to complaints about the physical amenity of council areas–they do not make the residents of the 1965–70 areas any more eager to agree with demolition proposals. 'After viewing from my window in Pennywell the desolate acreage of mud, scrub grass and abandoned, dilapidated machinery, I can only surmise that this must have been the result of enemy bombing. . . .'[3] 'Some council tenants at Farringdon, Sunderland, have decided to begin a rent strike today because they say they are living next door to Corporation slums!'[4]

What of the social aspects of the neighbourhood? 'Community feeling', 'sociability' and the cohesiveness of the traditional urban working-class locality are notions which have been prominent in discussions of housing and planning policy.[5] It may be that in some quarters the study of neighbourliness is regarded as the sociologist's special skill and that devices for increasing interpersonal contacts is his professional stock-in-trade.[6]

In the areas covered by the 1965–70 slum-clearance proposals neighbours were, indeed, valued by some families as people with whom to 'pass the time of day' and as the occasional providers of certain services. 'My wife is handy for laying out. People know where to come.' 'O, they're good round here! I look after two of the old folk, chop sticks. Two old widows. I don't know about the young people who are coming to the street, they are strangers, but I've gone in and out of next door

for nearly forty years. "Here's the lodger, give him his dinner!" '
'They all speak to you no matter wee it is. When I sit at the
door they all come round and talk to uss.' 'If there's any
trouble you're all in one! No one sits over you, they don't
interfere, but if you're in trouble they'll help you. We do it.
We go messages for the old people without asking, if we know
they are poorly.' Eighty-two per cent of the informants in the
Hendon area, 79 per cent in the Millfield (Deptford Road) area,
78 per cent in the Southwick (Wayman Street) area and 76 per
cent in the Millfield (Booth Street) area said their neighbours
were 'sociable'. More than half of all the informants in the
Hendon, Deptford Road and Wayman Street areas (55 per cent,
52 per cent and 52 per cent) said their neighbours were 'very
sociable'.

More prominent in the interview responses than statements
about sociability and helpfulness, however, were expressions of
satisfaction with neighbours who simply caused no disturbance.
'I wouldn't let anyone come up against my privacy and they're
very reserved anyway. Nobody bothers us at all.' 'I've never
bickered with any of them.' 'They are reserved people.' 'They
suit us! I'm like them, reserved.' 'People keep themselves to
themselves.' 'I'm used to the neighbours. They are trustworthy,
you can leave the house and not bother.' 'Thirty-odd years and
never had a wrong word with them—eh? That takes a lot of
beating.' 'All the people are working-class.' 'People don't bother
me.' 'The neighbours are the same as ourselves.' Some researchers have suggested that the council house carries a social
stigma. Some groups, that is, would reject a council address
because for them it is an announcement of one's second-class
citizenship.[7] There is little evidence of a generalised feeling of
this kind among the families affected by the 1965–70 proposals.
There is, however, some apprehension that they may be
allocated a dwelling among neighbours uncongenial to themselves.

It all depends when we gaan where they put waa. When they pull
it down you got to go where they say. There is that many people
mixed up! Half of them are making slums of them already. You
can't pick and choose. They dinnit seem to bother. They seem to
mix the good'uns with the bad'uns—so we'll probably try to get a
house of our own when this comes down.

We hope we'll get amongst nice clean people—but we won't!
We'll be put among dirty people to give them an example!

Neighbours will be important if you get a maisonette—for
keeping it clean. But there is a fifty-fifty chance of getting bad
neighbours.

We know the new houses are nice, but it's who you get beside.

That these fears are not irrational is shown by the fact that the
proportion of informants in council dwellings[8] who said they
liked their neighbours 'very much' was as low as 18 per cent
at High Ford, 16 per cent at Pennywell and only 9 per cent
at Thorney Close (Diagram 16.A) while among the 1965–70
slum-clearance areas the proportion was 32 per cent even at
Hendon, which was, as usual, the least favoured of the slum-
clearance areas. The 1965–70 area with the highest proportion
of informants 'very satisfied' with their neighbours was at
Southwick (Wayman Street), heavily populated with miners
working at Wearmouth colliery. (Table 16.1.)

More than the loss of actual social contacts, therefore, it
seems that informants feared the loss of a neighbourhood in
which all families embraced a similar style of life.[9] Those
families who already felt 'at home' in their present localities
had doubts about the capacity of a new neighbourhood to
provide them with the same benefit. Some families were so
badly housed in other respects that they were willing to
sacrifice this benefit for the compensating advantages of a
council tenancy. The housing circumstances of others were
such, however, that they opposed demolition. It was not worth
their while to risk finding themselves among neighbours who
did not suit them so well. 'Better a morsel of dry bread and
peace than a house full of banqueting and quarrels.'

Kinship, especially the relationship between the married
daughter and her mother is another topic which is popularly
supposed to be of particular interest to the sociologist. The
investigations by the Institute of Community Studies of the
extended family in Bethnal Green, Debden and Woodford are
well known.[10] Other studies have been carried out in south
London, in Soho,[11] and in Swansea.[12]

Although there are signs of spontaneous changes[13] the
conclusion of these studies is that planning policy still has the

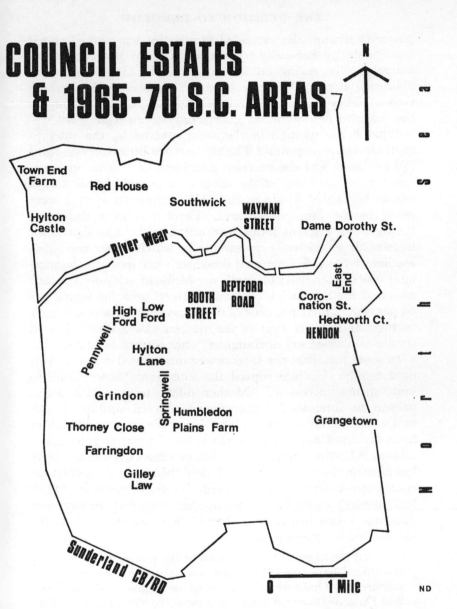

COUNCIL ESTATES
& 1965-70 S.C. AREAS

N

Town End Farm

Red House

Southwick

WAYMAN STREET

Dame Dorothy St.

Hylton Castle

River Wear

East End

DEPTFORD ROAD

BOOTH STREET

Coro-nation St.

Hedworth Ct.

HENDON

High Ford

Low Ford

Pennywell

Hylton Lane

Springwell

Grindon

Humbledon Plains Farm

Grangetown

Thorney Close

Farringdon

Gilley Law

Sunderland CB/RD

0   1 Mile

Diagram 16.A

seas

north

ND

power to disrupt the extended family 'by separating related households by impossible distances' and to prevent its re-emergence 'by taking no account of family circumstances in allocating housing'.[14] They echo the authors of the Bethnal Green studies in warning that the effect of planning policy on the extended family can be ignored only at our social peril.[15]

What is the position in the areas covered by the 1965–70 slum-clearance proposals? The mothers of a little over one-third (36 per cent) and the married daughters of a little over one-quarter (28 per cent) of the wives of household heads and of female household heads in the SHN sample (n = 115) were living in the Sunderland area. There was little difference between the different slum-clearance districts. The figures for households in the 1965–70 sample in which either the wife's mother or the wife's married daughter were living in Sunderland was 61 per cent; for both the Millfield (Deptford Road) area and the Southwick (Wayman Street) area the figure was 65 per cent. Thirty per cent of the married daughters saw their mothers and 28 per cent of the mothers saw a married child (either a married son or daughter) once a week or more.

In some instances the interviewer interrupted a family visit or a family visit interrupted the interview. 'Sister came to visit during interview.' 'Mother-in-law from Plains Farm present at interview.' 'Interview conducted upstairs in his mother's flat.' 'Grants me an interview while her granddaughter from Hylton Castle (who works in the Town) is getting her dinner.'[16] In other instances kinsfolk or affines lived in the same building or close by. 'Niece upstairs.' 'Sister lived upstairs for twenty-two years; now it is her sister's son and his wife.' 'They [neighbours] would help if we needed them but we have our daughter-in-law just near at hand.' 'My mother lives in the street. I see her every day.'

> I need me Mam to help me a lot at the minute with shopping and that. I have two kiddies and you can see that I'm expecting another one. That's why I'm dreading they'll give me one at Town End Farm or Downhill Estate or somewhere like them. I couldn't manage without her.

> The 84-year-old informant lives alone. But her daughter also has a cottage in the street and comes down every night to sleep with her mother.

If I couldn't get where I wanted to be, the bairns would be a drawback, because I'd be tied with them on some estate well out of the way. Here, if I want to go out I have the family all round. There I couldn't get out on a night with me husband. We'd have to take the children all over with us.

Proximity to relatives was, however, only rarely mentioned[17] as the best point about living in the area. Losing contact with relatives was mentioned even less rarely[18] as the main disadvantage of living on a council estate. These two perhaps surprising findings may be linked. It is possible to speculate that because of Sunderland's history and the distances involved (certainly as compared with the distance from Bethnal Green to Debden, though not as compared with distances in Swansea) rehousing does not seriously affect the more important kin contacts; neither the inner-town nor the suburban location, therefore, is particularly significant from this point of view.

Associated with the question of social interaction—its complement—is 'privacy'. *A priori* analyses of the social implications of urbanism,[19] studies of the isolated conditions of residents in 'the deep city' and others at the nadir of civil life, or of specialised reactions to those conditions,[20] as well as classic statements in sociology of 'the disenchantment of the world',[21] the replacement of community-type relationships by associational-type relationships[22] and the growth and consequences of egoism and *anomie*[23]—all these led to a preoccupation with the attempt to increase free and easy sociable contact over and above those required by the division of labour.

Privacy, a not very well-analysed concept, was considered a problem only in so far as there was excessive emphasis on it as a value,[24] or in so far as privacy was in fact unwanted isolation.[25]

In recent years, however, privacy for working-class families in public housing projects has been re-instated as a value to be seriously defended.[26] The problem of shared dwellings has been redefined as one of inter-family privacy; the problem of overcrowding in the home has been redefined as one of intra-family privacy.[27] Ethological writings, in particular, have become popular, and the importance of 'territoriality' among animals has obvious, if speculative, implications for 'privacy' among human beings.[28] Some writers have pointed out that architects have always been aware of the wrongness for themselves of regarding space as something to be used for other things and never to be enjoyed as territoriality–as a symbol and guarantee of individual privacy.[29] It is only now that they are beginning to assume that the same applies to council tenants.

When privacy is considered, then, what were the potential gains and losses for the families included in Sunderland's 1965–70 slum-clearance proposals? The main source of apprehension was the loss of privacy in two-, three- or four-storied flats.

> I like cottages better with being used to being on my own. I've never been in a tenanted house. If I am rehoused I am bound to go into a tenanted building.[30]

> In a cottage you have more privacy than anywhere. You can lock your own door here and no one sees what's going on.

> With the window being right on the pavement, passers-by don't get the chance to look in. They are past too quickly.[31]

> Your privacy has gone in flats. You can't have a noisy party. You don't know who you are going to get next to you. If I got someone on either side of me I don't like here, it wouldn't matter to us. I wouldn't have to pass them on the stairs every day.

> Hendon! Because there are only flats and maisonettes. I don't see the point. It means I will only be going out of one of these [a Tyneside flat] and going into one of them. My mother is in a council flat–there are more rows than anything else in my mother's block.

> A friend of mine was rehoused at Town End Farm. She got into a very low way. There were six families in the building. She took to wandering. Her man used to find her sitting in the station at South Shields. She has now bought a cottage in Cleft Street.

Among the 1965–70 families, of those in single-family houses (n = 19), 84 per cent said they were 'very satisfied' with the degree of privacy enjoyed; almost the same proportion, 82 per cent, of those in Sunderland cottages (n = 71) were very satisfied; in other forms of accommodation (flats and shared dwellings etc., n = 26) only 50 per cent were very satisfied.

It is sometimes argued that responses such as these are unreliable if they are used to prognosticate a family's reaction to rehousing. The family may be satisfied or dissatisfied with its present dwelling as far as privacy is concerned, but (it is said) whatever may be the scale along which it is rating its satisfaction, it is not one of 'better' or 'worse' than any alternative, for they nave not experienced the alternative.

While it may have some validity generally, there are three things to be said against that view. Sunderland, in the first place, is a town with a settled population, experiencing emigration, but little immigration. It therefore has a low proportion of newcomers unfamiliar with the town's housing stock and unrelated to their fellow townspeople who are familiar with it. Among the 39 large towns of England and Wales, indeed, Sunderland has the lowest proportion of foreign-born residents. (Table 16.2.) In Sunderland, secondly, a high proportion[32] of the population is already in council houses. At the time of the 1966 sample census 53 per cent of all four- and five-person families were in council houses and no fewer than 74 per cent of all six-person families were in council houses. Very many people, therefore, have relatives, ex-neighbours, friends or other acquaintances in various types of council dwelling, and receive reports on their merits and defects.

Probably the strongest argument, however, comes from an analysis of the responses to questions about privacy among families in council dwellings as well as families in the proposed slum-clearance areas. The highest proportion of informants 'very satisfied' with the privacy of their dwelling was in one of the areas of multi-storied council flats (93 per cent).[33] The Deptford Road area of Millfield was second (90 per cent 'very satisfied'). Two other areas of multi-storied council flats were third and fourth (88 per cent and 82 per cent). Among the 1965–70 slum-clearance areas the lowest proportion of informants very satisfied with regard to privacy was at Hendon (45 per cent), with its high proportion of shared dwellings. There were, however, ten council housing estates which had lower percentages than this. In the case of two large estates, the East End and Farringdon, each with a high proportion of two- three- and four-storied flats, the percentages very satisfied with their privacy were very much lower (22 per cent and 15 per cent). (Table 16.3.)[34]

The slum-clearance families who place a high value on privacy and feel that it may be diminished if they were to be rehoused appear, therefore, to be supported in their fears by these data. If they find themselves rehoused in the highly-ranked council districts the chances are that their privacy will not suffer.[35] But, *judging by the experience of people already there*, the likelihood is that as far as privacy is concerned they will find their new accommodation less satisfactory than their previous dwelling.

The final factor in the housing situation to be considered is the difficulty or ease of access to local and town facilities: shops, places of entertainment, the beaches of Roker and Seaburn, schools, hospitals, churches, the swimming baths, parks, work-places and so forth.

One of the peculiarities of the dwelling as a commodity is the fact that each is unique in its location. To some families–those composed only of retired or permanently unemployed people–access to workplace is irrelevant. To families without children access to school is unimportant. Some people like to be able to get to the town centre easily, others like to have a garden and be close to Hylton Woods. Some want to be close to the Royal Infirmary, others want to be close to a favourite pub. One group of families encountered in the course of the study had for many years bathed regularly in the sea between the North pier and the jetty (some of the men in winter and summer); the fact that they were within walking distance of the sands and were able to buy crabs and fish fresh from the boats on their way home was a matter of great importance to them.

The uniqueness of their dwelling's location is a fact which applies to all families, whether the dwelling is in good condition or bad condition or well- or ill-equipped. It also applies to all locations, suburban as well as inner-urban.

All families are not, of course, ideally situated from their own point of view. Overall those families with most power in the market can claim the location they prefer; the next richest segment of the population can claim their preferred locations from what remains; the poorest are left in the situation of 'least choice'. All families, rich as well as poor, must weigh one locational advantage against another. 'Within the range of choices open to me, how much further from the shops am I willing to move in order to be how much closer to the factory?' Location itself, furthermore, is only one element in the housing situation. 'How much convenience of access am I willing to sacrifice in order to obtain what additional household amenities and in order to obtain how much improvement in structural condition?'

Families vary in their attitude to location. There are those to whom it is very important; on the other hand there are those (for example, young couples without children and with personal transport) for whom it is quite unimportant. There are those who wish to cling to their inner-urban location; there are others who strongly desire to live on the outskirts of the town. What is true of them all, however, is that only the family itself can judge (i) how important locational factors are to its members and (ii) how satisfactory its present location is when compared with the range of possible alternatives which may result from compulsory clearance and rehousing.

To what extent, then, would rehousing make it more or less difficult for families in the areas proposed for slum-clearance between 1965 and 1970 to reach the places they want to get to?

All seven of the informants in the Millfield (Booth Street) area who had a worker in the family said that access to work was 'satisfactory'. Eighty-eight per cent of those families with workers in the Millfield (Deptford Road) area said that work access was satisfactory. In the Booth Street, Deptford Road and Wayman Street areas seven out of ten of the informants found work access 'very satisfactory'. Fifteen of the respondents in 1965–70 sample said that the ease of getting to work was the best point about their present housing situation. The lowest percentage of slum-clearance families saying that access to work was satisfactory was in Hendon (81 per cent).

In seven of the largest estates there were smaller percentages of families satisfied with access to work. At Farringdon the percentage finding access to work 'satisfactory' was only half of the percentage satisfied at Hendon, the least favoured of the slum-clearance areas from this point of view. (Table 16.4.)

Forty-one of the informants in the 1965–70 clearance areas said that access to shops was the best point about their housing situation. 'The shops are near and they are open until ten o'clock.' 'Shopping. Smashing! Handy and cheap!' 'Right on top of them!' 'Champion! Just out the back for the shops.' 'Only a couple of minutes to the shops in Hendon Road, Nobles

Bank Road and Villette Road.' By contrast, the difficulty of getting to shops for everyday needs was regarded by many informants as the main disadvantage of a council district.

In two of the slum-clearance areas all the informants regarded access to the shops as being 'satisfactory'. Ninety-six per cent of the informants in the other three slum-clearance areas regarded access to the shops as satisfactory. In both the Millfield (Deptford Road) area and the Southwick (Wayman Street) area 83 per cent of the informants were very satisfied.

In the slum-clearance areas the lowest proportion of informants saying they were very satisfied with local shopping facilities was 73 per cent in the case of Hendon. By contrast only 17 per cent of the informants at Town End Farm estate thought that access to shops was satisfactory. (Table 16.5.)

Forty-one of the slum-clearance informants said that the best points about their present housing situation was ease of access to the central business district ('the Town'). 'It is easy to get into the Town.' 'It is within walking distance of the Town.' 'It is very near the Town.' 'It's handy for the Town.' 'It is nice and central.' Ninety per cent of the informants in 'slum-clearance districts elsewhere' regarded access to the town centre as very satisfactory and 83 per cent of the informants in the Millfield (Deptford Road) area regarded access to the Town as very satisfactory. The main disadvantage of a council district for many people was, on the other hand, its distance from the Town. 'The only disadvantage would be the distance from the Town if it was an outlying estate.' 'You'd be away from the Town.' The slum-clearance area with the lowest proportion of respondents who regarded access to the Town as satisfactory was Hendon (96 per cent); but the housing estate with the lowest proportion of respondents who regarded access to the Town as satisfactory was Town End Farm (36 per cent). (Table 16.6.)

The above pattern of response is repeated when other facilities are analysed. The experience of residents in the slum-clearance areas, that is, is more favourable than that of the majority of residents in housing estates and much more favourable than the experience of those residents in such housing estates as Town End Farm. Ninety per cent or more of all the informants of the four main clearance areas regarded access to medical services—doctors, hospitals, clinics and so forth—as satisfactory. This was the response of only a little over half of the informants at both Pennywell and Town End Farm.[36] (Table 16.7.) The responses of those families with school-children on ease of access to school are shown in Table 16.8. The figures relating to satisfaction with access to places of entertainment are shown in Table 16.9.

Look at Town End Farm and Millfield! There's only one place for a drink at Town End Farm, the Club. If it is crap at the Club then you have to travel to the Caad Lad at Hylton Castle or the Shipwright's at Red House. There's no pub at all at Downhill. There are a lot of Hendon people at Town End Farm. They go to the Catholic Club at Tatham Street. They all want to be home at quarter-past ten, so there are terrific queues for that Town End Farm and Red House buses. It's quicker to get to Newcastle by the express bus from Sunderland than it is to get to Town End Farm.

If it's a crap night at the Willow Pond, in five minutes you can walk to the Buffs in Rutland Street or to the Mountain Daisy or the Railway or the Millfield Club.

It would be all right for me, I would get my own transport. But me Dad can't walk and he can only get as far as the Buffs. If you put him out to Town End Farm you might just as well shoot him up in a rocket and let him orbit in outer space.

Jevons and Madge in their study of Bristol families giving up council tenancies in the two years 1935–6 showed that distance from work, central shops, and the central hospital was very important in their decision to move: 'second only to irritation caused by neighbours was that due to excessive distance from work'.[37] This study looks at the problem from the other side, that of families who already enjoy good access and fear losing it:

Excellent! Bred and born here. I used to gan to the church ower the road when I was a little lass. It's good for getting down Hendon Road into the town. When the snow is on the ground I'm pinned in. I have arthritis of the spine.

Work? Just right! Shops? Couldn't get any better than this for anything like that! School? Just out of the backdoor! Church? Just down the street! Pubs and clubs? All around us! Town centre? Only a thruppenny bus ride!

The thing I bought this house for was because it was handy. It suits me fine, that's why I picked this district.

Everything is handy. Shops, entertainment, and church. I just like it around here, that's all.

Farringdon? It just seems that far away and awkward to get to.

Town End Farm? I'd lie down and die up there!

In all council areas, therefore, access is satisfactory for a high proportion of the residents; there are some areas of council housing where access to desired locations is as good as in the slum-clearance areas; and the 1965–70 areas rarely rank first en bloc in the tables of satisfaction with access. But it appears quite clearly in the above analysis, as from analyses of other housing factors, that on relocation the *chances* are that families from the areas included in the 1965–70 proposals would find it more difficult to reach places in the neighbourhood and in the town as a whole.

Not only are local facilities, work places and the town centre closer to the people in the slum-clearance districts than they would be if they were rehoused in the peripheral housing estates, the public transport system is, for them, much better. This can be shown by an examination of the availability of buses in each of the major traffic zones of Sunderland.[38] (See Diagram 16.B.) Zone H, which includes the two slum-clearance areas Millfield (Booth Street) and Millfield (Deptford Road) had no fewer than 3,007 buses per day leaving the zone. At the other end of the scale, there were only 569 buses leaving zone A (Town End Farm, Hylton Castle and Red House) each day. (Table 16.10.)

It might be supposed that with fewer buses, longer and therefore more tedious and expensive journeys, fewer journeys would be made by residents in peripheral housing estates. In fact, because of the absence of local facilities as compared with slum-clearance districts, far more journeys were made. A sample survey of families transferred from the Dock Street clearance area (1960–5) to Town End Farm estate showed that the total weekly journeys increased by 231 per cent. (Table 16. 11.) 'One family makes 122 bus journeys per week, against twelve in the old area. There are many other similar cases.'[39]

What is more, bus services, though more necessary to the housing-estate resident, are less frequent than in slum-clearance

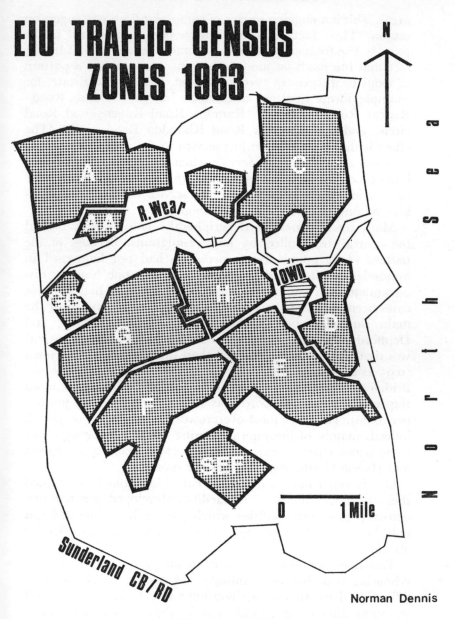

EIU TRAFFIC CENSUS ZONES 1963

N

A

AA

R.Wear

B

C

CC

H

Town

G

L

D

F

E

SEF

North Sea

0   1 Mile

Sunderland CB/RD

Norman Dennis

Diagram 16.B

areas. This is a nagging source of complaint from passengers on estates. 'These facts have not always been appreciated in the past.'[40] The frequency of buses is sometimes cut in half by the fact that the roads on modern housing estates make a pattern of loops to discourage through traffic. Red House Estate, for example, forms a pattern of three circles, the Rhodesia Road–Redcar Road circle, the Ramilles Road–Ravenswood Road circle, and the Ravenna Road–Rhondda Road circle. 'The effect is that a six minute bus service to the area immediately becomes a twelve minute service when it divides with alternate buses on each side of the estate.' Town End Farm has a similar lay-out and there a twelve minute service becomes a twenty-four minute service round each loop.[41]

Many towns experienced peripheral rehousing only to find the central areas filled by new in-migrants. Because of the pattern of its population growth this had not happened in Sunderland. What had happened was that one housing disadvantage of a central location, overcrowding, had in most cases been removed. In 1961 of the four wards containing the main slum-clearance districts, Park, Colliery, Bridge and Deptford, only Park (roughly the Hendon slum-clearance area) was significantly more crowded than the average for the town (0·95 as compared with 0·83 persons per room). Colliery and Bridge were near the median (0·89 and 0·85 persons per room respectively) and Deptford was below average (0·79 persons per room). The three most overcrowded wards were composed, indeed, mainly of peripheral housing estates: Thorney Close (1·03 persons per room), Pennywell (1·02 persons per room) and Hylton Castle (0·99 persons per room).

On the other hand families in central locations had retained the advantage of access to facilities developed for a much denser population–facilities which were still maintained not only by the local population but also by families now further afield.

This does not affirm or deny in any way that peripheral rehousing is or has been mistaken or avoidable. Nor does it affirm or deny that those housing-estate residents who find transport difficult and local facilities deficient do not greatly prefer the total 'package' of the council house and the estate location to their previous circumstances. The extent to which and for whom either of these propositions is true is a separate issue. What these data *do* suggest is that the families in the 1965–70 slum-clearance areas enjoyed great ease of accessibility. The housewives had access to better, more varied and more numerous shops than housewives on housing-estates. The men and women in employment were nearer to their work and, for example, could easily reach home for their mid-day meal. 'To be able to have my dinner with the wife and kids is worth £10 a week to me.' For shift-workers in particular the journey to and from work can be very tedious if it means a walk of two or three miles to an outlying estate in the early hours of the morning. The slum-clearance areas were nearer to the main shops, libraries, parks, cinemas, bingo-halls, clubs, public houses and the general excitement and free spectacle of the town centre.

In itself, then, superior access was an element in the housing situation of the 1965–70 families. Some were willing to forgo this advantage for the sake of others which a council tenancy would give them. For others, however, it was an element which made them look unsympathetically at council rehousing proposals. They had too much to lose and not enough to gain.

NOTES TO CHAPTER 16

1 Completed in 1965 for 209 tenants.
2 'Town Caretaker Assaulted By Car Vandals: Pillaging Rife At Hahnemann Court', *Sunderland Echo*, 19 January 1968.
3 *Sunderland Echo*, 17 May 1967.
4 *Sunderland Echo*, 28 February 1968 and *The Journal* (Newcastle), 28 February 1968.
5 Norman Dennis, 'The Popularity of the Neighbourhood Community Idea', *Sociological Review*, 6, 2, December 1958.
6 Norman Dennis, 'Community and Sociology', *Community Organisation in Great Britain*, Ed. Peter Kuenstler, London 1961, pp. 130–31.
7 Peter C. Collison, *The Cutteslowe Walls: a Study in Social Class*, London 1963. James Tucker, *Honourable Estates*, London 1966. (Correspondents in the *Echo* (presumably like correspondents in other local newspapers) direct a fairly steady stream of abuse at council tenants, mainly on the grounds that they are rich spongers. 'I know of one family in a council home with £100 per week going in and still have one's rent subsidised.' *Sunderland Echo*, 1 March 1967.)

8 In addition to the one-in-fifteen survey of the slum-clearance areas, a ten per cent sample survey was carried out in centrally located areas of council accommodation and in a suburban council estate, built in the early 1960s. One in thirty of the households in the rest of the council's stock of dwellings were also interviewed. The particular question under discussion here was not asked of the informants at Town End Farm.

9 'We have found that neighbourhoods flourish best in small clusters containing between forty and sixty houses, all at the same rent and with the same type of tenant.' Norman Williams, *Population Problems of New Estates* [Norris Green], Liverpool 1939, p. 48. Jevons and Madge in their study of Bristol's inter-war housing policy conclude that mixing different family types in very close proximity was resented for many reasons, and 'these difficulties can only be avoided by grouping tenants of similar habits in small though coherent sub-units'. Rosamund Jevons and John Madge, *Housing Estates*, Bristol 1946, p. 69. Morris and Mogey in their study of Berinsfield, South Oxfordshire, come to the same conclusion. They suggest that local authorities should ensure that compatible families are housed together in groups of between ten and 25 adult members. Ray Morris and John Mogey, *The Sociology of Housing*, London 1965.

10 Michael Young and Peter Willmott, *Family and Kinship in East London*, London 1957; Peter Townsend, *The Family Life of Old People*, London 1957; Peter Marris, *Widows and their Families*, London 1958; Peter Willmott and Michael Young, *Family and Class in a London Suburb*, London 1960.

11 Raymond Firth, (Ed.), *Two Studies of Kinship in London*, London 1956.

12 Colin Rosser and Christopher Harris, *The Family and Social Change*, London 1965.

13 Rosser and Harris put this point in its extremest form: 'The traditional working-class community is simply out of date for all its old-fashioned virtues – and our informants were certainly not slow to recognise this basic fact.' Rosser and Harris, *op. cit.*, pp. 298–99. None of the 49 tables in the book, unfortunately, gave any indication of the proportion of informants who did regard the out-of-dateness of the working-class community as such a basic fact.

14 *Op. cit.*, p. 298.

15 *Op. cit.*, pp. 298–99.

16 Shortly after this interview the letter from 'Karen' appeared in the local press. (See p. 293 below.) The points made in the letter make it seem likely that the granddaughter was stimulated by the questions and answers of the interview to state her grandmother's case.

17 Four cases.

18 Two cases.

19 Louis Wirth, 'Urbanism as a way of life', *American Journal of Sociology*, July 1938.

20 The work of the so-called Chicago school provides probably the best-known examples: Nels Anderson, *The Hobo*, Chicago 1923; Frederic

M. Thrasher, *The Gang*, Chicago 1927; Ernest R. Mowrer, *Family Disorganisation*, Chicago 1927; Louis Wirth, *The Ghetto*, Chicago 1928; Harvey Zorbaugh, *The Gold Coast and the Slum*, Chicago 1929; Paul G. Cressey, *The Taxi-Dance Hall*, Chicago 1932; Walter C. Reckless, *Vice in Chicago*, Chicago 1933; Norman Hayner, *Hotel Life*, Chapel Hill 1936; Robert E. L. Faris and H. Warren Dunham, *Mental Disorders in Urban Areas*, Chicago 1939.

21 Schiller's phrase, often quoted by Max Weber: see for example 'Science as a Vocation' (1919), in H. H. Gerth and C. Wright Mills, *From Max Weber*, London 1948, p. 155.

22 Ferdinand Toennies, *Community and Association* (1887), Trans. Loomis, London 1955.

23 Emile Durkheim, *The Division of Labour* (1893), Glencoe 1947; *Suicide* (1897), London 1952.

24 It might be guessed without concrete evidence, that reference to devices to protect privacy, privet hedges, lace curtains, and so forth are even now generally scornful.

25 See Paul Halmos, *Solitude and Privacy*, London 1952.

26 See, for example, Leo Kuper, 'Blueprint for Living Together', in *Living in Towns*, by Leo Kuper and others, London 1953. Kuper demonstrates the extent to which post-war housing neglected privacy in the search for sociability. See especially 'The Neighbour on the Hearth', *op. cit.*, pp. 11–27. It ought to be noted, however, that the 1967 Reith lecturer forcefully reasserted the view that 'we turn the whole problem back to front: we worry about privacy rather than loneliness'. Psychologists, doctors, schoolmasters and clergymen are described as putting over 'soppy' propaganda about the virtue of a united family life. 'Far from being the basis of the good society, the family, with its narrow privacy and tawdry secrets, is the source of all our discontents.' A society 'something like an Israeli kibbutz perhaps or a Chinese commune', the lecturer suggested, may be preferable. Edmund Leach, 'Ourselves and Others', *The Listener*, November 1967.

27 MHLG, *Homes for Today and Tomorrow*, HMSO 1961, Fourth Impression, 1966 (The Parker Morris Report).

28 Robert Ardrey, *The Territorial Imperative*, London 1957. Konrad Lorenz, *On Aggression*, London 1966.

29 'They cannot bear to forego the *dimensions* of their Victorian rectories or Pimlico drawingrooms.' Diana Rowntree, 'Design for Space', *The Guardian*, 23 June 1965. (Emphasis added.)

30 By 'tenanted' the informant means 'tenemented'.

31 This was an interesting and unexpected discovery. It may be *prima facie* obvious that 'privacy space' in front of houses will have the effect of increasing privacy. It appears, however, that residents in cottages opening directly onto the pavement feel less overlooked than residents on council estates with gardens. The front room can be seen only from right across the street or from the near pavement. The distraction of a view across the street as well as the distance is detrimental to either accidental or deliberate visual intrusions on privacy. On the near-side

pavement the room is in the line of vision of a passer-by for a very short time, and then only if his head is turned at 90 degrees. What is more, the passer-by is so close to the window that the reflected light makes it into a mirror; all that is needed for complete visual privacy is a bunch of flowers on a small table.

32 Forty-six per cent of the households in Sunderland CB were in local authority accommodation in 1966. GRO, *Sample Census 1966*, HMSO 1967.

33 As indicated above (Chapter 14), privacy is protected in Sunderland's multi-storied flats by resident caretakers. In one block of flats crudely printed notices read, 'Sightseers are not welcome. This means you. Please leave the building', and another notice informed commercial callers to report first to the caretaker. Privacy is further protected by the fact that tenancies are restricted to families without children under twelve.

34 The frequency and quality of contact which leads informants to state they are 'satisfied' with their privacy is affected, of course, by a multitude of factors. Children are more likely to violate privacy than are adults, and satisfaction with privacy is likely to be related, therefore, to the proportion of children in the neighbourhood. Invasions of privacy by adults, on the other hand, are probably less easily tolerated. The same action will be defined as an invasion of privacy in one set of circumstances and as a friendly gesture in another. Families in the 1965–70 areas who are participating in long established patterns of neighbouring, for example, will have relatively few social contacts they define as 'intrusions', i.e. as social contacts outside the range they have come to define as acceptable to themselves. On housing estates such settled patterns are less common and the chance is therefore higher of contacts being defined as intrusions.

35 The slum-clearance family might have other objections to being rehoused in those areas. They may dislike the idea of being supervised to some degree by the resident caretaker (some families see such supervision as 'regimentation'); they might be afraid of using lifts; they might object to living in a traditionally low-status area such as Coronation Street; young couples might find unattractive the idea of building up a home only to leave it when they have a baby; and so forth.

36 The difficulty of accepting that people have their own scale of preferences, and that these may be as rational as one's own can be illustrated by an extract from the notes taken at an early interview: 'It appears that this area will never be free from noise, dirt, and dust in the air. As the informant points out, the house is bordered on two sides by the Glass Works and a cement factory. She suffers a great deal from arthritis and although she would be better off in a council house where there would be no dampness, *she does not want to have to make the slight extra effort of travelling to the hospital once or twice a week*.' (Emphasis added.)

37 Rosamund Jevons and John Madge, *Housing Estates*, Bristol 1946, pp. 70–71.

38 The zones are those of the Economist Intelligence Unit census of traffic

in Sunderland in 1963. The study of bus availability is that of the Sunderland Town Planning Department, 18 September 1965.

39 Sunderland Corporation Transport Department, *People and Transport,* Sunderland 1964. The sampling fraction was one-in-ten.

40 *Ibid.,* pp. 29–30.

41 *Ibid.,* p. 30.

Table 16.1

Percentage of Informants who Like their Neighbours 'Very Much'

Rank Order	Area	per cent	One hundred per cent =
1	Low Ford	56	36
2	SOUTHWICK (WAYMAN ST.) AREA	52	23
3	Dame Dorothy Street*	49	37
4	MILLFIELD (BOOTH ST.) AREA	46	13
5	Hedworth Court*	43	40
6	MILLFIELD (DEPTFORD RD.) AREA	40	48
Joint 7	Hylton Castle	39	42
Joint 7	Grangetown	39	33
Joint 7	Springwell	39	28
8	Southwick	36	53
9	Hylton Lane	35	17
10	HENDON	32	22
Joint 11	Grindon	27	59
Joint 11	Plains Farm	27	30
Joint 11	Coronation Street*	27	15
12	Red House	25	76
13	East End	24	37
14	Farringdon	20	56
15	High Ford	18	28
16	Pennywell	16	82
17	Thorney Close	9	54

Source: Interview Analysis

* The sampling fraction was 1 : 10 in the council areas indicated by an asterisk. The sampling fraction was also 1 : 10 for Town End Farm, not shown in this Table. In all other council areas the sampling fraction was 1 : 30.

Table 16.2

Residents Born Outside England and Wales: Sunderland CB and Towns Comparable in Size 1961

	Residents born outside England and Wales per 1,000 enumerated population		Residents born outside England and Wales per 1,000 enumerated population
London AC and City	172	Southend on Sea	57
Coventry	133	Plymouth	57
Birmingham	105	Ipswich	57
Wolverhampton	91	Birkenhead	57
Manchester	90	Blackpool	53
Croydon	87	Oldham	50
Huddersfield	84	Bristol	49
Derby	83	Newcastle upon Tyne	48
Reading	78	Cardiff	48
Bradford	78	Liverpool	47
Leicester	72	Bolton	45
Bournemouth	70	Middlesbrough	44
Portsmouth	69	Stockport	43
Southampton	68	Sheffield	37
Nottingham	67	Walsall	35
Brighton	65	Norwich	31
West Ham	64	Swansea	29
Salford	64	Kingston upon Hull	27
Leeds	59	Stoke on Trent	26
		SUNDERLAND CB	24

Source: Census 1961

Table 16.3

Percentage of Informants for whom the Privacy of the Dwelling is Very Satisfactory

Rank Order	District	'Very satisfactory' per cent	One hundred per cent =
1	Coronation Street	93	15
2	MILLFIELD (DEPTFORD RD.) AREA	90	48
3	Hedworth Court	88	41
4	Dame Dorothy Street	82	39
5	SOUTHWICK (WAYMAN ST.) AREA	74	23
6	1965–70 S.C. (ELSEWHERE)	70	20
7	Low Ford	69	36
8	MILLFIELD (BOOTH ST.) AREA	62	13
Joint 9	Plains Farm	64	28
Joint 9	Springwell	64	28
10	High Ford	52	27
11	Town End Farm	49	197
Joint 12	HENDON	45	22
Joint 12	Southwick	45	53
13	Hylton Castle	43	46
14	Grindon	38	60
15	Hylton Lane	35	17
16	Red House	33	75
17	Thorney Close	28	54
18	Grangetown	24	33
Joint 19	Pennywell	22	82
Joint 19	East End	22	36
20	Farringdon	15	54

Source: Interview Analysis

Table 16.4

Percentage of Informants Satisfied with Work Access

Rank Order	District	per cent stating access 'satisfactory'	one hundred per cent =
Joint 1	Grangetown	100	26
Joint 1	MILLFIELD (BOOTH ST.) AREA	100	7
Joint 1	Low Ford	100	24
Joint 1	Coronation Street	100	9
2	Dame Dorothy Street	97	31
3	Hedworth Court	96	25
4	High Ford	95	19
5	Southwick	91	43
Joint 6	East End	90	30
Joint 6	Springwell	90	19
7	MILLFIELD (DEPTFORD RD.) AREA	88	35
8	ELSEWHERE	86	14
Joint 9	Hylton Lane	84	12
Joint 9	SOUTHWICK (WAYMAN ST.) AREA	84	12
10	Hylton Castle	83	36
11	HENDON	81	29
12	Red House	72	61
13	Plains Farm	71	21
14	Pennywell	61	67
15	Grindon	59	47
16	Thorney Close	51	39
17	Town End Farm	49	149
18	Farringdon	42	43

Source: Interview Analysis

Table 16.5

Percentage of Informants Satisfied with Access to Everyday Shops

Rank Order	District	per cent stating access 'satisfactory'	one hundred per cent =
Joint 1	ELSEWHERE	100	20
Joint 1	MILLFIELD (BOOTH ST.) AREA	100	11
Joint 2	Farringdon	96	56
Joint 2	MILLFIELD (DEPTFORD RD.) AREA	96	48
Joint 2	SOUTHWICK (WAYMAN ST.) AREA	96	23
Joint 2	HENDON	96	22
3	Grangetown	94	33
Joint 4	Dame Dorothy Street	92	39
Joint 4	Low Ford	92	36
5	Coronation Street	88	16
6	Hylton Castle	85	46
7	Hedworth Court	83	41
Joint 8	Thorney Close	81	54
Joint 8	East End	81	37
9	Southwick	76	54
10	Springwell	75	28
11	Plains Farm	66	30
12	High Ford	64	28
13	Red House	60	76
14	Grindon	57	60
15	Hylton Lane	47	17
16	Town End Farm	17	197

Source: Interview Analysis

Table 16.6

Percentage of Informants Satisfied with Access to the Central Business District

Rank Order	District	per cent stating access 'satis-factory'	one hundred per cent =
Joint 1	ELSEWHERE	100	20
Joint 1	MILLFIELD (BOOTH ST.) AREA	100	13
2	MILLFIELD (DEPTFORD RD.) AREA	98	48
Joint 3	Dame Dorothy Street	97	39
Joint 3	Low Ford	96	36
Joint 3	Plains Farm	96	30
Joint 4	SOUTHWICK (WAYMAN ST.) AREA	96	22
Joint 4	HENDON	96	22
5	Hedworth Court	95	41
Joint 6	East End	94	37
Joint 6	Grangetown	94	33
Joint 6	Coronation Street	94	16
7	Pennywell	86	82
Joint 8	Red House	83	76
Joint 8	High Ford	83	28
9	Springwell	82	28
10	Southwick	80	54
11	Farringdon	79	56
12	Hylton Lane	77	17
13	Grindon	73	59
14	Thorney Close	72	54
15	Hylton Castle	71	46
16	Town End Farm	36	196

Source: Interview Analysis

285

Table 16.7

Percentage of Informants Satisfied with Access to Medical Services

Rank Order	District	per cent stating access 'satisfactory'	one hundred per cent =
1	Coronation Street	94	16
2	MILLFIELD (BOOTH ST.) AREA	93	13
Joint 3	SOUTHWICK (WAYMAN ST.) AREA	91	23
Joint 3	HENDON	91	22
4	MILLFIELD (DEPTFORD RD.) AREA	90	48
Joint 5	East End	89	37
Joint 5	Low Ford	89	36
6	Plains Farm	83	30
Joint 7	Southwick	82	54
Joint 7	Hylton Lane	82	17
Joint 8	Dame Dorothy Street	80	39
Joint 8	ELSEWHERE	80	20
Joint 9	Hylton Castle	76	46
Joint 9	Hedworth Court	76	41
Joint 10	Grangetown	75	33
Joint 10	Springwell	75	28
Joint 10	High Ford	75	28
11	Grindon	69	60
12	Thorney Close	60	54
Joint 13	Red House	59	76
Joint 13	Farringdon	59	56
14	Town End Farm	57	194
15	Pennywell	51	86

Source: Interview Analysis

Table 16.8

Percentage of Informants Satisfied with Access to Schools

Rank Order	District	per cent stating access 'satisfactory'	one hundred per cent =
Joint 1	Dame Dorothy Street	100	13
Joint 1	Springwell	100	12
Joint 1	HENDON	100	7
Joint 1	Hedworth Court	100	7
Joint 1	ELSEWHERE	100	6
Joint 1	SOUTHWICK (WAYMAN ST.) AREA	100	4
Joint 1	MILLFIELD (BOOTH ST.) AREA	(1 case only)	
2	Southwick	97	26
3	East End	96	23
4	High Ford	93	14
Joint 5	Red House	92	38
Joint 5	MILLFIELD (DEPTFORD RD.) AREA	92	14
Joint 5	Thorney Close	92	27
6	Hylton Castle	90	21
7	Low Ford	88	9
8	Grangetown	87	23
9	Hylton Lane	86	7
10	Grindon	81	26
Joint 11	Farringdon	66	33
Joint 11	Plains Farm	66	9
12	Town End Farm	62	76
13	Pennywell	57	53

Source: Interview Analysis

Table 16.9

**Percentage of Informants Satisfied with Access to Places of
Entertainment**

Rank Order	District	per cent stating access 'satis-factory'	One hundred per cent =
Joint 1	Southwick (Wayman St.) Area	100	19
Joint 1	Coronation Street	100	16
Joint 1	Millfield (Booth St.) Area	100	10
2	Elsewhere	93	14
Joint 3	Millfield (Deptford Rd.) Area	90	40
Joint 3	Dame Dorothy Street	90	39
4	East End	89	37
Joint 5	Hedworth Court	85	41
Joint 5	Hendon	85	20
Joint 6	Southwick	80	54
Joint 6	Plains Farm	80	30
7	Grangetown	79	33
8	Low Ford	73	34
9	Pennywell	70	82
10	Farringdon	69	56
11	Hylton Lane	65	17
Joint 12	Grindon	64	60
Joint 12	Springwell	64	28
13	Red House	62	76
14	Hylton Castle	61	44
15	High Ford	60	28
16	Town End Farm	57	194

Source: Interview Analysis

Table 16.10

Availability of Buses
E.I.U. Traffic Zones September 1965

	Zone	Buses out of zone per day
H	Pallion–Millfield	3,007
C	Roker–Fulwell–Seaburn	2,008
B	Southwick–Marley Potts	1,641
E	Thornhill–Grangetown	1,469
G	Ford–Pennywell–Grindon	1,361
D	Hendon–East End	993
F	Thorney Close–Farringdon	870
A	Hylton Castle–Red House–Town End Farm	569

Source: Sunderland Town Planning Department

Table 16.11

Use of Bus Services Before and After Slum-clearance

	Dock Street families at Howick Street	Dock Street families after transfer to Town End Farm	Percentage increase
Total weekly journeys	1,282	4,247	231
Weekly journeys per family	14·7	49·0	220
Weekly journeys per person	4·9	16·6	240

Source: Sunderland Corporation Transport Department,
People and Transport, Sunderland 1964

CHAPTER 17

OPPOSITION TO THE SLUM CLEARANCE PROPOSALS 1965–70

IV. The Consumer's Preference Array

As early as 1908 Sidney Webb had recognised that once consumption in the society at large exceeded the level at which the under-consumer constituted a public nuisance by, for example, making himself particularly susceptible to epidemic disease and had risen above the level of actual discomfort, differentiated preference arrays would mean that great variety of provision would be inevitable.

> A regiment of naked men needs clothing too urgently to allow us to grumble that the standard sizes of the regimental contractor makes all the uniforms nothing better than misfits. The early Victorian community, bare of schools, or drains, or Factory Acts, had to get itself supplied with the common article of standard pattern. The most important business of twentieth century governments must be to provide not only for minorities, but even for quite small minorities, and actually for individuals. Every minority, every citizen, in fact, has to be supplied just as every soldier in the regiment has to have his pair of marching boots.[1]

At about the same time Patrick Geddes was insisting that the function of town planning 'is not to coerce people into new places against their associations, wishes and interests. Instead its task is to find the right places for each sort of people, to give people in fact the same care as we give when transplanting flowers'.[2]

In subsequent years this point of view became unfashionable. In 1966, however, the Ministry of Housing and Local Government carried out a study in Deeplish, a district of Rochdale. The report stimulated a new interest in the notion of a complex of housing values organised into a unique order of priorities by each individual family. The Deeplish study, indeed, went further than Webb and Geddes in that it did not take for granted that in relation to the consumer, the planner was some kind of army general, concerned with the ordnancing of his troops, or some kind of gardener, exercising his skill on un-resisting flora. The possibility that the consumer in mobilising his preferences into an ordered system could be acting rationally was admitted from the beginning. Speaking of the run-down residential districts which surround the centres of our industrial towns and cities the Minister of Housing wrote:

> The city planner, ambitious for wholesale redevelopment, eagerly writes them off as the slums of tomorrow and decrees a clean sweep. Yet on closer examination these 'twilight areas' are often found to contain hundreds of comfortable family homes in neighbourhoods of marked character and community feeling.[3]

Not everything that a family desires can be bought with its weekly income and scarcely any of its ends can be met as completely as its members would like. The house may satisfy the family's needs for rest and shelter; but it would like a home, perhaps, which would be more comfortable and convenient, a home that would look better and carry more prestige. If the family paid its whole weekly earnings in rent or mortgage it could have a much better house; but in that case there would be no money for anything else. A family's judgment upon its total housing experience is a matter of weighing up gains and losses in the light of the family's total circumstances. This is shown in various ways in the Deeplish study. A House Condition Index was devised in order to rate the dwellings in Deeplish against some notional 'new house of the same size'. The Deeplish houses were then placed in one of three categories: up to 30 per cent as good as a new house of the same size; from 31 per cent to 60 per cent as good; and from 61 per cent as good to just as good as a new house of the same size. The study showed that substantial numbers of respondents were very satisfied with even those houses in the poorest condition: poor physical conditions were outweighed by the satisfactions of owner-occupation, low cost and so forth. (Table 17.1.)

The study makes the same point about space standards. The manner in which house space fitted in to a family's hierarchy of housing values determined its level of housing satisfaction, rather than the objective provision of space itself. Forty-one per cent of the families whose space was 'less than standard' were nevertheless very well satisfied with the home and, by contrast, 16 per cent of the families enjoying the 'standard' space provisions were rather dissatisfied.

> Thus, while the houses were sometimes in a poor state structurally and more than half lacked the standard amenities, housing conditions were good in other respects. The households in Deeplish occupied their own houses without sharing, they generally enjoyed ample space standards, a high proportion were owner-occupiers and housing was cheap. Housing conditions of this kind were generally more important to the residents than the physical condition of the houses.[4]

Among the over-sixties living in the lowest quality housing when judged on the study's three indexes of condition, curtilage and environment, one-half were 'very well satisfied'. For older people, that is, the burden of moving home was judged more onerous than the defects of their present housing.

The process of balancing housing gains and losses and of placing the house within the context of other household circumstances is shown in the responses of the 1965–70 slum-clearance informants in Sunderland. For example, a cottager in Ogden Street, in expressing her opinion about the council's intention to demolish the area, said:

> We won't get put round here, we'll land up at Warden Law, miles away! We know new houses are nice, but it's who you get beside. I'd hate to be in a tenanted house [she meant tenemented house] because I've lived all my life in a cottage with my own front door. Buses and bus fares! (It's not so bad if there are workers in the house.) Shopping! I know there are vans, but the prices are extra. I wouldn't dare go into the sky scrapers: I'm frightened of heights and people are careless of cigarettes–I don't want to burn

292

to death. They are gorgeous inside, but more like dolls' houses, you are too much fastened in.

The same sort of listing and weighing of alternatives can be seen in some public statements of the problem:

> I understand that eight houses situated behind the Empire Theatre are being demolished. A simple sentence, but what heartache lies behind it. Nearly all the residents in this block have lived here for over fifty years; they are for the most part very old, and the younger residents in this small street help to make their lives a little easier. The uprooting at their age is bad enough, but some of the places suggested for them are ridiculous and disgusting. One person was sent to view a place and upon arrival found not only a house, but old furniture, a mouldy meal on the table and to complete the picture, a 'gusunder' complete. Others have been sent so far away that there is little hope of finding themselves able to get into the town, due to age, and others having to take places that are centrally heated, when their main comfort in life is their coal fires. KAREN.[5]

The following tables show both the extent to which Sunderland's 1965–70 slum-clearance programmes met the opposition of the families affected and which groups—defined by age, tenure, family type etc.—were most strongly attached to their 'slum' homes and districts. Table 17.2 shows that in the total sample over four out of ten families (42 per cent) were very satisfied with their current housing conditions (this may be compared with the 35 per cent who were very satisfied with their current housing conditions in the 1960–5 remainder). Among the small number interviewed in the Booth Street area (thirteen cases) nearly two-thirds (62 per cent) were very satisfied with their over-all housing conditions. Fifty-four per cent of the large adult families were very satisfied with their present living conditions. Fifty-five per cent of the mature single-person or two-person households were very satisfied.

Another indication of a preference for the existing dwelling and area is provided by the response to the question 'Say you were to be rehoused by the Council. Think of the sort of dwelling, good or not so good, where you expect you would actually go to if you were rehoused by the Council. All things considered, do you expect that you would be in a dwelling that would suit you better than this one or that it would not suit you as well as this one?' Table 17.3 shows the proportions of respondents who expected that they would *not* be better off in a council dwelling. This was the case with 54 per cent of the old single-person or two-person households. It was the case with 46 per cent of the informants in the Booth Street area. It was the case with 44 per cent of the owner-occupiers.

The picture is similar but the colours are somewhat stronger when one considers the expectations of the informants regarding the improvement in their conditions as a result of living in a council district. Sixty-eight per cent of the people in the Booth Street area did not expect to be better off in a council district. Fifty-eight per cent of the owner-occupiers did not expect to be better off in a council district. This was also the proportion for mature one-person and two-person families. (Table 17.4.)

Almost two-thirds of the owner-occupiers were not in favour of demolition. Fifty-four per cent of the old single-person and two-person families were not in favour of demolition and 42 per cent were very much against demolition. Forty-eight per cent of the respondents in the Deptford Road area were not in favour of demolition. (Table 17.5.)

The proportion of families who, at the time of the SHN interviews, had not filled in an application for a council house provides a final index to the extent and nature of opposition to rehousing. Owner-occupiers do not qualify for inclusion on the waiting-list for council dwellings and this question does not arise in their case; the percentages in Table 17.6 are heavily weighted, therefore, by the percentage of owner-occupiers in each sub-sample. Even when only the statistics for tenants of private landlords are considered, however, 45 per cent had not taken the voluntary step of applying for a council dwelling.

Two other housing features serve as rough indicators that the advantages and disadvantages have been such that on balance they have attached the informant to his existing dwelling and neighbourhood and made council accommodation relatively unattractive. The first feature is owner-occupation; the home has been attractive enough to buy. As has been shown, in the whole of the 1965–70 sample, just one-third (33 per cent) of the informants were owner-occupiers (as compared with 21 per cent in the 1960–5 remainder). The highest percentage was found in the Millfield (Deptford Road) area, where nearly one-half (46 per cent) of the informants were owner-occupiers. The lowest percentage was in Hendon where only 5 per cent of the informants were owner-occupiers.

The second indicator is length of residence: the house and area have proved their acceptability over a period of years. Sixty-five per cent of the mature single- and two-person families had lived in their present dwelling for twenty years or more; the proportion in the case of the old single- and two-person families was 62 per cent. In the Southwick (Wayman Street) area 61 per cent of the informants had lived in their present dwellings for twenty years or more. (Table 17.7.) Families can languish for years under adverse conditions and come to accept them resignedly. When long residence is combined with attitudes which are strongly favourable to the home and district, however, this represents the culmination of a process of self-selection and mutual adaptation: families have come and gone, staying if they found the social ecology of the area suited their needs and leaving if it did not.

This process of mutual accommodation by trial and error has been especially long in Sunderland as compared with other towns of comparable size. Sunderland grew dramatically in the last quarter of the nineteenth century (its population had been 88,000 in 1861 and it was 182,000 by 1901) but as we have seen, since 1901 its growth (to 218,000 by 1961) has been modest. Since 1901 growth has taken place, partly as a result of colliery developments in the villages which entered the borough in 1967 but mainly as a result of natural increase within the town itself, that is, the excess of births over deaths. Even in 1901 79 per cent of the males in the borough as it was constituted at that time originated in County Durham; 83 per cent of the females originated in County Durham. Only 6 per cent of the males in 1901 had not been born in England: 3·1 per cent were born in Scotland, 1·6 per cent in Ireland and 1·5 per cent in foreign countries. We have also seen that, as compared with other towns of comparable size (the eighteen larger than Sunderland and the eighteen smaller) an unusually low proportion of the population of Sunderland in 1961 was foreign born; put the other way, Sunderland's population is unusually indigenous and settled.

Another index of the homogeneity of the town's neighbourhoods is the percentage of seats uncontested in local elections. In the three years 1956–8 Sunderland had the fourth highest percentage of seats uncontested (74 per cent) of the 157 towns in England and Wales with a population of 50,000 or more.[6] Among the 39 largest towns of England and Wales councillors returned unopposed as a percentage of all councillors seeking re-election in 1961 was highest in the case of Sunderland. In nineteen of these towns no seats were uncontested; in Sunderland 61 per cent of the seats were uncontested; the next highest figure of uncontested seats was in Middlesbrough (47 per cent).

Attachment to a dwelling and a neighbourhood, which years of experience have shown to be at least not unsatisfactory, was expressed by residents in the following terms:

> We've been happy in this house, we've had 36 glorious years. That's what I'd feel about it when it came to break it up. It's been a happy home. That's the beauty. When you've lived in a house all your life since you've been married you dinnit want to move.

> When you've been born in the same bed as you are sleeping in, you take badly to having to move. I am the third generation in this house.

> When I saw it in the *Echo* I got a bit of a full feeling.

> Forty-six years – and we've got to get out.

> He was married out of here, and he'll be carried out of here! I could have had houses at Ryhope and I wouldn't go. Everything is good; there is nothing bad about it.

> I'm used to it. We know the people and they're all sociable; there is no fighting. I want to stop here the remainder of my days.

Long residence in the same place is not only an index of housing satisfaction, in itself it may be the source of such satisfaction. 'When asked specifically "What do you like about this house?", the housewives . . . showed attachment to the familiar home and identification of it with family life.' People tend to be attached to that place within which their own particular family experiences have been acted out.[7]

Some informants, whatever their housing conditions, considered that disturbance and change in themselves outweighed any prospective advantages of a council dwelling and district.

This was particularly so, of course, in the case of the elderly. Nearly one-third of the 1965–70 sample households contained at least one person aged 65 or older. This was true of over one-third (36 per cent) of the owner-occupier households. In the Southwick (Wayman Street) area nearly two-fifths (39 per cent) of the households in the sample contained one or two persons aged 65 or over. (Table 17.8.) At the other end of the age scale, the 1965–70 slum-clearance districts (with the exception of Hendon) did not house large numbers of young children. Seventy-two per cent of the households contained no children aged 0–4 years old and 75 per cent contained no children aged 5–15 years old. (Table 17.9 and Table 17.10.) A frequently stated view in the slum-clearance districts was that when the family was at an earlier stage of its development a council house had been sought unsuccessfully. Now that there was no desire for it and perhaps hostility towards it, a council house was being forced upon the family:

> No good giving me a council house now, they should have promised me a house in my younger days.

Objections based upon change as such were most common, as might be expected, among old people:

> When you are getting on in years you can't be bothered shifting.

> We are getting on in years. We'd say, 'Leave them up'.

> When you get on you don't want to be disturbed.

> I wouldn't could settle in a building estate because I never lived on an estate, I've always lived in a private house. I go to see my sister on Red House and I don't like the atmosphere. I feel out of the way, I feel shut away, you might as well be in prison.

> If they'd only let us stay. No one wants to go. We are not young, he (the informant's husband) will only last five years. That's what he says, 'If they'd only let us stay'.

> It's not right for old people. They say the new houses kills off the old people. It was the same with my mother and father at —— Street. They were the last ones to go. My mother died just a year ago, a stroke through worrying about the new house. My father is now in Cherry Knowle,[8] he went out of his mind with it. A woman in Wreath Quay Road got a flat at Town End Farm, she went funny as well, wandering about.

To planners, fulfilling their statutory duties and carrying into practice their professional doctrines, 'the house' is acceptable or unacceptable, ready for demolition or suitable for conversion, in so far as it contributes, for example, to the good appearance of the town or is so disposed in relation to other dwellings that pedestrian safety can be furthered. To a landlord 'the house' is a commodity and concerns him in so far as it secures for him a return on his capital; for him the house is a matter of so many years' purchase.

It appears from this analysis, however, that to the owner-occupier or the tenant the house represents an exceedingly large and complex range of values. A home and neighbourhood which are felt to be satisfying by the inhabitants are necessarily the creation of a long period of accommodation and adjustment. As Edmund Burke said in another connection, the high level of satisfaction in areas like Millfield is the result of 'a choice not of one day or one set of people . . . it is made by the peculiar circumstances, occasions, tempers, dispositions and moral, civil, and social habitudes of the people which disclose themselves only in a long space of time'.[9]

What the dwelling and the neighbourhood 'are', then, is not a question to be easily answered by reference to a physical milieu. Mediating between perception and environment are assumptions, needs, expectations.[10]

On one side lies the comparatively homogeneous group which is seeking to alter the physical environment. To a greater or lesser extent they have independently committed themselves to the objectives towards which control is directed. Belief in the value of the objectives (and the suitability of various means) has been inculcated in the course of professional training. Whatever their original view, furthermore, and no matter how effectively they may have been indoctrinated while becoming qualified, their career constrains them to accept the *Weltanschauung*, the social philosophy, of their colleagues and of their superior officers.

On the other side there is a variety of individuals and family types. All perceive and respond to the environment according to its relevance for the attainment of the ends they themselves value. The interests of many of them match those implied by the 1965–70 slum-clearance proposals. They perceive the environment as something which, given the alternatives, they wish to abandon or substantially modify. Others, however, judge that in their current and foreseeable circumstances what they have is better than anything they expect would result from municipal intervention.

Within the first frame of reference Millfield, for example, is a collection of shabby, mean and dreary houses, derelict back lanes, shoddy-fronted shops and broken pavements, the whole unsightly mess mercifully ill-lit.[11]

Within the second frame of reference, that, say, of a sixty-year-old woman who lives there, the same scene may convey messages of quite another kind, mawkishly sentimental though they may be, and backward-looking and trivial to the point of absurdity. Millfield for her is Bob Smith's, which she thinks (probably correctly) is the best butcher's in the town; George McKeith's wet-fish shop and Peary's fried-fish shop about which she says the same, with equal justification; Maw's hot pies and peas, prepared on the premises; the Willow Pond public house, in which her favourite nephew organises the darts and dominoes team; the Salvation Army band in a nearby street every Sunday and waking her with carols on Christmas morning; her special claim to attention at the grocer's because her niece worked there for several years; the spacious cottage in which she was born and brought up, which she now owns, has improved and which has not in her memory had defects which have caused either her or her neighbours discernible inconvenience (but which has some damp patches which make it classifiable as a 'slum dwelling'); the short road to the cemetery where she cares for the graves of her mother, father and brother; her sister's cottage across the road—she knows that every week-day at 12.30 a hot dinner will be ready for her when she comes from work; the bus route which will take her to the town centre in a few minutes; the homes of neighbours who since her childhood have helped her and whom she has helped; church, club and workplace within five minutes' walk; and, in general (as is said), 'every acre sweetened by the memory of the men who made us'.

The same sight meets the eyes of both these observers, but there is no resemblance in the symbolism of the images. The first is able to perceive Millfield objectively. His jejune freshness of vision has been skilfully supplemented with a set of stereotypes to which he can quickly assimilate his observations. The perception of the second, the sixty-year-old woman, is ir-remediably distorted by a host of peculiar and private associations.

However desirable it would be for her to see home and neighbourhood through the eyes of the planner and share his vision, however, the likelihood of it happening must be recog-nised as being of a low order. Eventually, indeed, it may be necessary for the planner to begin to make an effort of imagin-ative understanding to see her own symbolic world as she herself sees it. Certainly, if that were to happen, the planner would receive some support in social psychology. The physical environment is never simple—that is a tiresome but ineluctable feature of the human condition. It is important only in so far as it is perceived and it is perceived only to the extent that it is important for the achievement of ends. Objects in the physical world affect human behaviour only as percepts, and percepts are, in Mead's phrase, nothing but 'summaries of action'.[12] 'To sweep away the past entirely, even, perhaps, all the dirty and dilapidated past, is to diminish that heritage of symbols which makes society human.'[13]

When length of residence is taken into account, therefore, and when this is combined with continued attachment,[14] a cost-benefit balance, to the extent that the welfare of concrete human beings are to figure in it, must give some weight to the value in human terms of continuity as such.

The Presentation of the Alternatives

For some old people this complex of housing satisfactions, 'the home', may have the appearance of unity and simplicity; to them their present home, warts and all, may appear not as instrumental to other purposes but as a final, ultimate and supreme value in itself without being a means to any other end. With this exception borne in mind, it is nevertheless clear that for the majority of householders their support of or opposition to rehousing is not a matter of any single, overriding value. The question that lies, consciously or unconsciously, behind the consumers' acceptance or rejection of the local authority's proposals is, Will I be better off with what I expect to be offered?

Some local government officers tend to dismiss all objections to slum-clearance proposals as factitious. Objections come only from owner-occupiers and landlords, and the sole basis of the objections is the desire to extract higher compensation from the Corporation.

The prospects of generous or niggardly compensation payments do affect attitudes to demolition. In most cases compensation is expected to be below that level which would lead to a voluntary sale on the part of the owner. This would be so even if the majority of owners received the full 'market value', for the market price brings forward only the most willing sellers. The product 'is worth only what the market will bear, and the exchange value of the least useful part of the supply fixes the exchange value of all the rest'.[15] Even those with properties which they expect will be sold to the local authority at market value, however, do not usually receive market value. In the first place, slum-clearance proposals generally precede demolition by several years. The market value of the cottage after years of planning blight is usually felt, therefore, as being below the 'true market value', that is, the price the cottage *was* worth and would still be worth but for the proposals of the local authority itself. Compulsory purchase at market price constitutes, in effect, an extra tax paid by the unwilling vendor of an amount equal to the difference between the market price and the price at which the vendor would have been prepared to part with his property under ordinary market conditions.[16]

Secondly, the 1965–70 proposals were formulated by the local authority in the expectation that very few dwellings would be acquired at a cost as high as that of the market. Apart from certain very small areas at least 90 per cent of the properties in the districts of the 1965–70 programme were to be acquired as 'unfit properties'. (Table 17.11.)

Not unnaturally the one-third of the householders who were owner-occupiers suffered from a sense of deprivation. At best they would receive market value for their homes. It was possible that they would receive an ex gratia payment of an amount which would not be fixed until demolition was imminent, the so-called 'well-maintained grant' for unfit properties which had been kept in a state of good repair. In all likelihood, however, they would receive no compensation for the acquisition of their cottages by the local authority, but payment only for the land on which the dwelling stood.

In the Millfield area, indeed, this feeling of injustice stimulated the parish priest to publicly condemn the council's recent slum-clearance activities as 'legalized robbery and exploitation of the people'.[17] The vicar raised another point in connection with the alternatives offered the families which were to be rehoused. 'I consider that many of them have been treated like animals. They are told where they must live and threatened that if they refuse so many keys, they will find themselves on the street. What right has anyone to dictate to these people who have not asked for council houses?'[18]

There was a widespread apprehension in the 1965–70 slum-clearance areas that what would be offered as alternative accommodation by the council would be inferior in various respects to the residents' existing accommodation.

> My sister-in-law is in the grave through this. They took her house in Crowtree Road. She asked to be rehoused in Azalea Terrace as she had always lived near the centre of the town. She was offered a house at Farringdon twice [a housing estate on the outskirts of Sunderland]. In the end she never got a house. She was so poorly with worry that she decided to go in with her sister. She only lived one-and-a-half years after that. It wasn't fair. She moved out, so did her tenant—and two days later a family of nine was put in! The house is still standing.

> If they have their aan way they might put us out in the wilderness.

> There's a lot of roughnecks up at Farringdon in some parts— at the top end, where the terminus is. Phew! Where the big blue flats are.

> We are hoping they won't put us in a flat. But you are only allowed one refusal now. Saw it in the *Echo* a couple of months ago.

> There were so many people refusing up at Williams Street [the Peacock Street West slum-clearance area] that you are now put off the list if you refuse a second time. It's the law. You only get one chance now, then you have to find a place of your own with a friend or a relation.

The last two quotations referred to a council minute of 14 July 1965, which dealt with applicants on the waiting list and not with the problem of rehousing families from slum-clearance areas. The minute instituted the rule that an applicant on the waiting list who refused more than two offers of a council tenancy automatically lost his accumulated points. At the end of August 1967, the chairman of the Housing Committee held a Press conference in order to point out the difficulties which fuller choice of council dwelling would entail:

> I realise that housing is a human question and people want to remain near their friends and relations. We would never want to be heartless, but at the same time, I think some people go a bit too far in picking and choosing. We have asked the Housing Officer to take a very serious view of this matter. We can't go on condoning this insistence all the time by people on the waiting list that they must always be housed in a particular area.[19]

On this occasion, as in the case of the council minute referred to, the statement was confined to applicants on the waiting list and excluded slum-clearance families.

But at a lower level in the administrative structure the distinction between the volunteers on the waiting list and the pressed men in the slum-clearance areas has tended to blur. 'Refusals! Refusals were unheard of twenty years ago! Now no-one will take re-lets; everybody wants only a new house! What will happen to the re-lets? Will we have to pull them down because nobody wants them? The trouble is they are told too much. If they were just told that they were being moved out to a certain house—but they are pandered to.' The following letter was sent to a 77-year-old widow in her owner-occupied cottage in a slum-clearance area and may serve as an illustration of the administrative action which follows from such attitudes:

> You will be aware that the houses in the above area must be demolished as soon as possible because they are unfit to live in. To enable demolition to take place the Housing and Estates Manager has made you two offers of alternative suitable accommodation which I understand have been refused by you. I hereby give you notice that the offer will remain open for acceptance by you until —— and if you do not accept by that date, no more offers of accommodation will be made and steps will be taken, without further notice to you, to have you evicted from the

303

property to enable the same to be demolished as required by the Minister of Housing and Local Government. I will advise you in your own interest to accept this final offer immediately.

The sensitivity of residents in slum-clearance areas to such attitudes provoked a number of outspoken protests in the local newspaper:

I was one of those people forced out of my own home, but I was not lucky enough to be able to turn three keys down. We have been driven nearly insane in eight months. So I don't blame anyone for turning down what they don't want. I wish I had the chance.[20]

May I remind the people on the Housing Committee that the public are at liberty to disobey so-called 'orders'. I do not live in a council-owned house, but the look of the flats brings to my mind they look like barracks. Social security has never come my way, but I suppose when rehoused I will reluctantly become an applicant. Meanwhile I will sit tight, dreading the day when I have to move.[21]

Since home, to most of us, is the most important part of our lives, why shouldn't we wish to live near our friends and relations? Why should people be sent to live at Gilley Law if their hearts are in Hylton Castle, Fulwell or Grangetown? And why should a quiet, respectable family be forced to live among rough, noisy and destructive people?[22]

The residents of this particular area who tend to be rather choosey are those people who by stint of hard work and thrift have bought their own homes and who find they are going to lose them through no fault of their own. Who can blame them for refusing to accept re-let council houses which have been left in a deplorable and dirty state when all their lives they have striven to better themselves?[23]

It's the people's rights to refuse being put on these God-forsaken places. For one thing half the houses are like rabbit hutches, not enough room to swing a cat. It also means that people who have worked hard for their homes, have to sell their furniture before going into a council house. There are quite a lot of people also who can't manage stairs. Most women rely on their mothers for health reasons, and mothers rely on them too. I for one have my own cottage but expect to have it taken away because the land is wanted. But I'm not just going to go where I am told to go and like it. I like peace and quiet, which I get now, and I don't see why I should be put next door to someone who likes a lot of noise or who can't mind their own business.[24]

Letters such as these appear whenever freedom of choice for the slum-clearance families is threatened. A family had claimed that a room was required for their son's piano practice. It was reported that this boy was subsequently interrogated without the parents' knowledge or permission as to whether or not he was a pianist:

> I feel impelled to write to your paper after reading the article about the boy pianist who was interrogated at the behest of the housing authorities. I would not like to think the council stepped in and took my home after the struggle my husband and I had to get it, doing without holidays and many other things and then pour salt into open wounds and offer us accommodation that was unsuitable to our requirements. I am not one to stand in the way of progress, although I do think some consideration should go a long way to heal the breach of losing one's home and friends all in one go, without having to also suffer the indignities she and her family seem to have undergone through no fault of their own.[25]

NOTES TO CHAPTER 17

1 Sidney Webb, *The Necessary Basis of Society* [Address to the Social Political League, London, 14 May 1908], Fabian Society Tract 159, 1911.

2 Jacqueline Tyrwhitt (Ed.), *Patrick Geddes in India*, London 1947.

3 Foreword by Anthony Greenwood, MHLG, *The Deeplish Study: Improvement Possibilities in a District of Rochdale*, HMSO 1966.

4 *Op. cit.*, p. 26.

5 *Sunderland Echo*, 24 August 1965.

6 Claus A. Moser and Wolf Scott, *British Towns: A Statistical Study of their Differences*, London 1961.

7 *The Deeplish Study*, p. 24.

8 Cherry Knowle is a local hospital for patients with mental disorders.

9 Edmund Burke, 'Reform of Representation in the House of Commons', in *Works*, Vol. VI, p. 147.

10 I am indebted to my colleague David C. Russell for drawing my attention to the points made in the rest of this chapter. See his 'Psychology and Environment', *Planning Outlook*, VI, 2 (old series), 1964, for a fuller discussion of the contribution of social psychology to housing and town planning.

11 Russell has previously made this same point in a similar way, contrasting two views of Bigg Market, Newcastle upon Tyne, *op. cit.*, p. 37.

12 George Herbert Mead, *Mind, Self and Society*, Chicago 1934.

13 Russell, *op. cit.*, p. 36.

14 'Continued attachment' is, of course, a crucial datum. Long residence is not always associated with feelings of satisfaction. See Vereker and Mays, *Urban Redevelopment and Social Change*, Liverpool 1961, Chapter VI.

15 Sidney Webb, *Fabian Essays*, 1889.

16 The basis of compensation for property compulsorily purchased in connection with unfit properties in a clearance area is to be found in the Land Compensation Act, 1961. Briefly, owners of such properties are entitled to current market value, discounting the depressing effects on market value of the local authority's own proposals.

17 The Rev. W. J. Taylor, 'To be or not to be?' *The Magazine of St. Mark's Parish*, November 1967.

18 *Ibid.*

19 *Sunderland Echo*, 31 August 1967.

20 *Ibid.*, 7 September 1967.

21 *Ibid.*, 4 September 1967.

22 *Ibid.*, 5 September 1967.

23 *Ibid.*, 5 September 1967.

24 *Ibid.*, 4 September 1967.

25 *Ibid.*, 14 October 1967.

Table 17.1

Dwelling Condition and Consumer Satisfaction: Deeplish, Rochdale 1966

	Rating of Dwelling on House Condition Index		
Degree of Satisfaction	Dwellings up to 30 per cent as good as a new house of the same size per cent	Dwellings from 31 per cent to 60 per cent as good as a new house of the same size per cent	Dwellings from 61 per cent as good to just as good as a new house of the same size per cent
'Very well satisfied'	28	58	77
'Find it all right'	33	34	19
'Rather dissatisfied'	39	8	4
	n=67	n=179	n=99

Source: *The Deeplish Study*

Table 17.2

Families 'Very Satisfied' with their Present Living Conditions: Sunderland CB Slum Clearance Programme 1965–70

Sub-sample	Per Cent 'very satisfied'	Total number in the sub-sample (= 100 per cent)
1965–70 Programme	42	125
Millfield (Booth Street) area	62	13
Millfield (Deptford Road) area	45	47
Southwick (Wayman Street) area	43	23
Hendon	27	22
Elsewhere	35	20
Twenty years or more in present dwelling	61	49
One year but under 5 years in present dwelling	30	23
Under one year in present dwelling	25	12
Mature single-person or two-person families	55	20
Adult large families	54	24
Old single-person and two-person families	50	34
Young large families	29	14
Young small families	20	30
Owner-occupiers	50	42
Tenants of private landlords	36	72
Single-family cottages	50	70
Single-family houses	42	19
Flats	18	22

Source: Interview Analysis

Table 17.3

Families Expecting They Would Not Be Better Off in a Council Dwelling: Sunderland CB Slum Clearance Programme 1965-70

Sub-sample	Percentage expecting they would not be better off in a council dwelling	Total number in the sub-sample (=100 per cent)
1965–70 Programme	29	125
Old single-person and two-person families	54	34
Mature single-person and two-person families	35	20
Adult large families	22	23
Young small families	10	31
Young large families	7	14
Millfield (Booth Street) area	46	13
Millfield (Deptford Road) area	36	47
Southwick (Wayman Street) area	30	23
Hendon	15	22
Elsewhere	20	20
Owner-occupiers	44	41
Tenants of private landlords	22	73
Ten-fifteen years in present dwelling	43	14
Twenty years or more in present dwelling	40	19
Under one year in present dwelling	16	12
Single-family cottages	40	70
Single-family houses	22	19
Flats	18	22

Source: Interview Analysis

Table 17.4

Families Expecting They Would Not Be Better Off in a Council District: Sunderland CB Slum Clearance Programme 1965–70

Sub-sample	Percentage expecting they would not be better off in a council district	Total number in the sub-sample (=100 per cent)
1965–70 Programme	55	125
Old single-person or two-person families	71	31
Mature single-person and two-person families	58	19
Adult large families	46	22
Young small families	42	31
Young large families	35	14
Millfield (Booth Street) area	68	12
Southwick (Wayman Street) area	59	22
Millfield (Deptford Road) area	51	46
Hendon	43	21
Elsewhere	48	19
Owner-occupiers	58	38
Tenants of private landlords	50	71
Single-family cottages	61	66
Single-family houses	42	19
Flats	37	22
Twenty years or more in present dwelling	61	46
One year but under five in present dwelling	28	22

Source: Interview Analysis

Table 17.5

Families Not in Favour of Demolition: Sunderland CB Slum Clearance Programme 1965–70

Sub-sample	Families not in favour of demolition per cent	Number of families in the sub-sample (=100 per cent)
1965–70 Programme	47	123
Owner-occupiers	64	38
Tenants of private landlords	29	61
Old single-person or two-person families	54	26
Adult large families	54	22
Mature single-person and two-person families	40	15
Young small families	26	31
Young large families	17	12
Single-family cottages	49	60
Single-family houses	42	17
Flats	15	20

Source: Interview Analysis

Table 17.6

Families Who Had Not Applied to the Local Authority for Voluntary Rehousing (Waiting List)
Sunderland CB: Slum Clearance Programme 1965–70

Sub-sample	Families who had not applied to the local authority for voluntary rehousing	Number of families in the sub-sample (=100 per cent)
1965–70 Programme	67	125
Millfield (Booth Street) area	85	13
Millfield (Deptford Road) area	79	48
Southwick (Wayman Street) area	74	23
Hendon	36	22
Elsewhere	50	20
Old single-person and two-person families	82	34
Mature single-person and two-person families	80	20
Young large families	79	14
Adult large families	71	24
Young small families	32	31
Twenty years or more in present dwelling	82	49
One year but under five years in present dwelling	30	23
Single-family cottages	80	71
Single-family houses	79	19
Flats	36	22

Source: Interview Analysis

Table 17.7

Residence of Twenty Years or Longer in Present Dwelling: Sunderland CB Slum-Clearance Programme 1965–70

Sub-sample	Informants who have lived in present dwelling for twenty years or longer per cent	Number of families in the sub-sample (=100 per cent)
1965–70 Programme	39	126
Mature single-person and two-person families	65	20
Old single-person and two-person families	62	34
Adult large families	46	24
Young small families	10	31
Young large families	7	14
Southwick (Wayman Street) area	61	23
Millfield (Booth Street) area	54	13
Elsewhere	35	20
Millfield (Deptford Road) area	33	48
Hendon	23	22

Source: Interview Analysis

Table 17.8

Households Containing At Least One Person Aged 65 or Older: Sunderland CB Slum-Clearance Programme 1965–70

Sub-sample	Households containing at least one person 65 or older per cent	Number in the sub-sample (=100 per cent)
1965–70 Programme	29	126
Southwick (Wayman Street) area	39	23
Millfield (Booth Street) area	38	13
Elsewhere	35	20
Millfield (Deptford Road) area	25	48
Hendon	18	22
Owner-occupiers	36	42
Tenants of private landlords	26	73

Source: Interview Analysis

Table 17.9

Households Containing No Children Aged 0–4 Years Old: Sunderland CB Slum-Clearance Programme 1965–70

Sub-sample	Families containing no children 0–4 per cent	Number of families in the sub-sample (=100 per cent)
1965–70 Programme	72	126
Southwick (Wayman Street) area	91	23
Millfield (Booth Street) area	85	13
Millfield (Deptford Road) area	69	48
Elsewhere	65	20
Hendon	55	22
Single-family cottages	77	71
Single-family houses	74	19
Flats	50	22

Source: Interview Analysis

Table 17.10

Households Containing No Children Aged 5–15 Years Old: Sunderland CB Slum-Clearance Programme 1965–70

Sub-sample	Families containing no children 5–15 per cent	Number of families in the sub-sample (=100 per cent)
1965–70 Programme	75	125
Millfield (Booth Street) area	92	13
Southwick (Wayman Street) area	83	23
Elsewhere	79	19
Millfield (Deptford Road) area	71	48
Hendon	64	22
Tenants of private landlords	81	72
Owner-occupiers	67	42

Source: Interview Analysis

Table 17.11

Properties Expected to be Compulsory Acquired at Site Value Only: Sunderland CB Slum-Clearance Programme 1965–70

Area	Estimated number of unfit houses	Estimated number of fit houses	Percentage of houses to be acquired at site value only
Rosalie Terrace	58	0	100
Gladstone Street	39	0	100
Ocean Road	38	0	100
Harold Street	27	0	100
Eden Street (Newcastle Road)	10	0	100
Sans Street South	7	0	100
Thompson Street	129	1	99
Millfield (Booth Street) area	357	4	99
Southwick (Wayman Street) area	285	6	98
Southwick (Edward Burdis Str.)	91	2	98
Millfield (Deptford Road) area	626	62	91
Randolph Street	139	15	90
Millfield (Catherine Street W.)	91	12	88
Barrack Street	17	10	63
Total 1965–70 Programme	1943	113	94

Source: Sunderland CB, *Second Five Year Slum-Clearance Programme 1965–70*, 19 February 1965

SECTION V
The Decision to Demolish

CHAPTER 18

THE INTERESTS OF THE RESIDENTS IN THE SLUM CLEARANCE AREAS

The consumer's attitude to moving is the result of comparing the net gains and losses incurred by remaining in one place with the net gains and losses he expects to incur in the destination of the move. Wilkinson and Merry argue that the chief gains and losses likely to be considered by prospective movers are household amenities, family ties, local social ties and local environmental amenities. The relative importance of these sets of factors is likely to vary according to the needs and expectations of the individual family as determined by its composition, age structure and income. Within this framework, which the SHN study shares, the apparently conflicting experiences of slum-clearance programmes in, for example, Glasgow,[1] Liverpool,[2] and Leeds 'would all seem to be reconcilable'.[3]

Families (or, more strictly, whoever makes the decisions in families) vary in the precise list of items which they include on their list of housing objectives. As housing objectives are numerous and diverse, in exercising its preferences the family must also weigh and choose between the items on the list, and families differ also, therefore, in their systems of value. At least as important, however, are the differences between families in their underlying attitudes to their value systems. Does the family seek to maximize one or other of its housing satisfactions, even if the effort carries serious risks of complete failure? Or does the family look for some level of all-round satisfaction which is 'good enough over the long term'—a strategy of decision-making described by Simon as 'satisficing'.[4]

Or does it look, alternatively, for security, and thus seek to make the most unfavourable outcome of its housing decisions as acceptable as it can? Such a family would want the worst possible consequences of its decision-making strategy to be better than the worst consequences of other possible strategies— it minimizes maximum gains, perhaps, but (what is more important) it minimizes maximum losses.[5]

The study of the areas covered by the 1965–70 slum-clearance programme in Sunderland has shown that (with the exception of Hendon residents and families with young children), in their own terms, large minorities and in many instances substantial majorities of the families believe that on balance they would lose by being rehoused. The question therefore arises, on what grounds are their objections to be over-ridden? Are they to be unwillingly rehoused because that is the requirement of the law which officials have to implement, as their duty, without any conscious regard to its purposes in terms of human betterment? Is the justification, alternatively, that the opponents of rehousing are simply mistaken in their comparison of their present accommodation with the accommodation they are likely to be offered? Or is the justification of compulsory rehousing to be found in the benefits which will be reaped by other members of the community, either in the slum-clearance areas or elsewhere in the town, region or country?

The statutory basis of the 1965–70 programme was the same as that of the 1960–5 programme, namely, the Housing Act 1957. In February 1965 the MHLG asked the local authority to submit, by the end of April 1965, its 1965–70 slum-clearance programme in compliance with this legislation. The principal part in the preparation of all previous programmes had been taken by the public health inspectorate, and to some extent areas had been chosen by the residents themselves, in the sense that the first adumbration of a slum-clearance programme depended upon the frequency of complaints to the public health department about defective property. Internal inspections by district inspectors then provided data for a final decision on the boundaries of slum-clearance areas.

In 1965 Hendon still produced such complaints. This was not the case with any other extensive area. The public health inspectorate, furthermore, was short-staffed at this time. The establishment of district inspectors for a place as large as Sunderland might be expected to be in the region of ten. At the time of the MHLG's request there were two; to make matters worse, the section with particular responsibility for slum-clearance had recently lost key personnel. As a result interview responses included such statements as: 'I quite confess that I have not seen the inside of many of these properties'; 'Sheer guesswork I'm afraid'; 'The Minister approved the Peacock Street West CPO, the areas for 1965–70 were about this standard when judged roughly from the outside'.[6]

Such an accumulation of difficulties led the department to seek the assistance of the town planners. This profession has been under considerable attack. 'A large part of the trouble is that during the last fifteen years of relative inactivity in planning the muscular tone of discourse about planning has slackened intolerably. . . . We are now in a situation in which almost any planning theory, however crackpot, can gain support if advocated sufficiently loudly . . . the resources and the effects on human happiness involved are too great for it to be allowed to be carried on in a state of mental intoxication masquerading as imaginativeness.'[7] It is widely recognised, furthermore, that research has been lacking. 'All these factors point to the critical importance of increasing research effort into the planning field. There will need to be a much better understanding of the determinants of urban development and urban form and a much greater knowledge of the needs and aspirations of the community.'[8] It is therefore necessary to examine carefully the contribution of the town planning profession to the development of the 1965–70 slum-clearance programme in Sunderland.

In practical terms the procedure was as follows. All houses with a 'life' of under five years were identified from age and condition maps. The life of these buildings had been estimated on an 'intuitive' basis. No written criteria had been prepared, and the classification of each particular dwelling was the result of a visual external inspection, frequently from a moving vehicle, by personnel with little formal training in the relevant housing legislation and with only a layman's knowledge of building materials and structures.[9] The 1965–70 house-building pro-gramme was then examined and on the assumption that one-half of the new houses ought to be available for slum-clearance families, a further contribution of slum houses was made from the houses with a life of from five to ten years 'to make the numbers up'.[10]

Partly as a result of the SHN study, partly as a result of a change of control of the local council, door-to-door surveys were undertaken by the local authority. Properties were not entered or inspected – the intention to do either was publicly disclaimed. The survey was again carried out by town-planning and some public health staff. 'It will take the form of personal interviews . . . *and will not involve the inspection of the properties.*' The questionnaire covered only the following points: (i) the age and sex of members of the household; (ii) the number of rooms in the dwelling; (iii) whether there was a bath and a separate bathroom; (iv) whether there was a wash-basin; (v) whether there was hot and cold water on tap at the bath and wash-handbasin and (vi) whether the w.c. was inside or outside the dwelling. Interviews were typically completed in under two minutes.[11] According to the Chairman of the Town Planning Committee this survey was intended to provide guidance on the reassessment of the slum-clearance programme.[12] It is difficult to see, however, that this investigation could provide a set of data about slum-clearance or its legal justification. Not one of the items bears directly upon the compulsory powers of slum-clearance legislation. They are all related, rather, to Improvement Grant measures. Except for landlords when certain conditions are met under the Housing Act 1964, the use of Improvement Grants is voluntary.

The question of the internal water closet can be briefly examined as characteristic of the interplay of legal provision, professional beliefs and consumer preference. 'No indoor water closet' began as a convenient *indicator* of where *areas* of bad housing were to be found. By 1966 the indoor w.c. had found its way into the national sample census as one of the basic household amenities to be enumerated. Because an indoor w.c. is preferred by very many people, especially, of course, when the outdoor toilet was in a yard shared by other families, or when 'outdoors' meant actually in the street, legislation at first permitted local authorities to give a monetary grant towards its provision (1949). Later this grant became a right which the individual could require of the local authority if certain conditions were fulfilled. At the time of the SHN study official attitudes had progressed to the point where, in Sunderland, inter-war council houses were being provided with indoor w.c.s whether or not the tenants preferred their existing outdoor w.c. (A senior official closely concerned with this matter said, 'I don't understand it! When they were outside people wanted them inside. Now that we are bringing them inside they want them outside.') The local authority's questionnaire in the 1965-70 areas asked about the presence of an internal w.c. without asking about preferences. To a remarkable degree there was a failure on the part of the staff concerned to appreciate that legally householders are still free to be without an indoor w.c.[13]

The arbitrariness of town-planning judgments on present and prospective fitness for human habitation is also shown in the dramatic inconsistencies in and reversals of policy. All the stippled areas shown on Diagram 18.A were programmed for re-development within the fifteen years after 1957 i.e. by the end of 1971. In 1965, however, so-called Discretionary Grants were being allowed over much of this area. These can be legally authorised only in respect of properties with an expected 'life' of a further thirty years or more *after* 1965. Residents of cottages programmed for redevelopment within four-and-a-half years were told that this was an official judgment that could not be altered in the near future. But, the official added, '*Looking at it realistically*, a lot of the cottages had lives of up to thirty years'.[14]

What ideology, then, lies behind the 1965-70 slum-clearance decision? At its most benign there is merely agreement with Gordon Cosmo Lang: bad housing conditions work havoc on 'pure home life' and public opinion 'should be restlessly, resistlessly intolerant of so palpable and blatant an evil . . . scarcely any sacrifice, individual or corporate, civic or political, is too great for rolling away the reproach of conditions which to our grandchildren will seem as unbelievable as the facts and figures which confronted Wilberforce in his anti-slavery campaigns a century ago . . . cost what it may to any group or class or fellowship, we must bring it to an end. I do not scruple to say that its continuance in a Christian country is contrary to the Will of God.'[15]

This attitude takes for granted, that is, that demolition is

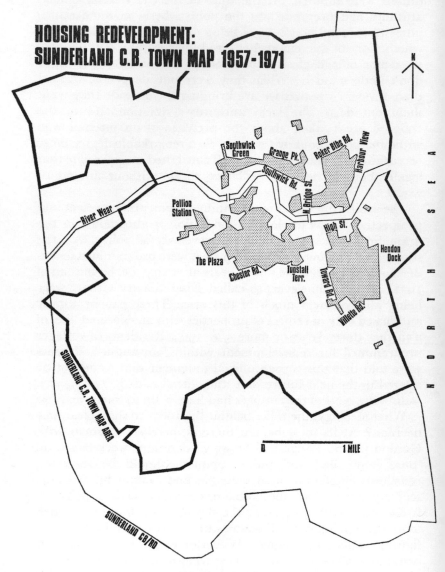

Diagram 18.A

generally desired by the inhabitants of slum-clearance areas and that the only thing which prevents the removal of an evil generally deplored is the public will to do so. That is a generous view which may have been valid in 1928 but which was not valid in Sunderland in 1965.

The data show that conditions in the 1965–70 slum-clearance areas cannot in general be described as baneful. The view expressed by a knowledgeable and sympathetic local government officer that 'for every one where it is a case of hardship, there are thousands that benefit', is not supported by detailed investigation. Another officer, who played an important part in the selection of the 1965–70 slum-clearance areas, categorised the residents in those areas in the following way. Most eager to be rehoused are those who had taken the slum-clearance houses because they wanted a year or two of cheap rent and then a 'free ride' to a council house. Next most eager are those who dislike the house, but who retain their tenancy in order to acquire a council house more quickly than would be the case if they depended upon a straightforward application. Lastly, there are a few who would rather stay, but 'the minority must be over-ruled by the majority'.

These views though factually incorrect, implicitly accept the view that the consumer is rational. The decisions are indeed to be justified because they meet the wishes of the residents. As Dicey says, they are the views of the man who favours government 'by the people in conformity to the broad common sense he attributes to ordinary citizens'.[16]

When the slum-clearance proposals were no longer an MOH's responsibility almost exclusively, however, a new and more powerful attitude appeared. It is to be expected that there will be opposition to slum-clearance proposals. The relative lack of development of 'housing need' among the working classes is a characteristic which has traditionally set them off from the upper classes.[17] A few instances may be found in the SHN survey which give colour to this view:

> This is the downstairs of a Tyneside flat. The whole of the front wall bulged and had to be rebuilt because of the danger to passers-by. There are no modern amenities: the fireplace is an old black range: the tap and the w.c. are outside. But she does not want a council house because, she says, the children on estates are always

fighting, breaking windows and generally misbehaving. Although her neighbour upstairs is haunting the housing department to get a council house, this informant is 'as happy as Chloë'. The living room is filthy.

Many of the houses lower down the street are now vandalised or used for the storage of the shipyards' timber. The cottage is in a deplorable condition. The rooms upstairs with dormer windows and teefalls cannot be used because of the damp, so both husband and wife have to sleep in the living room. The scullery is also very damp and 'the place is over-run with blacklocks and slugs'. The foodstuffs get foisty in the cupboard and often have to be thrown out. There is only one electric point—the television has many yards of flex from the outlet to the set. The family formerly lived in a council house at Hylton Castle. Her husband said that the air did not agree with him and when they had the chance of exchanging the council tenancy for this cottage they did so. It is nearer to the husband's work.

As old Hammond said in *News from Nowhere*, 'The great difficulty was that the once-poor had such a feeble conception of the real pleasure of life: so to say, they did not ask enough, did not know how to ask enough, from the new state of things'.[18] The families which oppose slum-clearance do so because they are incompetent to assess their own best interests; they have been reduced to such a pitiful and skinny existence that they scarcely know how to form a desire for any life better than that which they now endure.[19]

In interviewing individuals concerned with the slum-clearance decision a yet more radical view was elaborated. The empirical findings of the SHN study might, indeed, suggest that the opponents of slum-clearance are reaching rational decisions in the light of their own circumstances and value preferences. The value preferences themselves are inadmissible. It is true that from the point of view of the sociologist the most impressive aspect of modern society is the extent to which change rather than stability is normal. The rise of science and its associated technologies has become a guarantee of continuous social transformations with unprecedented consequences for each new generation.[20] There is also some evidence that to some degree, not yet carefully investigated, certain groups in certain kinds of poorer urban areas are undemanding and unaspiring.[21]

The protective role of the well-established locality is regarded with concern by some as inhibiting social mobility. Particular attention has been paid to this possibility by a group of social researchers at Liverpool.[22]

> It is apparent in our society, that life in a decaying area, especially a residual one, may be limited in the range of experiences and opportunities in which the individual may reasonably hope to share. Applications of decision theory to the study of social groups or strata have imputed the short-run hedonistic pattern of decision making, in which explicit future expectations play a negligible role, to the lower working classes in general, and the poorer urban classes in particular. This is a 'style of life', a narrowness of horizon, that is consciously or unconsciously experienced by many in areas such as these. The matrilocal structure, typical of the residual areas, has been seen as tending to reinforce this situation by inhibiting desires to break away. This state of affairs, more subtle and elusive of definition than the incidence of individual social phenomena, is regarded by some as *one of the most disquieting aspects of life in these areas*, being in violation of the principles currently accepted in our society, of social mobility and equality of opportunity. (Emphasis added.)[23]

Such researchers, however, although they recognise the intensely dynamic nature of modern society and may both personally disapprove of this value orientation and believe that it is disappearing under modern conditions rarely, if ever, recommend coercive measures in order to hasten its destruction. Still less would it be expected that they would recommend compulsory rehousing as the chosen instrument of such changes.[24]

The narrowness of the empirical base, however, and the dubiety of its political, social and moral basis have not prevented informants from advocating this policy. The desire to remain at a lower level of housing consumption than is technically possible reveals a 'cosy' outlook on life and this is inappropriate under modern conditions. In so far as it deals rudely with those who 'confine their voyages to the familiar creeks and havens, and never willingly forsake the shelter of the shore'[25] slum clearance fulfils a valuable function in ridding the community of backward-looking, sluggish elements.

Not only technical decisions but also moral judgments are properly in the hands of a skilled class of administrative officials and the destiny of slum-clearance families is to be decisively moulded, not by their own fallible judgment, but according to 'the intuitiveness of rare great minds'[26] and not according to their own scheme of morality but according to the edicts of an enlightened profession.

In arriving at a decision about the replacement of dwellings some informants give little weight to the likes and dislikes of the residents. Their approach is comprehensive, activist and progressive:

> All houses built before 1914 can and ought to be cleared in the next ten years. Their lay-out is obsolete; their yards are too small; they are badly orientated; there is bad ventilation within the house; and the sun-lighting is inadequate. None of these things is remediable. In America they reckon the life of a house as forty years. We ought to have cheap plastic houses that we can throw away after twenty years. Good God! We will be on the moon in 2000 and these houses were built when Charles Dickens was writing his novels.

The unambiguous desire is to encourage rapid deterioration and hasten the day of demolition; giving a 'life' to the dwelling of five, or ten years or fifteen years, or condemning it, is consciously conceived as a way of achieving this end. The fact that the official statistics are unreliable, that Welwyn Garden City is shown to have the same proportion of unfit houses as Stoke Newington; Cheltenham the same proportion as Swindon; Carshalton the same proportion as St. Pancras; and Trowbridge more slums than the Rhondda, is, for them, not an argument for caution. Their conclusion is that of the Town and Country Planning Association, that 'the figures of the number of unfit houses now standing is misleading. In fact, the assessment was made in 1954–5 on a standard which was not uniform. *The only sort of estimate which can therefore be reasonably made would be one which was made recently on the highest standards used by local authorities in the 1954–5 survey*'.[27] If this were done, the number of unfit houses would be more than doubled.

Merely to identify 'the inarticulate major premises' of the slum-area decision makers seems to be also an exposure of their weaknesses. The replacement of existing dwellings is a matter, however, which cannot be decided exclusively in terms of the residents. Some planners, when challenged on the question of

330

the neglect of the consumer, answer that 'controls are essential to protect the consumer from his neighbour, and his neighbour from him. The basic objective of town planning is to ensure the best use of land and property in the interest of the community, i.e. in the interest of the consumers *collectively*.'[28] It is necessary, therefore, to examine those interests which may be served by demolition, even where demolition is clearly admitted to damage the welfare of the residents themselves.

NOTES TO CHAPTER 18

1 Tom Brennan, *Reshaping a City*, Glasgow 1959.
2 C. Vereker and J. B. Mays, *Urban Redevelopment and Social Change*, Liverpool 1961.
3 R. Wilkinson and D. M. Merry, 'A Statistical Analysis of Attitudes to Moving' [Leeds], *Urban Studies*, May 1965.
4 Herbert A. Simon, *Administrative Behaviour* (1945), Second Edition, New York 1960, p. xxv.
5 For another recent study of the 'rationality' of superficially stupid and irrational decisions, see Michael Lipton's report on the agricultural strategies of peasants in the Indian village of Kavathe: *Assessing Economic Performance*, London 1968.
6 The observer's field-notes record that at a public meeting in November 1967 the Chairman of the Town Planning Committee stated that, because of the shortage of staff *inspections of properties could not be expected to precede the preparation of the slum-clearance programme;* the necessary inspection could only take place subsequently. A report of the meeting appeared in the *Sunderland Echo*, 16 November 1967.
7 Lewis B. Keeble, 'Presidential Address to the Town Planning Institute, 1965', *Journal of the Town Planning Institute*, November 1965.
8 Planning Advisory Group, *The Future of Development Plans*, HMSO 1965, p. 53.
9 This refers to, for example, inspections by someone in the final year of a three-year part-time evening town-planning certificate course. The author himself holds the same certificate and is therefore familiar with the content of the training.
10 The calculations may be found in Sunderland CB, *Second five-year slum clearance programme: 1965–70*, February 1965.
11 *Sunderland Echo*, 10 February 1968. (Emphasis added.)
12 *Sunderland Echo*, 1 February 1968 and 23 March 1968.
13 In Newcastle powers have been seriously sought to compel all owner-occupiers, tenants and landlords not only to provide an internal toilet, but also one with a low-level cistern! See Jon Gower Davies, *The Evangelical Bureaucrat* (forthcoming).

14 *Sunderland Echo*, 8 June 1967. (Emphasis added.) For a discussion of the development of and problems raised by executive discretion and the tension between 'the rule of law' (in Dicey's sense) and the administrative requirements of universal and comprehensive state welfare services, see Kathleen M. Bell, *Tribunals in the Social Services*, London 1969.

15 Introduction to B. S. Townroe, *The Slum Problem*, London 1928, p. ix. Lang was consecrated Archbishop of Canterbury in 1928.

16 A. V. Dicey, *Law and Public Opinion in England*, London 1926, p. lxxvi.

17 Maurice Halbwachs, *La Classe Ouvriere et les Niveaux de Vie*, Paris 1913, pp. 450–51.

18 William Morris, *News from Nowhere* (1890), Nelson's Classics Edition, p. 179.

19 *Idem.*, 'How I Became a Socialist', *Nonesuch Morris*, p. 659.

20 A. H. Halsey, 'The Sociology of Education', in *Sociology: An Introduction*, edited by Neil J. Smelser, London 1967, p. 389.

21 Norman Dennis, Clifford Slaughter and Fernando Henriques, *Coal is Our Life*, London 1956.

22 C. Vereker and John Barron Mays, *Urban Redevelopment and Social Change*, Liverpool 1961, pp. 118, 19.

23 Elizabeth Gittus, 'Sociological Aspects of Urban Decay', in John Parry Lewis and Franklin Medhurst, *Urban Decay*, Civic Trust for the North West (forthcoming).
    The decision theory referred to is J. M. Beshers, *Urban Social Structure*, Glencoe 1962, especially p. 31.

24 Colin Rosser and Christopher Harris, *The Family and Social Change* [Swansea], London 1965, p. 298.

25 C. F. G. Masterman, *The Condition of England*, London 1909, p. 55.

26 Alfredo Rocco, 'The Political Doctrine of Fascism', *Readings on Fascism and National Socialism*, Alan Swallow, Denver, Colorado, no date, p. 37. A startlingly clear revelation of official attitudes to consumer preferences is to be found in, J. E. Barlow and G. I. Ramsdale, 'Balanced Population —An Experiment at Silksworth Overspill Township for Sunderland', *Journal of The Town Planning Institute*, July 1966. It is interesting to see, incidentally, the choice of the term 'township', reminiscent of the 'decent little ghettoes' of Sophiatown and Mufakose.

27 TCPA, *Housing in Britain*, London 1964. (Emphasis added.)

28 R. S. McConnell, Review of *Town Planning: The Consumers' Environment* in *The Journal of the Town Planning Institute*, February 1966.

CHAPTER 19

THE INTERESTS OF THE
COMMUNITY

Four out of every ten families living in the 1965–70 clearance areas were very satisfied with their present living conditions; in some areas the proportion was as high as six out of every ten. Over half of the old single- and two-person families did not expect to be better off in a council dwelling; seven out of ten did not expect to be better off in a council district. Two out of every three owner-occupiers were not in favour of demolition.

What arguments can be marshalled to justify the use of the coercive powers of the state in order to rehouse them? The survey data of the SHN study does not support the view that officials are more capable than the families themselves of making valid assessments of a family's housing needs and circumstances. On the contrary, Jacob Burckhardt's strictures on the 'terribles simplificateurs' seem to apply to housing with particular force. The utterances of the officials on behalf of such families tend to be composed of a jumble of dry and contradictory formulas, assembled according to the needs of the moment and the demands of professional orthodoxy.

Is it possible to argue, however, that the interests of these large minorities or actual majorities must be subordinated to the interests of other people in the community–that their losses are outweighed by benefits accruing to other families?

Historically the welfare of the wider community has been a matter of public health. Directly, slum areas were centres of epidemic disease. Indirectly all families in the community had to bear the cost of attending to tubercular cases, bronchial cases and sufferers from other diseases which originate in or are exacerbated by slum conditions. 'The fear of epidemics and consequent higher rates has made the before-all-things money-collecting Briton become willing that the human machine that makes his money should be better housed.'[1] It had been noticed, too, that as well as disease, crime and vice accumulated in the labyrinths of the slums. 'The police and the priest were as unable to penetrate as the sunshine.'[2]

> In these horrid dens the most abandoned characters of the city are collected, and from thence they nightly issue to pour upon the town every species of crime and abomination.[3]

Clearly these traditional justifications for coercion have lost all force. The same may be said about the argument that, because high density central development was too favourable to revolutionary activity, the packed centres of our towns must be emptied and their under-privileged populations dispersed in suburban estates. Town planning was at one time, but is no longer, conceived of as 'the third alternative' to the old order or to Bolshevism.[4]

The 'community' argument which has tended to replace 'the third alternative' is that of the importance of aesthetics.[5] The nineteenth-century industrial town produced nothing beautiful. As an early and still influential exponent of planning ideas put it, it was nothing but 'a spreading sore, swallowing up with it loathsomeness field and wood and heath without mercy and without hope'.[6] London and the great cities were 'mere masses of sordidness, filth and squalor'.

> Forget six counties overhung with smoke,
> Forget the snorting steam and piston stroke,
> Forget the spreading of the hideous town,
> Think rather of the packhorse on the down,
> And dream of London, small and white and clean,
> The clear Thames bordered by its gardens green.[7]

The values which would justify coercion in the interests of visual appearance are not confined, of course, to any particular profession. This orientation is very clearly that of many laymen:

> All these rights extend beyond the bounds of Millfield. Millfield is a disgrace, a blot, a decaying, rotting canker and the rest

334

of the proud natives of Sunderland have equal claim in their desire to see all such areas completely renewed as quickly as possible.[8]

It is extremely doubtful, however, whether the exponents of this viewpoint, trained or untrained, pay sufficient attention to the nature, extent and intensity of the losses suffered by the unwillingly rehoused families on the one hand, and on the other the nature, extent and intensity of the aesthetic benefits (if any) derived from demolition and replacement.[9]

Rapid population growth combined with low residential densities in certain areas is another possible argument for compulsory replacement of property. 'As some members of the household die off, as grown-up children move away, the remaining members do not move into smaller accommodation. They stay in the old buildings, sometimes rattling round like peas in a bucket.'[10] In an expanding town (it might be argued) low densities in in-town areas place too heavy a burden upon the peripheral population.

Given the particular population history and prospects of Sunderland, however, this argument has little validity: the town is experiencing a net loss of population, not an increase in population. Furthermore, if the space argument were at all central to the case for replacement, it would have to be shown that it was equitable to place the whole burden of saving scarce space upon one section of the population. Obviously, in a town such as Sunderland there is very low density development in certain centrally located residential areas. If powers existed to acquire, for example, The Cedars, a large (at present inviolate) area would be made available at the cost of disturbing relatively few families.

In terms of the benefits which citizens outside the proposed 1965–70 clearance areas could be expected to derive from demolition it is difficult, then, to find cogent arguments for creating a class of *Ausgewiesene*.[11] Is compulsory eviction and rehousing justified by the interests of those suffering from poor housing conditions within the proposed clearance areas? Given certain of the cultural postulates of our society, most people, perhaps, would be inclined to answer this question partly on the basis of fact. They would especially want to know the numbers involved on the one side or the other. It is clear that

335

some of those who were principally connected with the slum-clearance recommendations believe implicitly that the number of reluctant movers is negligible. The example quoted above (p. 327) was given in the following context:

> It is not a myth that estates kill old people. We know it is going to happen I quite accept it. As we go round, an old lady will say, 'It'll take two years? Well, it doesn't matter to me, I'll be underneath by then.' We had cases of suicide: one man threw himself off the bridge over the Deptford clearance. *But for every one where it is a case of hardship, there are thousands that benefit.* (Emphasis added.)

The SHN data throw the strongest doubt upon the factual content of statements which imply that only a small minority are opposed to eviction: the problem is not one of large majorities pitted against a negligible few who are comfortably and well housed or who are simply obstructive, selfish and misguided. Overall, those wanting to be rehoused outnumber those who want to retain their present homes: but the latter are not overwhelmingly outnumbered and in some areas and parts of areas the position is reversed. Under these conditions policies which have been formulated prior to surveys of the circumstances and preferences of the consumer, and which recommend clearance without discrimination between sub-areas and different dwellings cannot, *prima facie*, be justified by using the concept of 'minority' and 'majority'.

It is necessary to consider, finally, one particular group of beneficiaries from slum-clearance policies–the policy makers themselves. Sociologically this has been described as the problem of 'the persistence of aggregates'. Once an organisation has been brought into existence, the interests of its members in the income, power and prestige which are derived from their position in it will ensure that even when its original function becomes emasculated it will continue in existence. In the particular case of Sunderland, where since the end of the second world war more houses per thousand families[12] have been built than in any other town of comparable size (Table 19.1), large organisations have been built up in order to meet the town's housing needs. As de Tocqueville pointed out, one danger of public provision is that officials might come to act more and more 'as if they thought themselves responsible for the actions and private condition of their subjects' and, what disturbed him even more, that private individuals would grow more and more to look upon the supreme power in the same light, to see themselves as a flock of timid and industrious animals of which the government is the shepherd.[13] Following de Tocqueville many writers have become preoccupied with the question of the rule of law in modern society.[14] The rule of law can be maintained if officials are prevented from usurping political and legislative functions. Officials, however, whatever their personal qualities, are impelled by the requirements of their social position to modify right-granting laws in such a way as to facilitate the work of their departments.[15]

The tendency for departments to seek large resources in order to carry out what they define as their functions and to define their functions in such a way as to command large resources has meant that insufficient attention has been paid to the effects of their activities. As Weber said, the position can easily arise in which the question can no longer be asked, ought a public department to carry out this particular task? but only, given that this will be carried out by a public depart-ment, how can we ensure that it will be carried out humanely?

> The passion for bureaucracy is enough to drive one to despair. It is as if we were deliberately to become men who need order and nothing but order. That the whole world should know no men but these: it is in such an evolution that we are already caught up, the great question is, therefore, not how we can promote and hasten it, but what can we oppose to this machinery in order to keep a portion of mankind free from this parcelling out of his soul, from the supreme mastery of the bureaucratic way of life.[16]

The Interests of Posterity

It may be that the case for demolition depends more upon the welfare of posterity than upon the way it affects the present generation.

One argument has not been used by those responsible for the 1965–70 proposals but it needs to be considered. Not only the physical health but also the preparation of the child for his place in adult society is affected by housing conditions. This process takes place in many different contexts: the juvenile gang, the school, the church, as well as in the family itself. Some societies favour the informal experiences of the extended kin group and the neighbourhood as means of socialising the child. Our society, by contrast, places a great deal of emphasis on providing more or less similar experiences for all children within the framework of official institutions, principally the school.

The effectiveness of these official agencies is lessened if alternative value patterns are presented to the child in his home and in his locality. It is therefore important that each family should be open exclusively to the official agencies of social control and socialisation and that the child should not be contaminated by his family's participation in a local sub-culture. Lack of contact with other people in the same locality shakes the child and the parent loose from local standards of achievement and aspiration and this has the important functional consequence of aiding social mobility. In this way all potential talent is available for recruitment to the demanding roles of a complex society, without hindrance from local example and parochial culture. These social objectives are obviously incompatible with the necessity to share a dwelling with another family. They are also incompatible with settled, homogeneous neighbourhoods.

Two questions arise. The first is a question of value and it will be put without being answered: if families are in shared dwellings and if families are ensconced in a sub-culture which fails to embrace whole-heartedly the dominant values of our society, is it desirable that they should be 'shaken free' in the interests of the children?

Second, the question of fact: how many families are in shared dwellings and how many children are affected by the slum-clearance proposals? Seventy-one per cent of all the families in the 1965–70 programme are in single-family occupation of either a house or a single-storied Sunderland cottage. Of those not in single-family occupation fifty-six per cent are in the Hendon district, which contributes only 17 per cent of all families in the 1965–70 programme. While only two of the families in the Hendon sub-sample (n = 22) and only six of the families in 'slum-clearance areas elsewhere' (n = 20) are in single-family occupation, single-family occupation is almost universal in the other areas. Where families do share their dwelling with one or more families the moral problem raised by the cultural priorities of our society in the field of education do not arise, because the families themselves generally desire to be rehoused for many reasons unconnected with this. Similarly, in those areas where the situation is not one of shared dwellings but rather of a solidified pattern of adjustment, the facts suggest that the moral and social problem under discussion at this point does not arise in a sharp form. Over one-quarter (27 per cent) of the families in the total 1965–70 sample were classified as 'old single- and two-person households', 16 per cent were classified as 'mature single- and two-person households', and a further 19 per cent were classified as 'adult large households'; all these family types are beyond the stage at which child-rearing is part of their normal functioning.

One argument which features 'the benefit of posterity' is particularly popular with some town planners. They argue that the quality of a town's housing stock is an important part of its 'image' and the image of a town in this sense influences to a significant degree the location decisions of industrialists. An extreme version maintains that the very fact of demolition and replacement has a tonic effect upon economic and social structure:

> It is in the climate of rapid reconstruction and expansion that a city prospers and attracts the most imaginative and courageous minds. This is seen time and time again after the blanket destruction of cities in war. The more demanding the challenge the more vigorous the response to reconstruct. The Victorian industrial terraces and decay are there but disappearing daily. This city [Teesside] bids fair to change the image of an industrial nation and of showing that an industrial city of the twenty-first century, with its aesthetic grace of stacks and towers breaking the skyline, can be as beautiful as anything our medieval forefathers built.[17]

It may be that these intuitions are sound. It may be that factually they would be supported by research findings and that the moral implications would not prove to be problematical. Further comment would be premature as research on the hypothesis underlying such statements has not been undertaken nor have the implications in terms of political and social philosophy been explored. Superficially, however, it would seem difficult to justify clearance proposals, as they would affect specific individuals in the here-and-now, by appealing to benefits so indefinite and diffuse.

The appeal to the future also takes the following form. 'I acknowledge that people today find these houses quite pleasant and that they don't realise that they are outworn. They want a television set rather than pay more rent for their houses. I sometimes think that they would be better off if they lived in their motor cars.'[18] Such houses must be cleared 'on the postulate of rising housing standards'. They are not deficient in structure but 'society does not want such houses any more'.[19] At 1955 values the national annual income per head was £250; in 1965 it was £325; if the National Plan[20] assumption is accepted, that the economy will grow at a rate of four per cent per annum, then the figure will be £1,000 per head by the year 2000. In 1962 the length of the average working week was 47 hours; by the year 2000 the average working week will be 30 hours. In 1953 there were 3,500,000 car owners; by the year 2000 there will be 30 million car owners.[21]

When these changes come about it is predicted that a type of house will be required different from those which at present exist.[22] A similar argument is found in The Deeplish Study. Clearances now, even against opposition, are necessary because of what might happen in the future:

> As old people, used to low standards, die off, the houses will be acceptable only to the poor. Those who have acquired more wealth and possessions will move out or not take houses in the area, which will come to be inhabited exclusively by the poor and the old.[23]

This argument and the practical consequences of basing policies upon them are fully dealt with elsewhere.[24] Briefly, however, it may be said that, on the side of fact, it would be hazardous to prepare now for a degree of material prosperity that may look probable at one stage but improbable a few years later. It would also seem inappropriate to impose on sections of the population which actually receive only low wages or state pensions standards which have been devised because national averages are high and rising. On the side of value, how far is it equitable to impose on present day population standards which may be consonant with the conditions of some future time, but which are obviously and admittedly not suitable for present needs and circumstances? This argument, that a higher standard of housing consumption must be forced on recalcitrant families because in the future such higher standards will be universally and willingly accepted if expected social changes take place, would, it seems, need to be worked out in more detail before it could be completely understood and accepted.

Posterity, finally (it is argued), is the gainer from 'comprehensive' redevelopment rather than redevelopment which tinkers with the problem in a piecemeal manner. Comprehensive, here, means redevelopment on a scale large enough to ensure that unit cost is low and that it can be carried out by building firms suited to reconstruction rather than renovation,[25] that utilities (sewers etc.) are provided at an optimal level, that the roads form an efficient pattern of movement and pedestrian safety and that neighbourhood amenities such as shops, public houses and community buildings can be suitably located in sufficient numbers.

Although comprehensive is a word often heard, there are several reasons for treating it with circumspection. There is little evidence, in the first place, that consideration has been given to establishing the boundaries of the slum-clearance areas with these objectives in mind. Secondly (and this raises a more important and general point) what does comprehensive mean when used in this connection? It means large enough to achieve the few objectives enumerated above. But the social and personal ends which are pursued and secured in a viable locality are infinitely more numerous than those which feature in comprehensive development plans. Experience has shown that great losses of benefits frequently accompany gains made from a comprehensive approach. 'They make a wilderness and call it comprehensive redevelopment.'[26] In order to provide, for example, retailing facilities at convenient centres the fabric built up over generations – of particular shops, paying particular (low) rents,[27] providing particular ranges of goods, not just a pork butcher, but a pork butcher supplying favourite polonies, not just a baker, but a baker supplying special types of bread and cakes for the known demand in the neighbourhood, shopkeepers who are patient and kind to the second and third generation buying their penny novelties, all perhaps slightly comical to the outsider but of not negligible importance for the families in the areas under threat of clearance–may be destroyed in the name of comprehensiveness. The same applies to a life lived among mutually acceptable and congenial neighbours and to patterns of mutual aid between relatives.

Comprehensiveness, in this light, may be recognised as a misnomer. It becomes almost a synonym for superficiality; for the truly comprehensive approach would necessarily take into consideration all the important interests affected and not just a handful of them.

NOTES TO CHAPTER 19

1 R. Williams, *The People The Nation's Wealth*, London 1895.
2 Marian Bowley, *Housing and the State*, London 1945, p. 2.
3 S. Laing, *National Distress: It's Causes and Remedies*, London 1844, p. 11.
4 'Towards the Third Alternative', *Sociological Review*, XI, 1, 1919.
5 For a discussion of the historical roots of this emphasis, see William Ashworth, *The Genesis of Modern British Town Planning*, London 1954, p. 194.
6 William Morris, 'Art and Socialism' (1884) in *Architecture, Industry and Wealth*, London 1902.
7 Morris, *The Earthly Paradise*.
8 *Sunderland Echo*, 23 November 1967.
9 It must be recognised, however, that this is a problem of social value and it is quite possible to take the view that quite large losses elsewhere are not too high a price to pay for even small gains in appearance. Such a judgment, indeed, has been commonly made wherever totalitarian tendencies have gained an upper hand, as in Renaissance Europe, Haussmann's Paris and in Mussolini's Italy.
10 Norman Macrae, *To Let*, pp. 28–30.
11 Migrants who have been 'shown the door', as distinct from migrants fleeing for their liberty or their lives, *Fluechtlinge*.
12 New houses built 1 April 1945–30 June 1964 per thousand families (private households 1961).
13 Alexis de Tocqueville, *Democracy in America* (1835), The World's Classics, London 1946.
14 'The interests of the community' as a reason for exercising executive coercion, especially in so far as it bears on the problems of adjudication in disputes between private citizens and public authorities are discussed in, for example, the Report of the Committee on Ministers' Powers (Cmd. 4060, HMSO 1932 ('The Donoughmore Report')) and in the Report of the Committee on Administrative Tribunals and Enquiries (Cmnd. 218, HMSO 1957 ('The Franks Report')). The Donoughmore Report

sought to distinguish 'judicial' issues (p. 74) from issues concerning 'what it is in the public interest to do' (p. 114), and stressed the importance in judicial issues of unimpeded access to the ordinary courts (pp. 113–14). Twenty-six years later, in considering very much the same problems (though in a vastly changed context of state welfare provision), the Franks committee's terms of reference restricted it to a study of the constitution and working of tribunals and inquiries and it did not consider the role of the courts at all. Tribunals were recommended where the 'judicial' element was strong. Inquiries with Ministerial decision were recommended where it was desirable 'to preserve flexibility of decision *in the pursuance of public policy*' (para. 31). (Emphasis added.) It is interesting to see, therefore, that in disputes between the householder and the local authority arising from slum-clearance proposals adjudication is by inquiry and Ministerial decision and not by tribunal, however weak the 'public policy' element may be. (See Kathleen Bell, *op. cit.*)

15 For a full discussion of the attempt by Newcastle CB to extend compulsory purchase powers of Section 4(4) of the Town and Country Planning Act, 1962 ('bad layout and obsolete development') to secure internal improvements to dwellings, and thereby bypass the multitudinous precautions of the Housing Acts, see Jon Gower Davies, *op. cit.*

16 Max Weber, in a debate at the 1909 Convention of the Verein für Sozialpolitik. Quoted in Reinhard Bendix, *Max Weber,: An Intellectual Portrait*, London 1960, p. 464.

17 Franklin Medhurst, 'Visionary City Can Change Image of Industrial North', *The Times*, 20 October 1967.

18 Wilfred Burns, Address to the Northumberland and Newcastle Society, 17 October 1966.

19 Burns, *Ibid.*

20 DEA, *The National Plan*, Cmnd. 2764, HMSO 1965.

21 Burns, *Ibid.*

22 Burns's estimate is that 4,500 dwellings remain which could be cleared under the Housing Act 1957. Using the above argument, however, he estimates that a further 15,000 dwellings ought to be demolished in Newcastle over the next twenty years. Burns, *Ibid.*

23 *Op. cit.*, p. 70.

24 Jon Gower Davies, *The Evangelical Bureaucrat* (forthcoming); see also Davies, 'Pollution by Planning', *Official Architecture and Planning*, 32, 2, June 1969.

25 'The Urge To Knock Down', first leader of *The Times*, 19 April 1967.

26 'The quotation "They made a desert and called it peace" might well have been applied to some of our post-war redevelopment schemes. It is, I think, a reflection on *the immaturity of our techniques of redevelopment* that the phrase "Comprehensive Development Area" is almost becoming an insult.' Colin Jones, 'The Renewal of Areas of Twilight Housing', RIBA Conference, *Living in Britain*, July 1967. (Emphasis added.)

27 Jane Jacobs, *The Death and Life of Great American Cities*, London 1962, Chapter 10.

Table 19.1

Total New Houses Per Thousand Families: Sunderland CB and Comparable Towns

	New houses per thousand families		New houses per thousand families
SUNDERLAND CB	382	*Newcastle upon Tyne	231
Coventry	339	Brighton	230
Southampton	320	*Sheffield	228
Middlesbrough	291	Bristol	222
Swansea	286	Bournemouth	215
*Portsmouth	272	Blackpool	215
Wolverhampton	270	Nottingham	210
Stoke on Trent	260	*Liverpool	207
Cardiff	256	Bradford	197
Plymouth	252	*Manchester	189
Birkenhead	244	Kingston upon Hull	176
Leeds	243	*Birmingham	175
Leicester	240	Bolton	137
Southend on Sea	238	Salford	105

Source: Census 1961, Table 3; and MHLG,
Housing Return, 30 June 1964, Appendix

* County boroughs with over 1,000 local authority dwellings outside the local authority area. These are not included in the above figures.

CHAPTER 20

PUBLIC PARTICIPATION IN THE DECISION-MAKING PROCESS

The interests of the consumer, individually and collectively, played, then, a minor part in the formulation of the 1965–70 slum-clearance proposals. To some extent his interests were considered relevant to the decision, but no attempt was made to ascertain what those interests were: the decision was reached by using an incorrect and outdated stereotype of the slum family, eager and impatient to be granted improved accommodation. To a large extent, however, the consumer's self-perceived interests were regarded as a miscalculation, pernicious to himself and as a datum worthless to the official. The consumer does not know enough about either his own conditions or those he will be offered. Partly, this is a straightforward matter of the consumer's ignorance. Partly it is a matter of the consumer's active preference for what is objectively inferior.

In the light of this neglect of the consumer's point of view it would be expected, perhaps, that the affected parties would make vigorous use of their local councillors, M.P.s, the local planning machinery and so forth, in order to ensure that the decision would be altered so as to take their concerns more seriously into account. The SHN study, indeed, included questions on the topic of citizen participation in the decision-making process. Informants were asked whether they were favourably or unfavourably disposed to the demolition of their dwelling. Those who expressed some degree of disapproval were then asked two further questions: 'Do you expect you will be doing anything about stopping it being demolished?' and 'What do you expect you will do?' The interviewers and the director of the research were soon puzzled by the fact that while many informants expressed strong attachment to their homes and unequivocal opposition to demolition, often in vivid and forceful language, these questions were almost without exception met with something amounting to incomprehension. The impression frequently left was that it would be as meaningful to talk about doing something to prevent the ebb and the flow of the tides.

> I went to the Town Hall about it, but they want it, so that's the end of it. There's nothing more we can do. It seems as if they are stuck on it, they said word had come from London that they had to come down.

> The Corporation takes no notice of the opinion of people like us. They'd ask the directors of Joblings, but not us.

> We wouldn't stand a chance. It's up to them with their own houses to see about it. They wouldn't ask me nothing. I'm just a tenant.

> You could sign a petition, but what's the use? You can't go up against the Law.

These findings are interesting for two reasons. First, when provision is compulsory as distinct from voluntary, 'feed-back' from the consumer or potential consumer is the only method of judging the appropriateness of what is provided. Ford Motors may produce an Edsel, an automobile which theoretically matches the motorist's wishes, both conscious and unconscious. Whether it does so is immediately tested by the 'votes' of the consumers in the market place: the car is either bought or remains unsold in the showrooms. (As a matter of fact, the Edsel was one of the most expensive failures in the history of the automobile industry.) Where consumption is compulsory, however, the market mechanism has been quite deliberately suspended; if public comment is either absent or ignored, what can be the criterion of success? It can only be an abstraction, 'the true interests of the consumer' either in the present or the future or both, as defined by the decision-maker within the framework of the social values to which his profession is committed. Where a profession recognises that its activities are soaked with value judgments and political significance, there might be disagreement with its particular evaluations, but within its own terms its efficiency could be measured. Where the profession touches social values at every point, however, and yet is sociologically and politically naïve, the reaction of 'the toad beneath the harrow' is its only guide.[1]

The second reason for interest in the SHN findings on the lack of confidence of slum-clearance families in their own effectiveness is the fact that our society is partly committed to a democratic ideology. Not only is public participation required for the sake of efficiency, in order to monitor the items involved in compulsory consumption; democracy elevates it to the position of a virtue in its own right and in some degree fundamental to the culture of the nation. The failure of the planning system to secure public involvement has been recently recognised as a defect to be remedied. The group commissioned to advise the government on the future of development plans begin their report with the words: 'We have approached the review of the planning system with the following as *our main objectives*: to ensure that the planning system serves its purpose satisfactorily both as an instrument of planning policy and *as a means of public participation in the planning process.*'[2] Whether some measure of democracy in one form or another is the appropriate form of social organisation for a large, complex society, or for all or most of the organisations within it, is a question not raised here. What is under discussion is how large a part the consumer should play in those particular decisions which affect his own home. Nor is the discussion about the consumer or the home in the abstract, but consumers with the range of material and mental resources actually to be found in particular homes, in particular districts, in a particular town, at a particular time. When this becomes the frame of reference, then the claims of the consumers to a predominant role in decisions about their own housing destiny may be strengthened and the case for coercive powers may begin to look more fragile.

It has been shown that the intrusion of the ordinary citizen into housing decisions is regarded in some quarters as at best irrelevant and as likely, indeed, to bring harm to both himself and others. For those who regard autonomy or, failing that,

347

some form of democracy as practically and spiritually valuable, however, the SHN findings are an indication that the problem of public participation is one of Sunderland's outstanding housing needs. It is necessary, therefore, to explain and understand why, when autonomy is threatened, the devices of democratic activity lie unregarded and comparatively unused by the opponents of slum clearance.

The Problem of Public Apathy

Popular participation is both a fact and a value. As a value it rarely meets an open challenge. It is an aid to the provision of suitable public services: only the wearer knows where the shoe pinches. It is indispensable for the sound decisions of policy: 'The truth of any great practical question is too large for any one mind to contain it. The adjustment of partial truths to each other takes place, not in the isolation of individual minds, but "by the rough process of a struggle between combatants fighting under hostile banners". '[3] Thirdly, in the words of the same writer, local administrative institutions are the chief instrument of 'the public education of the citizens'.[4]

As a fact, however, its weakness is frequently the cause of disappointment and dismay. The attempt by the local planning authority in Sunderland to follow the recommendations of the Planning Advisory Group[5] elicited a negligible response. Its 'action plan' for north-west Sunderland, an area with a working population of 20,000, was submitted to the public by way of a pamphlet and an exhibition. 'One purpose is to make the public aware of the proposals that are envisaged for their locality and to allow all concerned to make their comments at an early stage and thus participate in the general planning of their area.'[6] Only thirty-six observations on the proposals were submitted.[7]

At its most general the explanation of apathy may lie in a basic feature of the life-style of the industrial wage-earner. Too few studies have been carried out in this country to allow this to be anything more than a tentative suggestion, but from everyday observation it may be inferred that he is, on the whole, more 'passive' than say, the salaried professional man. The world presents the working-class family with situations to which it must adapt. The middle-class family is more likely, by com-

348

parison, to view any situation as something amenable to its control.

The middle-class family, in the first place, has reached middle-class status precisely because it is more adept, either because of the inherent capacities or social training of its members, at manipulating the world to suit its own purposes. Secondly, it has more frequent experiences of successful control of its environment. Middle-class work involves greater independent activity and/or control of other people. That is essential to the concept of 'the middle class' as distinguished from the concept of 'the working class'. In the domestic dealings with tradesmen, doctors, the daily help, the children's schoolteachers and others with whom she comes into contact the initiative lies more firmly and more usually in the hands of the middle-class housewife than is the case with the working-class housewife.

This difference of approach is carried over into dealings with public authorities. The working-class family has a low expectation that it will be influential in any negotiations. The middle-class group is likely to be more knowledgeable about and active in the pursuit of opportunities for self protection:

> Large property companies and groups of landowners are already appointing valuation officers to represent their interests in negotiation with the Government's promised Land Commission. This is expected to make even more acute the Commission's difficulty in finding enough experienced valuation officers and surveyors to work the official scheme. These new appointments are being offered at very high salaries, with which the Inland Revenue cannot compete. This trend may leave the Civil Service seriously short not only of qualified valuation officers but also of experts in other aspects of land development and planning procedures.[8]

A celebrated case, that involving the Packington Estate,[9] was typically formulated and pressed by residents and absentee owners whose 'life-chances' had equipped them with the necessary verbal and organisational skills as well as imbued them with the confidence that the expenditure of their energies would not be futile. 'The inability of the poor to protect themselves' has long been recognised as a problem in housing provision. 'When notice is given they never seem to appreciate the fact that their homes are about to be destroyed until the workmen come to pull the roof from over their heads. Lord Shaftesbury described how the inhabitants have been seen like people in a besieged town, running to and fro, and not knowing where to turn. The evidence of the inability of the poor to protect themselves in this and other particulars is conclusive.'[10]

There are other disincentives to public participation specific to the slum-clearance situation. First, the residents are not presented in the early stages with proposals that need to be faced as an issue. Ever since 1957 the 1965–70 areas have been programmed for 'redevelopment' by the end of 1971.[11] (See page 236.) When this programming was being discussed in the early 1950s, what might happen in the late 1960s no doubt seemed an excessively remote problem. The next reaction is generated when the slum-clearance proposals are publicised as a news item in the local press. The date of slum-clearance is placed between one and five years in the future. The backlog from previous programmes gives rise to the supposition that the time lag between announcement and execution will be longer than the time stated. At this stage, also, the attitude that 'it might never happen' is easily adopted. The threat is not immediate enough to form a basis for organised opposition and there is in any case no machinery for consultation.

Those most likely to respond are the alert and well-informed residents. From this point onwards their housing decisions will be made with a lively sense of the impermanence of their tenure. Their place is taken by an entirely different sort of family which comes into the area precisely because its stay will be short-lived and because the end result will be the allocation of a municipal dwelling.

' "Planning blight" refers to the depressing effect on existing property of proposals which imply public acquisition and disturbance of the existing use. The effect of planning blight can be to make property that is likely to be affected by a scheme either unsaleable or not saleable at the price it would have fetched apart from those proposals and it can also, through uncertainty, affect the standard of maintenance and improvements, capital investment, mortgages and the operation of businesses.'[12] Blight, which has been an incipient problem under the provisions of the 1957–71 development plan, especially in the later stages, now begins to appear on a larger scale. Modernisation is abandoned. Maintenance is held at the lowest level compatible with comfort and self-respect. Interior decorations are allowed to deteriorate. Eventually spring cleaning may be regarded as not worth the trouble. Public spaces are neglected. Pavements are patched rather than renewed. Streets remain cobbled while all other town roads are asphalted. In design and efficiency all such items as lamp standards fall behind. The decay of the physical environment and changes in the area's social composition adversely affect the area's morale. People are ashamed when their friends visit them.

It is only as the scheduled time of demolition approaches that the accumulation of such grievances leads to protest. The protest now, however, is based on the desire to accelerate demolition. Conditions for many families have become intolerable.[13]

Slum-clearance may be, therefore, to some extent a self-fulfilling prophecy. In some areas the descent to slumdom can be traced directly to a single cause: the slum-clearance proposals themselves. The prophecy tends also to be self-vindicating because the coincidence of a sufficient number of heavily charged grievances borne by a large enough number of people tends to occur only towards the end of the process and to take the form of demands that demolition be hastened.

A second specific source of public apathy in the early stages of a slum-clearance scheme is the sheer magnitude of the change. For some people who do wish to retain their house and remain in the area, slum-clearance is an appalling disaster. Its meaning and psychological effect can be clarified by contrasting it with public response to 'environmental revitalisation' proposals. Under such proposals families know, for example, that they will have to park their cars in the back lane instead of in the newly pedestrianized front street. This is a definite and certain inconvenience. It is just one more inconvenience in life, against which they are asked to set some promised indefinite future convenience. The choice of the residents may be badly or well judged, but the choice itself is simple to comprehend.

Slum-clearance, by contrast, means a total change in circumstances, the possible ramifications of which may be too complex to grasp and too obscure to be contemplated. One reaction to this state of affairs is analogous to that which arises when war breaks out. The pattern of the future will be completely disrupted. All the known irritations of workaday life will be at any rate halted. Another reaction is analogous to the state of shock; the residents' state of mind can be that of stunned disbelief.

A third specific source of apathy is the feeling that demolition and replacement are inevitable. The word 'slum' carries the connotation of undesirability. No one can favour the retention of slum property. Once the description has been affixed to a particular area a fight against such a damning social judgment may well seem hopeless. As Burke says, 'Those who are subjected to wrong under multitudes are deprived of all external consolation. They seem deserted by mankind, overpowered by a conspiracy of their whole species.'[14]

Finally, there is the effect of the planning machinery and the behaviour and attitudes of the planning personnel. Whatever the intention, the effect of certain statements by planning officers is to engender a sense of helplessness. The following incident illustrates this. A planning officer was asked by a councillor in committee for a firm indication of the future prospects for some cottages in Pallion. The councillor was told 'they were in the approved development plan, which had the force of a statutory document, and a lot of them were planned for redevelopment by 1972'.[15] The cottages were not in a slum-clearance area. The officer was saying quite clearly that the town council did not have it within its power to prevent the cottages being demolished. Because the programme map of the development plan showed the cottages as likely to be 're-developed' by 1972, he implied, statutory obligations were in operation which would force the council to go ahead with demolition whatever the state of the cottages and whatever councillors decided. In truth, however, the programme map, while it is a statutory document, places no obligation whatsoever on the council to carry out any of the redevelopment which it describes.

Behind disappointment with the level of public participation, lies the unwarrantable assumption that techniques such as town-planning exhibitions carry an intrinsic virtue which somehow will overcome these formidable obstacles and enable them to raise popular participation to a high level. If they fail to do so, the fault lies with the public, not with the device.

In addition to the general arguments for democracy which were mentioned at the beginning of this chapter, however, some degree of participation by the 1965–70 slum-clearance families in those decisions which affect their own homes and neighbourhoods may be regarded as particularly desirable. In the first place they are knowledgeable about their own housing and local conditions in a way and to an extent which can not be matched by the outside decision-maker or his advisers no matter how robust may be the claims and no matter how impressively these claims may be authenticated and certified by professional or party bodies. In the second place, the technical problems of housing (and of town-planning to the extent that it relates to housing) are much less profound and difficult than the problems of social value, and the decision-maker has no way of knowing anything at all about the social values which are embedded in the situation except by familiarising himself with them through the words and other symbolic behaviour of the people concerned. Thus, on the physical side, the decision-maker and his adviser may have considerable knowledge of the externally observable structures and they will certainly possess technical knowledge and skills the inhabitants lack. Participation on this plane means tapping the additional stores of knowledge lying with the residents. On the sociological side, however, the decision-maker and his adviser must, in the field of housing, receive his information from the only 'experts' available, the people themselves.

At its most indispensable, most simple and least controversial, 'popular participation' means, then, public contributions to a particular fund of knowledge: knowledge of the physical and social factors which are relevant to a particular decision. When this is understood then the comparative failure of existing methods designed to encourage participation becomes a matter of discovering more effective methods rather than to excuse the professional's 'contempt for the consumer'.

Public meetings, exhibitions, M.P.'s 'surgeries', complaints or comments to local councillors, voting procedures, letters to the press and so forth are not without value as channels for the transmission of this knowledge. For some groups they can be extremely useful. But 'we now know that members of the ignorant and unpropertied masses are considerably less active politically than the educated and the well-to-do. By their propensity for political passivity the poor and uneducated disfranchise themselves'[16]—and we also know that in housing we cannot afford to allow this passivity to deprive decision-makers of essential information.[17] The most effective technique for securing the participation of families who are unable or unwilling to contribute in middle-class ways is to approach them individually. Their value orientations and the knowledge which they uniquely hold can be most economically, efficiently and assuredly gathered, that is, by sociological methods.

It must be stressed finally, however, that participation means something more than knowledge fed to a decision-maker for him to examine or neglect according to the play of his own interests and energies, and use or discard as he sees fit. It also connotes control of the decision-maker to ensure that the values which are incorporated in any scheme are those of the people affected by it. The necessity of control by the people affected exists whether their numbers are large or small and whether they are concentrated at the point at which the scheme will be physically located or widely dispersed from it.

To secure public participation in this 'controlling' sense is a much more intractable problem than public participation in the 'informational' sense. The political arena, the battle-ground of conflicting interests, is shunned by the great majority of the residents of the Sunderland clearance areas. As Dahl suggests, it would clear the air of a good deal of cant if instead of assuming that politics is a normal and natural activity, one were to make the contrary assumption that whatever lip-service citizens may pay to conventional attitudes politics is remote and alien.[18] In particular, it would mean recognising that the problem is not to suppress and fear such limited political activity as may emerge from slum-clearance proposals. Such political activity is not only legitimated by the democratic *mores* of our society; given the existing structure of decision-making and the informational and ethical content of slum-clearance schemes it also may, and indeed is likely to be related more closely and effectively to the issues of social justice than is the decision-making machinery of the local authority itself.[19]

354

NOTES TO CHAPTER 20

1 In this connection, the Planning Advisory Group, when it considered the future of development plans in 1965, stated that 'the main defects of the present [planning] system' flow from the stress laid in the 1947 Planning Act *on map-making rather than policy matters*. It is interesting to compare the 1947 Act definition of a development plan with the wording in the first draft of the Bill where it was defined as 'a plan *indicating the general principles* upon which development will be promoted and controlled'. (Emphasis added.)

MHLG, *The Future of Development Plans: A Report by the PAG*, London, HMSO 1965, pp. 5, 6.

2 *Op. cit.*, p. 2. (Emphasis added.)

3 John Stuart Mill, *On Liberty* (1859), Chapter II, Para. 36.

4 John Stuart Mill, *Representative Government*, Chapter XV.

5 MHLG, *The Future of Development Plans*, London, HMSO 1965.

6 Sunderland CB, *Southwick: A Plan for the Future*, 1967. Introduction by the Chairman of the Planning Committee.

7 *Sunderland Echo*, 27 October 1967.

8 James Margach, 'Landowners Scoop the Civil Service', *Sunday Times*, 3 October 1965.

9 *Hansard*, 9 February 1966, Cols. 402–08; 'Planning Inquiries', *The New Law Journal*, 116, 5221, 17 February 1966; Richard Davy, 'Mr. Crossman's Crichel Down?', *The Spectator*, 18 February 1966; *Hansard*, 2 March 1966, Cols. 1311–80; 'Comment', *Public Law*, Spring 1966; R. L. C. Jewell, 'The Packington Estate Case', *Journal of Planning and Property Law*, April 1966; *The Annual Report of the Council on Tribunals for 1965*, London, HMSO 1966, Appendix A, p. 25.

10 The Royal Commission on the Housing of the Working Classes, *First Report*, London, HMSO 1885, p. 21.

11 Sunderland CB, *Development Plan Programme Map*.

12 MHLG, *The Future of Development Plans*, London, HMSO 1965, p. 50.

13 Though very different in its degree of seriousness, the resemblance of this process to 'the betrayal funnel' for e.g., prospective mental patients or concentration camp victims is obvious. See Erving Goffman, *Asylums* Anchor Books 1961, pp. 140–41; David Boder, *I did Not Interview the Dead*, Urbana 1949, p. 81; and E. A. Cohen, *Human Behaviour in the Concentration Camp*, New York 1953, p. 32 and p. 37.

14 Edmund Burke, *Reflections on the Revolution in France*, World Classics edition, London 1950, p. 138. On the damage to self-respect of such 'mirroring effects' see Goffman, *op. cit.*, p. 149.

15 *Sunderland Echo*, 8 June 1967.

16 Robert A. Dahl, *Preface to Democratic Theory*, Chicago 1956, p. 81.

17 It is interesting to note that the lack of *local* interest in the Southwick

plan failed to disturb the responsible authorities. Their public stance, rather, was that the plan had aroused *international* interest and that requests for copies had come from as far afield as Tokyo and Johannesburg. See *The Journal* (Newcastle), 14 May 1968, p. 8.

18 Robert A. Dahl, *Who Governs?*, London 1961, p. 279.

19 For a discussion of the question, 'Where, then, do the decision-makers get their ideas from?', see Norman Dennis, 'Mass Housing and the Reformer's Myth', *Planning Outlook*, New Series, 6, Spring 1969.

Since this book was written the Town and Country Planning Act, 1968, has been passed. Part I, section 7, lays certain obligations upon planning authorities to take 'such steps as will in their opinion' give adequate publicity to local plans and afford adequate opportunities for 'representations' from persons who may be expected to want to make them. Also, shortly before this book goes to press the Parliamentary Committee on Public Participation in Planning (the Skeffington Committee) has reported. (MHLG, *People and Planning*, HMSO 1969.) An account of participation—against this background—by the residents of Millfield since November 1967 (see p. 302) is in preparation.

CONCLUSION

The initial framework of the research was that suggested by the county borough of Sunderland. The director of the research had a background in local government.[1] It was recognised from an early stage, however, that the important issues might turn on the definition of the problem. Indeed, the choice of a university researcher rather than some other worker or agency presumably implied the local authority's wish to 'question the questions'. Certainly, freedom to examine basic assumptions was fundamental to the willingness of a university researcher to undertake such a project. As was partly foreseen, the main interest of the research did involve such basic preconceptions, and it will be the business of the concluding chapter, in the light of this study, to comment upon them.

Housing Replacement as a Public Issue

One assumption with which the research started out was that housing replacement is a community issue. In the course of research, however, the question was raised, 'To what extent and under what conditions does housing replacement become a public issue?' On analysis the phrase 'public issue', as it applies to housing replacement, is seen to carry three separate meanings, and three separate answers are therefore required.

It can mean that, to the extent that it proves detrimental to the interests of other people or prevents other people enjoying benefits of convincing weight and attainability, a person's freedom to retain his own home must be limited: a person's freedom to have a home which is a breeding ground of epidemic disease, a person's freedom to stunt and cripple his

357

children in cramped, dark and airless quarters, his freedom to prevent road improvements or reservoir construction. Restrictions of such liberties have been resisted in the past, and the rights and wrongs of particular issues will always leave room for debate; in principle, however, the right of the public to intervene in such matters through its chosen agencies is widely ceded in our society. Housing demolition is everywhere a public issue in the sense that the widespread benefits to be derived from, for example, the construction and realignment of roads constantly requires the dispossession of the individual householder; everywhere, also, buildings will continue to be condemned because they are structurally unsafe or constitute a public health hazard. These, however, are grounds for the demolition of only a small portion of the houses covered by the proposals for slum-clearance in Sunderland in the years after 1965.

The particular 'public interests', in this first sense, however, which are now invoked are much more tenuous than these. A family's right to remain in its existing home must be abrogated, the argument runs, either if the dwelling is judged ugly or if the competent officer rules that the dwelling will at some unspecified time in the future adversely affect the business decision of some unknown entrepreneur. Of these it may be said that aesthetic judgments, *par excellence*, depend upon discrimination, taste and a fine sense of differences; and connections between housing and economic behaviour must be based to a large extent upon guesswork. The 'public' consequences of private housing decisions have become, that is, much more intangible and the evidence which would establish the relationship between them becomes more difficult to find; so that the professional's demand for wider powers on the grounds of 'the public interest' in this sense is seen to grow more insistent at the same time as the case for control by the professional becomes more difficult to substantiate.

The term 'a public issue' has a second and quite different meaning. Sewers, roads, and airports are 'public' facilities. They are indivisibles. There is no way in which a part of a main sewer can be allocated for the beneficial use of a particular person or family. A motorway runs from A to B; it makes no sense to build two miles of road, leave two miles of fields, and recommence with two further miles of road. An airport operates as a coherent whole; each of the millions of passengers makes use of the total complex of equipment, personnel and administrative structures. In making the claim for extended powers of demolition, an attempt is made to assimilate areas of housing to such public installations and so make demolition 'a public issue' in this second sense.[2]

Areas of housing do indeed depend upon certain indivisibles. But the indivisibles relevant to comprehensive housing development can be and, of course, are frequently renewed without demolition. A special case has, therefore, to be made out on those occasions when improvements of, or alterations and additions to indivisible amenities *do* require the demolition of dwellings. The failure to clarify the concept of 'a public issue' has meant, however, that it is rarely thought necessary to make out such a case. On the contrary, the assumed public nature of dwelling replacement has meant that demolition powers have frequently been claimed by referring to the neglect of such clearly public matters as the state of the roads, the standard of scavenging, the adequacy of street lighting and so forth.[3]

The claimants of power over standards of housing consumption beyond the level at which the public element is clearly discernible view the home, that is, as if it were a public property in this second sense, like an airport. The design and location of a major airport, however, is a matter which affects millions of passengers very directly. It is so socially and technically complex that it cannot be created except by a large team of highly trained experts. It is difficult, however, to accept the home as 'public' in this sense at all. The home is the paradigm of all that is broken from the public world and absorbed into the pattern of the private and unique life of each family. As Laski argues, the home lies at the core of a man's autonomy. Once above the level of public nuisance the right to choose one's own housing standards is, in Laski's view, the culmination of socialist control, of 'planning for freedom':

> The reward each citizen earns must be his own to do with as he will. He may choose, as is so typical of America, to sacrifice the creature-comforts of his home to the possession of a motor-car; or he may wish, as in the case of many Londoners, to endure the

359

discomfort of a long railway journey for the pleasure of cultivating a garden. The more a man is tempted to experiment with his own standards of consumption, the better it is for society. The one thing we want to avoid are those long rows of villas with identical wall-paper, identical books, and identical standards of pleasure. Life is an art which we can know only by experience. And the experience must be fully our own, shot through with the texture of our unique personality, if we are to realise the things within us which makes us different from our fellows. If this be true, a society is well advised which avoids controlling the standards of consumption which exist.[4]

'A public issue' also means public concern for members of the community who are suffering in some way. The pain of disease, the humiliation of poverty, the burden of ignorance, the degradation of squalor, the hopelessness of enforced idleness and the multitudinous frustrations of bad housing–whether or not other people are affected, whether or not, that is, these happen to be also public issues in the first sense, they may become public issues in this third sense.

On these grounds public intervention is simply meant to make life more pleasant for the people who are otherwise at a disadvantage. Obviously, then, this sort of argument for replacement is plausible only if life *is* made more pleasant for the inhabitants of the condemned dwelling. The best judge (some would say the only possible judge) of whether a change of circumstances has this result is the person himself. There can be little sense in a policy which is justified by reference to its beneficial effects, if the 'beneficiaries' experience the results as hardship.

Naïve lay support for public housing-policies continues to depend largely upon the acceptance (more or less willingly) of the view that it is the responsibility of the community to assist those who have failed to secure decent accommodation for themselves. Whatever the strength of any public arguments in the first two senses general support would be difficult to muster if it were thought that for those whose homes were being demolished the consequences were harsh. When they are faced with the reality of local opposition by a survey such as the SHN study, demolition policies are vindicated by councillors and their professional advisers by community arguments in the first two senses; but public sympathy can only be maintained by obscurely allowing community arguments of the third sort to enter their rhetoric.

In summary, demolition can be for the benefit of either the public or the inhabitants of the clearance areas. If the latter, then proposals must clearly appear attractive enough to result in their voluntary acceptance by the residents. If the former, those who lose in the clearance areas for the public good must not be expected to bear an inequitably large share of the cost.[5] They ought, in particular, to be properly compensated in financial terms and rehoused with meticulous regard to their own wishes.

Housing Replacement as a Technical Problem

The second assumption which originally underlay the research programme was that housing replacement is principally a technical matter. A dwelling, physically, aesthetically, or in some other way, either reaches a more or less measurable standard or it does not. If it fails to reach the current standard it must be demolished. So conceived, the problem is 'technical' in Weber's sense of the word.[6] The ends are given; only the appropriate means remain to be chosen.

This is the local authority's basic and hitherto largely un-questioned approach to housing replacement. One of the main tasks of this book has been to examine its validity. The evidence strongly supports the conclusion that the ends which are taken for granted are not only grossly oversimplified, but that they are also outdated, having originated in conditions which have now been superseded.

So long as there was agreement on what constituted 'unfit property' or 'slum dwellings' the ends served by housing replacement were indeed 'given'. They were given by public opinion itself. In Sunderland, largely as a result of vigorous housing policies, this consensus has evaporated; and the end of consensus ends also the pre-eminence of the technical expert. In housing replacement the situation is no longer that of a set of agreed goals which the technical officer is commissioned to reach with as much expedition and with as little cost as possible. The value of what is being destroyed is being increasingly canvassed; doubt is increasingly being cast upon the value of what he is attempting to achieve and actually achieving.

As Galbraith points out,[7] all human beings qua human beings share the same interest in having certain elementary physical sensations served: they wish to avoid being hungry, they want to be protected against cold, they need to be provided with shelter, pain needs to be suppressed. But in economically advanced societies such needs come to comprise a small and diminishing part of what people consume. Most goods come to be enjoyed because of some mental, social or emotional response to their possession or use. When this state of affairs is reached then the problems of psychological adjustment come to be as important as further improvements in the level of material comfort.

The failure to recognise the extent to which they are impregnated with unexplored and crude value premises lies, it may be suggested, at the root of the widespread opposition, as revealed in the SHN interviews, to the local authority's 1965–70 slum-clearance proposals.

Providers of services can no longer give absolute priority to the few desiderata which they are professionally trained to accomplish. In the present connection, what is urgently needed is an acknowledgement of the fact that for large numbers of people in slum-clearance areas the physical and aesthetic level of their accommodation is not so low that everything else must be sacrificed to raise it. For them, as the South American *seigneur* says, *La hacienda no es negocio*: one's home is too precious to be treated like other possessions.

Housing Replacement as a Panacea

The third assumption which this study has questioned is closely related to the second. Conversations with officers and councillors indicate that among those who are influential for policy a council house is thought to be almost universally sought after by working people. Given their present dwelling and the present quality, location and rent of council houses, nearly all of them would take a council tenancy if it were to be offered to them. The only thing that prevents such a change in their housing situation is the fact that they fail to qualify under the local authority's allocation scheme. This study shows that this view is in poor correspondence with the facts.

The SHN findings make it clear that many families do suffer from housing stress of one sort or another and passionately hope to be rehoused by the council. The problem in such cases retains its technical complexion. Most, if not all, of the remaining families in the area covered by the 1965–70 proposals also suffer from some form of housing stress. Some of these, if they were more knowledgeable or more rational, would recognise that they too would be better off in a council dwelling. But the majority of those who object to demolition and reject alternative accommodation are expressing, on the whole, sound and rational preferences. Instead of monolithic policies of clearance, therefore, the problem at the present time in Sunderland seems to call for responses as heterogeneous as the problems.

One of the reasons why families which desire to be rehoused cannot be allocated a council dwelling is that unwelcome council tenures are being forced upon families which would prefer to stay where they are. Some families, secondly, wish to have their home demolished, but not at the price of losing the convenience of their neighbourhood amenities and their place in an established network of neighbours and relatives. Such families ought to be rehoused elsewhere temporarily and given priority in their 'own' area when it has been redeveloped. Although lip-service is frequently paid to this concept, it has been put into practice in only very limited ways in Sunderland. Much more could be done, too, to retain the proven advantages of lay-out by sensitively and imaginatively reconstructing cottage streets or parts of streets rather than engaging in wholesale demolition.

A striking feature of so-called adventurous and forward-looking official schemes for housing renewal has been, in fact, the poverty and narrowness rather than richness and variety of their underlying conception of the problem. What is needed, above all, is an awareness of the valued and valuable things which are being sought and sacrificed in slum-clearance proposals. As it is, one is reminded of nothing so much as Butler's *Erewhon*:

> These evils had long been apparent and recognised; until at last a benevolent reformer devoted his whole life to effecting the

necessary changes. He divided all illnesses into three classes—those affecting the head, the trunk and the lower limbs—and obtained an enactment that all diseases of the head should be treated with laudanum, those of the body with castor-oil, and those of the lower limbs with an embrocation of strong sulphuric acid and water. It may be said that this classification was not sufficiently careful, and that the remedies were ill-chosen; but it is a hard thing to initiate any reform, and it is necessary to familiarize the public mind with the principle by inserting the thin end of the wedge.[8]

'Planned' Housing Replacement

The fourth assumption concerns the concept of 'planning'. In the ordinary sense of the term, planning implies a decision or collection of decisions which can be taken at one time and which can then form the dependable framework for other decisions in the future. The notion of dependability is here sufficiently wide to include the necessity of 'contingency planning'. Planning introduces relative certainty and order in place of anarchy, friction and doubt.

By describing their own activities as 'planning', certain groups concerned with housing replacement in Sunderland have succeeded in creating the impression that word and substance are the same thing. In clearance policies this is close to being the opposite of the truth. In the absence of 'planning' householders would be ceaselessly making decisions about when and how and to what extent they should renovate, repair or improve their dwellings, whether they should stay in the district or sell their house and move away and so forth. These decisions would be made in the light of the family's own expectations about future income, housing requirements and other relevant factors. When 'planned demolition' enters the picture no decisions can be made; because instead of knowing more about the future course of events householders now know much less.

The dwelling will be demolished—at some indefinite time in the future. The house might or might not be defined as unfit for human habitation. The householder might receive compensation—he has no way of guessing the amount. What the family will be offered in return for their existing home is completely unknown.

Dwellings in clearance areas have been, therefore, placed hitherto in a decision-making limbo. In those cases where slum clearance *has* been justified and accepted, therefore, an outstanding housing need in Sunderland is to introduce 'planning' in the ordinary sense of the term, that is, a framework of public policies within which the citizen can hope to organise his own affairs more effectively than he could in the absence of planning. Up to the present time, it is not too much to say, 'planning' has meant keeping all the options open to the local authority, i.e. it has enabled it to postpone pressing decisions in the here-and-now, while preventing decisions being taken in the here-and-now by everyone else. 'Planning' that is, has been close to being a synonym for confusion.

The solution, obviously, is for the local authority to seriously consider an overhaul of its attitudes to, and its procedures for transmitting information to the public. (See footnote 19, p. 356.)

Housing Replacement and Research

The fifth assumption concerns the need for knowledge. There is no doubt that replacement decisions have been reached in what is virtually a data vacuum. In the early stages of the research it was believed that ignorance of life in clearance areas and even of the physical state of the dwellings was due exclusively to shortage of staff: that, naturally, if staff had been available data would have been collected. It was, therefore, something of a surprise to discover that this was by no means the whole story– that on the contrary, it was assumed in some quarters that such information would be of no help in arriving at sound and valid policy judgments. The assumption was that, in order to determine whether an area should be demolished or not, sufficient *could* be learned from a brief visit and from a moving vehicle.

This attitude can only be held by decision-makers or advisers whose view of slum clearance is excessively restricted and who wish to use and are confident in the efficacy of their powers of compulsion. For those attempting to achieve a smooth transition and to elicit the energies and loyalties of the citizens, however, the reasons for the connection between housing and behaviour, the values implicated in housing decisions

365

and the reason for intangible obstacles and discords, all need to be understood, and understanding must depend upon knowledge. 'We cannot develop the social arithmetic of housing unless we are prepared to study the needs of people and the results of policies.'[9] The need to carry out research and justify policies at the local level is being slowly recognised in the planning profession,[10] but until the importance of data and some awareness of the problems of social philosophy are accepted as the *sine qua non* of decision-making in the realm of human affairs, planning will continue to exhibit, as has been said, the 'vigour of a clumsy giant crushing with heavy hoof things of whose value he has no conception'.

My thoughts and attitudes have been radically reoriented as a result of the three years which have gone into the preparation of this book. Edmund Burke has been quoted more than once on previous pages. No concluding words seem more apt than his:

> If circumspection and caution are part of wisdom, when we work only on inanimate matter, surely they become part of duty too, when the subject of our demolition and construction is not bricks and timber, but sentient being. The true lawgiver ought to love and respect his kind, and to fear himself.[11]

NOTES TO CONCLUSION

1 At the time of his appointment the director was employed by a county planning authority during leave of absence from the University of Birmingham.

2 The construction of such public installations *incidentally* involves the demolition of dwellings. This is quite a separate issue and lies outside the scope of this chapter.

3 See the *Sunderland Echo*, 12 December 1967, where an example is given of such arguments. 'Twenty-nine East End Houses Unfit. A Corporation planning officer told the inquiry that the East End as a whole still contained a conglomeration of mixed land uses, declining industries, outdated buildings and derelict sites, all of which gave an air of decay, dirt and drabness.' All this may well be true, but it is difficult to see its relevance to a decision about the fitness for human habitation in the legal sense of the twenty-nine houses in question.

4 Harold J. Laski, *A Grammar of Politics* (1925), London 1938 edition, pp. 199–200.

5 Least of all should they be treated as if someone was doing them a favour. For someone who objects strongly to being moved that is very hard to bear.

6 Max Weber, *The Theory of Social and Economic Organisation*, edited by Talcott Parsons, London 1947, p. 162.

7 John Kenneth Galbraith, *The Reith Lectures*, Third Lecture, November 1966. (Printed in *The Listener*, 1 December 1966. See especially p. 795.)

8 *Op. cit.* (1872), Florian Library Edition, pp. 129–30.

9 Richard M. Titmuss, Preface to Alvin L. Schorr, *Slums and Social Insecurity*, London 1964, pp. xi, xii. Schorr is very critical of the lack of research in planning. In his discussion of the shift over from New Towns of the Crawley type to those of the Cumbernauld type he writes: 'The hour has seemed to go to the best new adjective. Virtually no studies have been conducted.' p. 138.

10 'The policy statement should not be limited to a bald statement of proposals . . . but should include a reasonably full summary of the reasoning that led up to the proposals derived from survey and analysis.'

MHLG, PAG, *The Future of Development Plans*, HMSO, London 1965, p. 17.

'Slowly' is an important qualifier. The door-to-door survey carried out after the SHN study had been presented to the Corporation as a report was commenced some time after 10 February 1968. The relevance of the survey to policy has been discussed (see p. 324 above). Its quality can be judged from the fact that, using only office staff who could be spared from their other duties, the survey of no fewer than 8,000 dwellings was claimed to have been completed a little over a month later. (*Sunderland Echo*, 18 March 1968.) In only 'a few cases', said a Planning Department spokesman, were people not in when the surveyor called —surely an unprecedented phenomenon in door-to-door interviewing.

11 Edmund Burke, *Reflections on the Revolution in France* (World Classics edition, 1950), pp. 186–87. Burke, who was notorious for his phrase 'the swinish multitude', reads today like a champion of the oppressed.

BIBLIOGRAPHY

BOOKS

ANDERSON, Nels. *The Hobo*, Chicago: University of Chicago Press, 1923

ARDREY, Robert. *The Territorial Imperative: a personal inquiry into the animal origins of property and nations*, London: Collins, 1967

ASHWORTH, William. *The Genesis of Modern British Town Planning: a study in economic and social history of the nineteenth and twentieth centuries*, London: Routledge and Kegan Paul, 1954

BARNES, Harry. *Housing: the facts and the future*, London: Ernest Benn, 1923

BEER, Samuel H. *Modern British Politics*, London: Faber and Faber, 1965

BELL, Kathleen M. *Tribunals in the Social Services*, London: Routledge and Kegan Paul, 1969

BENDIX, Reinhard. *Max Weber: an intellectual portrait*, London: Routledge and Kegan Paul, 1966

BESHERS, J. M. *Urban Social Structure*, Glencoe: The Free Press, 1962

BIRCH, A. H. *Small Town Politics: a study of political life in Glossop*, London: Oxford University Press, 1959

BIRD, James. *The Major Seaports of the United Kingdom*, London: Hutchinson, 1963

BODER, David Pablo. *I Did not Interview the Dead*, Urbana: University of Illinois Press, 1949

BOWLEY, A. L., and BURNETT-HURST, A. R. *Livelihood and Poverty: a study in the economic and social conditions of working-class households in Northampton, Warrington, Stanley and Reading [and Bolton]*, London: Bell, 1915

BOWLEY, A. L. *Wages and Income in the United Kingdom since 1860*, Cambridge: Cambridge University Press, 1937

BOWLEY, Marian. *Housing and the State: 1919–1944*, London: George Allen and Unwin, 1945

369

BRENNAN, Tom. *Reshaping a City*, Glasgow: Grant, 1959

BRIGGS, Asa. *Victorian Cities*, London: Odhams, 1963

BURKE, Edmund. *Reflections on the Revolution in France and Other Writings*, (1790–91), London: Oxford University Press, 1907

BURNETT, James. *History of Sunderland: the history of the town and port of Sunderland, and the parishes of Bishopwearmouth and Monkwearmouth*, Sunderland: J. F. Burnett, 1830

BUTLER, Samuel. *Erewhom: or over the range*, (1872), London: Cape, 1932

CLANNY, W. Reid. *Hyperanthraxis: the cholera of Sunderland*, London: Whittaker, Treacher and Arnott, 1832

COHEN, Elie A. *Human Behaviour in the Concentration Camp*, New York: Grosset and Dunlap, 1953

COLLISON, Peter C. *The Cutteslowe Walls: a study in social class*, London: Faber and Faber, 1966

COURT, W. H. B. *A Concise Economic History of Britain from 1750 to Recent Times*, Cambridge: Cambridge University Press, 1954

CRESSEY, Paul G. *The Taxi-Dance Hall*, Chicago: University of Chicago Press, 1932

CULLINGWORTH, J. B. *Housing Needs and Planning Policy: a restatement of the problems of housing need and "overspill" in England and Wales*, London: Routledge and Kegan Paul, 1960

—. *Housing in Transition: a case study in the city of Lancaster 1958–62*, London: Heinemann, 1963

DAHL, Robert A. *Preface to Democratic Theory*, (Charles R. Walgreen Foundation Lectures), Chicago: University of Chicago Press, 1956

—. *Who Governs?: democracy and power in an American city*, New Haven: Yale University Press, 1961

DALE, Thomas Lawrence. *Towards a Plan for Oxford City*, London: Faber and Faber, 1944

DAVIES, Jon Gower. *The Evangelical Bureaucrat: a study of planners and "revitalization" in Rye Hill, Newcastle upon Tyne*, [forthcoming]

DENNIS, Norman, SLAUGHTER, Cliff, and HENRIQUES, Fernando. *Coal is our Life*, London: Eyre and Spottiswoode, 1956

DEPARTMENT OF PHILOSOPHY, UNIVERSITY OF COLORADO. *Readings on Fascism and National Socialism*, Denver: Alan Swallow, no date

DICEY, Albert Venn. *Law and Public Opinion in England in the Nineteenth Century*, (1905), London: Macmillan, 1914 (reprinted 1926)

DONNISON, David V. *The Government of Housing*, Harmondsworth: Penguin Books, 1967

DURKHEIM, Emile. *The Division of Labour in Society*, (1893), Glencoe: The Free Press, 1947

—. *Suicide: a study in sociology*, (1897), London: Routledge and Kegan Paul, 1952

ENGELS, Friedrich. *The Condition of the Working Class in England in 1844*, (1845), London: George Allen and Unwin, 1892

EVERSLEY, David E. C., JACKSON, Valerie J., and LOMAS, G. M. *Population Growth and Planning Policy*, Birmingham: West Midlands Social and Political Research Unit, 1965

FARIS, Robert E. L., and DUNHAM, H. Warren. *Mental Disorders in Urban Areas: an ecological study of schizophrenia and other psychoses*, Chicago: University of Chicago Press, 1939

FAY, Charles Ryle. *Great Britain from Adam Smith to the Present Day: an economic and social survey [1700–1949]*, (1928), London: Longmans, Green, 1950

FIRTH, Raymond, (Editor). *Two Studies of Kinship in London*, London: Athlone Press, 1956

FORTUNE Editors (Editors). *The Exploding Metropolis: a study of the assault on urbanism and how our cities can resist it*, New York: Doubleday, 1957

FRIEDMAN, Milton, and STIGLER, George. *Roof or Ceilings?*, (Popular Essays in Current Problems, I, 2: The Current Housing Problem), New York: Foundation for Economic Education, 1946

GERTH, Hans H., and MILLS, C. Wright, (Translators and Editors). *From Max Weber: essays in sociology*, London: Routledge and Kegan Paul, 1948

GOFFMAN, Erving. *Asylums: essays on the social situation of mental patients and other inmates*, New York: Doubleday, 1961

HALBWACHS, Maurice. *La Classe Ouvrière et les Niveaux de Vie: recherches sur la hiérarchie des besoins dans les sociétés industrielles contemporaines*, Paris: Alcan, 1913

HALMOS, Paul. *Solitude and Privacy: a study of social isolation, its causes and therapy*, London: Routledge and Kegan Paul, 1952

HARVEY, Audrey. *Tenants in Danger*, Harmondsworth: Penguin Books, 1964

HATT, Paul K., and REISS, Albert J. Junior. *Cities and Society: a revised Reader in urban sociology*, Glencoe: The Free Press, 1957

HAYNER, Norman S. *Hotel Life*, Chapel Hill: University of North Carolina Press, 1936

HOPKINS, C. H. G. *Pallion 1874–1954: Church and people in a shipyard parish*, Sunderland: Wearside Printing Co., 1954

JACKSON, J. N. *Surveys for Town and Country Planning*, London: Hutchinson, 1963

JACOBS, Jane. *The Death and Life of Great American Cities*, (1961), London: Cape, 1962

371

JEVONS, Rosamund, and MADGE, John. *Housing Estates: a study of Bristol Corporation policy and practice between the wars*, Bristol: J. W. Arrowsmith [for the University of Bristol], 1946

KUENSTLER, Peter. (Editor), *Community Organization in Great Britain*, London: Faber and Faber, 1961

KUPER, Leo, and others. *Living in Towns*, London: The Cresset Press, 1953

LAING, Samuel the younger. *National Distress: its causes and remedies*, (Atlas Prize Essay), London: Longmans, 1844

LASKI, Harold J. *A Grammar of Politics*, (1925), London: George Allen and Unwin, 1938

LEWIS, John Parry, and MEDHURST, Franklin. *Urban Decay*, [for the Civic Trust for the North West], Macmillan, [forthcoming]

LIPTON, Michael. *Assessing Economic Performance: some features of British economic development 1950–65 in the light of economic theory and the principles of economic planning*, London: Staples, 1968

LOCKE, John. *Two Treatises of Civil Government*, London: Dent, 1924

LONDON AND NORTH EASTERN RAILWAY. *Seaports on the North Eastern Railway: Sunderland*, Edinburgh: 1898

LONGMATE, Norman. *King Cholera: the biography of a disease*, London: Hamilton, 1966

LORENZ, Konrad. *On Aggression*, London: Methuen, 1966

MCGONIGLE, G. C. M., and KIRBY, J. *Poverty and Public Health*, London: Gollancz, 1936

MARRIS, Peter. *Widows and their Families*, London: Routledge and Kegan Paul, 1958

—, and REIN, Martin. *Dilemmas of Social Reform: poverty and community action in the United States*, London: Routledge and Kegan Paul, 1967

MARX, Karl. *Capital: a critical analysis of capitalist production*, (1867), Moscow: Foreign Languages Publishing House, 1958

MARX, Karl, and ENGELS, Friedrich. *Selected Works*, Volume I, Moscow: Foreign Languages Publishing House, 1958

MASTERMAN, C. F. G. *The Condition of England*, (1909), London: Methuen, 1910

MEAD, George Herbert. *Mind, Self and Society from the standpoint of a social behaviorist*, Chicago: University of Chicago Press, 1934

MESS, Henry A. *Industrial Tyneside: a social survey*, London: Ernest Benn, 1928

MILL, John Stuart. *On Liberty; Representative Government; The Subjection of Women*, (1859, 1861, 1869), London: Oxford University Press, 1912

MITCHELL, William Cranmer. *History of Sunderland*, Sunderland: Hills, 1919

MORRIS, Ray N., and MOGEY, John. *The Sociology of Housing: studies at Berinsfield*, London: Routledge and Kegan Paul, 1965

MORRIS, William. *News from Nowhere: or an epoch of rest*, (1890), London: Nelson, no date

—. *Nonesuch Morris: Architecture, Industry and Wealth*, London: Longmans, 1902

MOSER, Claus A., and SCOTT, Wolf. *British Towns: a statistical study of their social and economical differences*, London: Oliver and Boyd, 1961

MOWRER, Ernest R. *Family Disorganization*, Chicago: University of Chicago Press, 1927

ONIONS, C. T. *The Oxford Universal Dictionary on Historical Principles* (1955)

POLITICAL AND ECONOMIC PLANNING. *Growth in the British Economy: a study of economic problems and policies in contemporary Britain*, London: George Allen and Unwin, 1960

POPPER, Karl. *The Poverty of Historicism*, London: Routledge and Kegan Paul, 1961

POTTS, Taylor. *Sunderland: a history of the town, port, trade and commerce*, Sunderland: Williams, 1892

RECKLESS, Walter C. *Vice in Chicago*, Chicago: University of Chicago Press, 1933

ROBERTS, David. *Victorian Origins of the British Welfare State*, New Haven: Yale University Press, 1960

ROBSON, Brian Turnbull. *Urban Analysis: a study of city structure with special reference to Sunderland*, Cambridge: Cambridge University Press, 1969. His Upper Hendon is roughly our Hendon. His Deptford, as described and specified in terms of Census EDS (p. 189), though *not* in terms of his map (p. 188), is roughly our Deptford Road area.

ROSSER, Colin, and HARRIS, Christopher C. *The Family and Social Change: a study of family and kinship in a South Wales town*, London: Routledge and Kegan Paul, 1965

ROSSI, Peter H. *Why Families Move: a study in the social psychology of urban residential mobility*, Glencoe: The Free Press, 1955

ROWNTREE, B. Seebohm. *Poverty: a study of town life*, (1901), London: Macmillan, 1902

—. *Poverty and Progress: a second social survey of York*, (1941), London: Longmans, Green, 1942

SCHORR, Alvin Louis. *Slums and Social Insecurity*, London: Nelson, 1964

SHARP, Thomas. *Town Planning*, (1940), New York: Pelican No. 66, 1942

SIMON, Herbert A. *Administrative Behaviour: a study of decision-making processes in administrative organizations*, (1945), New York: Macmillan, 1957

373

SINCLAIR, Robert. *Metropolitan Man: the future of the English*, London: George Allen and Unwin, 1937 [published in the United States under the title *The Big City*]

SMELSER, Neil J. *Sociology: an introduction*, New York: John Wiley, 1967

SMITH, J. W., and HOLDEN, T. S. *Where Ships are Born: Sunderland 1346–1946*, Sunderland: Thomas Reed, 1946

TAWNEY, R. H. *The Acquisitive Society*, (1920), New York: Harcourt, Brace, 1948

—. *Religion and the Rise of Capitalism*, (1922), Harmondsworth: Penguin Books, 1938

THRASHER, Frederic Milton. *The Gang: a study of 1,313 gangs in Chicago*, (1927), Chicago: University of Chicago Press, 1936

TOCQUEVILLE, Alexis de. *Democracy in America*, (1835), London: Oxford University Press, 1946

TOENNIES, Ferdinand. *Community and Association*, (1887), London: Routledge and Kegan Paul, 1955

TOMLINSON, William Weaver. *The North Eastern Railway: its rise and development*, (1914), Newcastle: Andrew Reid, 1967

TOWN AND COUNTRY PLANNING ASSOCIATION. *Housing in Britain: a survey commissioned by the Town and Country Planning Association and carried out by O. W. Roskill Industrial Consultants*, London: Town and Country Planning Association, 1964

TOWNROE, Bernard Stephen. *The Slum Problem*, London: Longmans, 1928

TOWNSEND, Peter. *The Family Life of Old People: an inquiry in East London*, London: Routledge and Kegan Paul, 1957

TUCKER, James. *Honourable Estates*, London: Gollancz, 1966

TYRWHITT, Jacqueline (Editor). *Patrick Geddes in India*, London: Lund, Humphries, 1947

WATERS, Robert Amor. *Hendon: past and present*, Sunderland: Hills, 1900

WEBB, Sidney. *Fabian Essays in Socialism*, (edited by George Bernard Shaw), London: Walter Scott, 1889

WEBER, Max. *The Theory of Social and Economic Organization*, (translated and edited by Talcott Parsons), London: Oxford University Press, 1947

WENDT, Paul F. *Housing Policy: the search for solutions*, Berkeley: University of California Press, 1962

WHELLAN, William and Co. *The History, Topography and Directory of the County Palatine of Durham*, London: Whittaker, 1856

WILENSKY, Harold L. *Organizational Intelligence: knowledge and policy in government and industry*, New York: Basis Books, 1967

WILLIAMS, Norman. *Population Problems of New Estates: with special reference to Norris Green*, Liverpool: Liverpool University Press, 1939

WILLIAMS, Robert. *The People the Nation's Wealth*, London: Reeves, 1895

WILLMOTT, Peter, and YOUNG, Michael. *Family and Class in a London Suburb*, London: Routledge and Kegan Paul, 1960

WILLMOTT, Peter. *The Evolution of a Community: a study of Dagenham after forty years*, London: Routledge and Kegan Paul, 1963

WIRTH, Louis. *The Ghetto*, Chicago: University of Chicago Press, 1928

YOUNG, Michael, and WILLMOTT, Peter. *Family and Kinship in East London*, London: Routledge and Kegan Paul, 1957

YOUNG, Terence. *Becontree and Dagenham: the story of the growth of a housing estate*, London: Pilgrim Trust, 1934

ZORBAUGH, Harvey W. *The Gold Coast and the Slum*, Chicago: University of Chicago Press, 1929

OFFICIAL PUBLICATIONS AND REPORTS

BOARD OF TRADE. *The North East: a programme for regional development and growth*, (The Hailsham Report), Cmnd. 2206, HMSO 1963

CENTRAL STATISTICAL OFFICE. 'Projecting the Population of the United Kingdom', *Economic Trends*, 139, May 1965

—. 'The Age Structure and Regional Distribution of the United Kingdom Population 1964 to 1981', *Ibid.*, 145, November 1965

—. 'Revised Projections of the Regional Distribution of the United Kingdom Population in 1971 and 1981', *Ibid.*, 157, November 1966

COMMISSIONERS FOR INQUIRING INTO THE STATE OF THE LARGE TOWNS AND POPULOUS DISTRICTS. *Second Report*, HMSO 1845

COMMITTEE ON ADMINISTRATIVE TRIBUNALS AND ENQUIRIES. *Report*, (The Franks Report), Cmnd. 218, HMSO 1957

COMMITTEE ON MINISTERS' POWERS. *Report*, (The Donoughmore Report), Cmd. 4060, HMSO 1932

COUNCIL ON TRIBUNALS. *Annual Report for 1965*, HMSO 1966

DAVIES WEEKS AND PARTNERS. *Washington New Town Master Plan and Report*, December 1966

DEPARTMENT OF ECONOMIC AFFAIRS. *The National Plan*, Cmnd. 2764, HMSO 1965

GENERAL REGISTER OFFICE. *Census* [1801–1966] [various Reports]

—. *Quarterly Return* for various quarters

—. *Registrar General's Statistical Review of England and Wales* for various years

GOVERNMENT ACTUARY'S DEPARTMENT (GAD). *Report on the First Quinquennial Review of the National Insurance Act, 1946*, House of Commons Papers No. 1, HMSO 1954

HANSARD for various dates

HOUSE OF COMMONS ESTIMATES COMMITTEE. *Fourth Report: Government Statistical Services*, HMSO 1966

INSTITUTE OF MUNICIPAL TREASURERS AND ACCOUNTANTS. *Housing Statistics* for various years

—. *Return of Rates* for various years

JOINT CONSULTATIVE COMMITTEE AS TO REGIONAL PLANNING: TECHNICAL SUB-COMMITTEE OF PLANNING OFFICERS. *Final Report of the Working Party on Method of Assessment of North East Housing Need*, [mimeographed], February 1965

LOCAL GOVERNMENT BOARD. *Report of the Committee on Building Construction in Connexion with the Provision of Dwellings for the Working Classes*, (The Tudor Walters Report), HMSO 1918

MINISTRY OF HEALTH. *Circular 61/47* [Standards of Fitness], HMSO 1947

—. *Health and Welfare*, Cmnd. 1973, HMSO 1963

MINISTRY OF HOUSING AND LOCAL GOVERNMENT. *Housing Return* for various dates

—. *Local Housing Statistics* [from January 1967]

—. *Housing: the next step*, Cmd. 8996, HMSO 1953

—. *Slum clearance: summary of returns including proposals submitted by local authorities under Section I of the Housing Repairs and Rents Act, 1954*, Cmd. 9593, HMSO 1955

—, HOUSING MANAGEMENT SUB-COMMITTEE. *Moving from the Slums*, HMSO 1956

—. *Homes for Today and Tomorrow*, (The Parker Morris Report), HMSO 1961

—. *Report of the Committee on Housing in Greater London*, (The Milner Holland Report), Cmnd. 2605, HMSO 1965

—. *The Future of Development Plans: a report by the Planning Advisory Group*, (The PAG Report), HMSO 1965

—, CENTRAL HOUSING ADVISORY COMMITTEE, SUB-COMMITTEE ON STANDARDS OF HOUSING FITNESS, *Our Older Homes: a call for action*, HMSO 1966

—. *The Deeplish Study: improvement possibilities in a district of Rochdale*, HMSO 1966

—. *Circular 69/67* [explanatory notes on standards of fitness under section 4 of the Housing Act, 1957], HMSO 25 October 1967

—. *People and Planning: report of the Committee on Public Participation in Planning*, (The Skeffington Report), HMSO 1969

MINISTRY OF LABOUR. *Northern Region Monthly Digest of Statistics* for various dates [mimeographed]

MINISTRY OF RECONSTRUCTION. *Housing*, Cmd. 6609, HMSO 1945

NORTHERN ECONOMIC PLANNING COUNCIL. *Challenge of the Changing North: a preliminary study*, HMSO 1966

ORDNANCE SURVEY. Maps, various dates, in archives of Sunderland museum

ROYAL COMMISSION ON THE HOUSING OF THE WORKING CLASSES, *First Report*, HMSO 1885

ROYAL COMMISSION ON POPULATION. *Report*, Cmd. 7695, HMSO 1949

—. *Papers of the Royal Commission on Population*, Volume II, HMSO 1950

SUNDERLAND C.B. COUNCIL. *Minutes* of various meetings

SUNDERLAND C.B. HEALTH DEPARTMENT. *The Annual Report on the Health and Sanitary Conditions of Sunderland* for various years

—. *Annual Report of the Medical Officer of Health* for various years

SUNDERLAND C.B. PLANNING DEPARTMENT. *Second Five-Year Slum-Clearance Programme 1965–70*, [mimeographed], 19 February 1965, [with the Health Department]

—. *Southwick: a plan for the future*, 1967

SUNDERLAND C.B. TRANSPORT DEPARTMENT. *People and Transport*, 1964

TOWN PLANNING INSTITUTE. *Planning Delays: memorandum presented to the Ministry of Housing and Local Government*, 5 June 1967

UNITED NATIONS, DEPARTMENT OF ECONOMIC AND SOCIAL AFFAIRS. Manuals on Methods of Estimating Population: *Manual III Methods for Population Projections by Sex and Age*, New York: 1956

—. *Government Policies and the Cost of Building*, Part I, Geneva: 1959

PAMPHLETS, ARTICLES, DIRECTORIES, Etc.

ABEL-SMITH, Brian. *Freedom in the Welfare State*, Fabian Society Tract No. 353, 1964

ASHWORTH, Herbert. 'Economics of Finance of Twentieth Century Housing', *The British Housing and Planning Year Book, 1954*, London: National Housing and Town Planning Council, 1954

BARLOW, J. E., and RAMSDALE, G. I. 'Balanced Population: an experiment at Silksworth Overspill Township for Sunderland', *Journal of the Town Planning Institute*, 52, 7, July 1966

BOWLEY, A. L., and WOOD, George H. 'Wages in Shipbuilding: non-trade union sources', *Journal of the Royal Statistical Society*, September 1905

377

CARMICHAEL, John. *Vacant Possession: a study of Britain's 50-year-old 'housing problem'*, Hobart Paper No. 28, London: Institute of Economic Affairs, 1964

COGDON, R. S. 'Civil Engineering in the Development of Shipyards . . . in the Port of Sunderland', Institution of Civil Engineers Northern Counties Association, *Chairman's Address, 1960–1*

COLLISON, Peter C. 'Occupation, Education and Housing in an English City', *American Journal of Sociology*, 65, 6, May 1960

CULLINGWORTH, J. B. 'Some Aspects of the Housing Problem', *Housing*, 1, 2, July 1965

DAVIES, Jon Gower. 'Pollution by Planning', *Official Architecture and Planning*, 32, 2, June 1969

DENNIS, Norman. 'The Popularity of the Neighbourhood Community Idea', *Sociological Review*, 6, 2, [New Series], December 1958

—. 'Mass Housing and the Reformer's Myth', *Planning Outlook*, 6, [New Series], Spring 1969

DONNISON, David V. *Housing Policy Since the War*, Occasional Papers on Social Administration No. 1, Welwyn: Codicote, July 1960

GALBRAITH, John Kenneth. *The Reith Lectures, 1966*, Lecture III. [Published in *The Listener*, 1 December 1966]

JEWELL, R. L. C. 'The Packington Estate Case', *Journal of Planning and Property Law*, April 1966

JONES, Colin. 'The Renewal of Areas of Twilight Housing', [mimeographed] RIBA Conference, *Living in Britain*, July 1967

KAIM-CAUDLE, Peter R. 'A New Look at Housing Subsidies', *Local Government Finance*, 68, 3, March 1964

KEEBLE, Lewis B. 'Presidential Address, 1965', *Journal of the Town Planning Institute*, 51, 9, November 1965

LEACH, Edmund. *The Reith Lectures, 1967*, Lecture III [Published in *The Listener*, 30 November 1967]

MACRAE, Norman. *To Let?*, Hobart Paper No. 2, London: Barrie and Rockliff, 1960

MARTIN, A. E. 'Environment, Housing and Health', *Urban Studies*, 4, 1, February 1967

NEEDLEMAN, Lionel. 'A Long-Term View of Housing', *National Institute Economic Review*, No. 18, November 1961

'Planning Inquiries', *The New Law Journal*, 116, 5221, 17 February 1966

ROBSON, Brian T. 'An Ecological Analysis of the Evolution of Residential Areas in Sunderland', *Urban Studies*, 3, 2, June 1966. [This paper and Robson's *Urban Analysis* are the only works listed which do not appear in the text. They both are, however, of too great an

interest to anyone studying the town from either a sociological or geographical standpoint for them not to be noted. There is, for example, a useful discussion of the relative pace of decline, in terms of ratable values, of Hendon and of the area south of Millfield. Only restriction of space prevented this material being utilized in the present study.]

RUSSELL, David C. 'Psychology and Environment', *Planning Outlook*, 6, 2, [Old Series], 1964

SCHNEIDER, J. R. L. 'Local Population Projections in England and Wales', *Population Studies*, 10, 1, July 1956

SHILS, Edward. 'The Intellectuals: Great Britain', *Encounter*, April 1955

SOCIOLOGICAL SOCIETY, CITIES COMMITTEE. 'Towards the Third Alternative', *Sociological Review*, 11, 1, [Old Series], 1919

SUNDERLAND. *Directory for the Parishes of Sunderland, Bishopwearmouth, Monkwearmouth and Monkwearmouth Shore*, Bishopwearmouth: Burnett, 1831

—. *Directory of Sunderland, 1865*, Sunderland: John Barnes, 1865

—. *The Borough Guide to Sunderland for 1913*, Cheltenham: Burrow, 1913

TAYLOR, W. James. 'To Be Or Not To Be?', *The Magazine of St. Mark's Parish, Millfield*, November 1967

WALKDEN, A. H. 'The Estimation of Future Numbers of Private Households in England and Wales', *Population Studies*, 15, 2, November 1961

WEBB, Sidney. *The Necessary Basis of Society*, [Address to the Social Political League, London, 14 May 1908], Fabian Society Tract No. 159, 1911

WILKINSON, R., assisted by MERRY, D. M. 'A Statistical Analysis of Attitudes to Moving: a survey of slum-clearance areas in Leeds', *Urban Studies*, 2, 1, May 1965

WIRTH, Louis. 'Urbanism as a Way of Life', *American Journal of Sociology*, 44, 1, July 1938

GENERAL INDEX

Accessibility, 153–4, 292–3, 302, 304, 341–2
  1960–5, 182–3
  1965–70, 268–75, 283–9
  Unfit by 1981, 237
  Council, 268–75, 283–9
Acts of Parliament,
  Sunderland Improvement Acts, 1809, 1826, 148
  Nuisance Removal Act, 1846, 148
  Town Improvement Clauses Act, 1847, 148
  Public Health Act, 1848, 148
  Artisans' and Labourers' Dwellings Improvement Act, 1875, 148
  Cross Acts, 1879, 1882, 148
  Housing of the Working Classes Act, 1890, 149
  Housing, Town Planning etc. Act, 1919, 149
  Chamberlain Act, 1923, 149
  Greenwood Act, 149–50
  Housing Act, 1936, 165
  Town and Country Planning Act, 1947, 355n.
  Housing Repairs and Rents Act, 1954, 120–1, 129n., 166
  Housing Subsidies Act, 1956, 166
  [Housing Subsidies Order, 1956, 166]
  Housing Act, 1957, 119, 128n., 180n., 322 ['Housing Act, 1957: Slum Clearance', MHLG Circular 69/67, 128 n.]

Housing Act, 1961, 172
  Town and Country Planning Act, 1962, 343n.
  Town and Country Planning Act, 1968, 356n.
Age groups (*see* Age and sex structure, Children, Elderly, Stage of family development)
Age and sex structure, 34, 81, 85–9, 93
  in 1931 and 1951, 82–3
  in 1961, 1971 and 1981, 83–4, 94, 97–8, 106
Allocation of council dwellings (*see* Housing list, Rehousing), 230–2, 250–2, 363
Amalgamated Society of Engineers, 136
Apathy, 348–54
Architects, 31, 76n., 119, 120, 239n.
Autonomy, 26, 237, 241n., 269, 275, 304–5, 327–8, 333, 345, 347–8, 357, 359–60

Backyards (*see* Curtilage)
Bartram's shipyard, 140n.
Basic amenities (*see* Internal facilities)
Batley, 120
Bethnal Green, 262, 264–5
Betrayal funnel, 355n.
Birkenhead, 122, 129–31, 216–19, 244–9, 253, 281, 344
Birmingham, 90, 122, 129–31, 138, 217–19, 228, 244–9, 253, 281, 344

380

Flats, 31, 73, 185, *Plate 15*, 214–15, 222n., 223n., 239n., 266–7, 292, 302, 304, 308–12, 315
Ford, 138
Ford Estate, 152
  High Ford, 262–3, 280, 282–8
  Low Ford, 263, 280, 282–9
Freedom (*see* Autonomy)
Fulwell, 170–1

Gardens (*see* Curtilage)
GRO, General Register Office, 35, 52, 57, 59–60, 62, 64–5, 66n., 67–70, 80, 89, 91n., 95, 112, 188n.
Gilley Law, 75, 214, 222, 240n., 263
Glasgow, 321
GAD, Government Actuary's Department, 59, 62–3, 91n.
Grangetown, 263, 280, 282–8
Grants (*see* Improvement, Subsidies), 191, 193
Grindon, 263, 280, 282–9
Guardian, 128n.

Hahnemann Court, *Plate 18*, 260, 275n.
Hailsham Report, 34, 38, 44, 61
Hall *v.* Manchester Corporation, 128n.
Hansard, 66n., 111n.
Hartlepool [West Hartlepool], 241n.
Health (*see* Public health), 151, 156, 195
Hedworth Court, 263, 280–8
Hendon, 80, 166–8, 170–1, 173, 195, 197, 199, 200–7, *Plates 10, 11*, 224, 226, 256–8, 262–3, 266, 270, 274, 280, 282–9, 297, 308–10, 312–16, 322, 338
Herrington, 138
Holland, Sir Milner [Milner Holland Report], 29, 121
House Condition Index, 291
Households (*see* Household fission, Household formation forecasting), 86–8, 106
  A/S/MC [age, sex, marital condition] groups,

in 1951, 86, 100, 102, 104
  in 1961, 101
  in 1971 and 1981, 87, 106
  concealed, 86–7, 103–5
  number of, 29, 77, 86–8, 106
    in 1951, 104–5
    in 1961, 85
    in 1971 and 1981, 87
  size of, 29, 77–8, 81, 87, 90, 93
  stage of development of, 81, 85–6, 102, 225
Household fission, 29, 77, 80, 85, 87–8, 107, 109, 117
Household-formation forecasting, 21, 81–91, 109–10
  HFF [household-formation factor], 85–7, 99–101, 105–6
  methods of,
    Walkden/MHLG's, 81–8, 91
    GRO's, 88
    Cullingworth's, 89
    Eversley's, 90–1
  reliability of, 88–91, 109, 117
  results of, 87–8, 106
House of Commons Estimates Committee, 91n.
Housing Associations, 29
Housing-demand units, 80–1, 83, 85–6, 109
Housing estates (*see* Council districts), 263
Housing list (*see* Allocation),
  1960–5, 180, 187
  1965–70, 206, 231, 250–2, 294, 312, 362–3
Housing,
  and the market, 21–2, 80
Housing needs, 29, 30, 81, 88, 109–110, 149, 165, *and throughout*
Housing Management Sub-Committee of MHLG, 118
Housing standards (*see* Internal facilities, Internal space, Neighbourhood amenity, Structural condition), 121, 123, 126–7
Housing stock, 80, 165, 336, 342n., 344
Huddersfield, 281

NAME INDEX

Abel-Smith, Brian, 241n.
Allen, Lady, 128n.
Allen, Walter, 136
Anderson, Nels, 276n.
Ardrey, Robert, 277n.
Ashworth, Herbert, 118, 119, 127n.
Ashworth, William, 342n.

Barlow, J. E., 332n.
Barnes, Harry, 156n.
Barnes, John, 139n.
Beer, Samuel H., 157n.
Bell, Kathleen M., 19, 332n., 343n.
Bendix, Reinhard, 343n.
Bendixson, Terence, 222n.
Beshers, J. M., 332n.
Birch, A. H., 140n.
Bird, James, 139n.
Boder, David, 355n.
Bolckow, Henry, 138
Bowley, A. L., 137, 140n., 209n.
Bowley, Marian, 342n.
Brennan, Tom, 331n.
Briggs, Asa, 140n.
Burckhardt, Jacob, 333
Burke, Edmund, 298, 305n., 352, 355n., 366, 367n.
Burnett, James, 134, 139n., 157n.
Burnett-Hurst, A. R., 209n.
Burns, Wilfred, 343n.
Butler, Samuel, 363

Carmichael, John, 110, 111n.
Chadwick, Edwin, 124
Chamberlain, Joseph, 124, 138

Churchill, Lord Randolph, 148
Clanny, W. Reid, 157n.
Cogdon, R. S., 140n.
Cohen, Elie A., 355n.
Collison, Peter C., 19, 238n., 275n.
Conrad, Joseph, 135
Court, W. H. B., 140n.
Cressey, P. G., 277n.
Cross, Richard, 148
Cullingworth, J. B., 89, 91n., 119, 127n., 191, 208n., 238n.

Dahl, Robert A., 354, 355n., 356n.
Dale, L., 124, 128n.
Davies, Jon Gower, 19, 331n., 343n.
Davies, Lord Llewelyn, 66n.
Davy, Richard, 355n.
Dennis, Norman, 19, 23, 25, 26, 275n., 332n., 356n.
Dicey, A. V., 327, 332n.
Disraeli, Benjamin, 124, 148
Donnison, David V., 208n.
Doré, Gustav, 125, 128n.
Dunham, H. Warren, 277n.
Durkheim, Emile, 277n.

Elder, John, 136
Engels, Frederick, 140n., 156n., 240n.
Eversley, David E. C., 90, 91n.

Faris, Robert E., 277n.
Fay, C. R., 140n.
Firey, Walter, 169n.
Firth, Raymond, 276n.

390